Here is another collection of Eric Sevareid's casually perceptive broadcasts, covering the period of the Eisenhower era. Mr. Sevareid speaks — for they were written to be listened to first — of the daily events that made the headlines as well as the feature stories. The pieces cover the catastrophic as well as the superficial, and in them you will find the familiar Sevareid touch — serious, wry, deft,

ALSO BY ERIC SEVAREID

In One Ear

(1952)

Not So Wild a Dream

(1946)

These are Borzoi Books published by
ALFRED A. KNOPF

Small Sounds

in

the Night

Eric Sevareid

SMALL SOUNDS

IN THE NIGHT

A collection of capsule commentaries

on the American scene

NEW YORK: Alfred · A · Knopf

WEST BEND PUBLIC LIBRARY

1956

L.C. catalog card number: 56-5799

© *Eric Sevareid, 1956*

THIS IS A BORZOI BOOK
PUBLISHED BY ALFRED A. KNOPF, INC.

COPYRIGHT *1956* by ERIC SEVAREID. *All rights reserved. No part of this book may be reproduced in any form without permission in writing from the publisher, except by a reviewer who may quote brief passages in a review to be printed in a magazine or newspaper. Manufactured in the United States of America. Published simultaneously in Canada by McClelland and Stewart Limited.*

FIRST EDITION

31,476   973.92   SE8

8 Aug. '56 Mc Clurg 2.45

FOR

Michael and Peter

ACKNOWLEDGMENTS

THANKS ARE DUE TO Alfred and Blanche Knopf for being brash enough to take a chance on a book of broadcasts; to Marjorie Geddes for doing the tiresome secretarial tasks; and to Lois, the perfect wife for a writer, who went right on knitting and didn't interrupt with a single helpful suggestion.

E. S.

❧ *Foreword*

You may remember the man who was enchanted to discover he had been speaking prose all his life. Well, I was happy to find with an earlier volume that the sounds coming nightly from my diaphragm so full of butterflies looked just like sentences and paragraphs when pinned to a page and mounted in a book.

I am not at all sure, however, that these "oral essays" amount to a new art form, as some lovable critics have alleged, partly because new art forms generally fall dead on the cash market and a surprising number of people paid good coin of the realm to read the first volume of what they had already heard on the air.

I wish I could say that, to a man, they pleaded for another volume, but that would sound too much like the hardy perennial of the politician—"so many of my friends have urged me to run again that I have reluctantly," etc. Besides, it wouldn't be true; they didn't *all* plead, and anyway I'm not a bit reluctant.

So here are more of the late evening CBS radio "analyses" already heard by night-duty bartenders, taxi-drivers, and insomniacs. It's possible these capsules can put other people to sleep in the printed form just as effectively as they did when taken by ear; so I recommend this as strictly bedtime reading.

It's not one of those book you can't put down. You can put this one down at any time, at any point in the text, any hour of the night. You don't even have to start at the beginning; you can sneak a look at the last page and not spoil a thing.

In other words, this is a real "peace of mind" book. It leaves you alone.

ERIC SEVAREID

Washington, D.C.

♦ Contents

xii

Contents

Small Sounds

in

the Night

Eric Sevareid

ALL IN THE FAMILY

[*July 4, 1951*]

M ost of us read the Declaration of Independence for the first time around high-school age; and most of us never read it again. It becomes fixed in our minds as a sacred parchment, a thing unto itself, having no relation to the sweaty struggles of fallible men. We think of the American Revolution, heralded by the Declaration, as a spontaneous, unanimous uprising of the pure and good against the corrupt and evil. So fixed is this illusion that some among us think of the American Revolution as the only noble revolt of men, and all other mass upheavals against authority as suspect, dangerous, and vulgar.

Perhaps the beginning of wisdom comes not only with the separation of the reality from the ideal, but with the understanding that the ideal is part of the reality; all men are moved by realities; the great men are moved by ideals; and the greatest of the great are those who infuse the two, drawing the noble ideal from the common condition, and expressing for common men the idealization of their struggle, which they cannot express for themselves. That is why

3

Jefferson and his Declaration are of enduring greatness; they gave form and meaning to a human struggle, which was passionate and just, but also confused, contradictory, sometimes cruel, and often stupid. The organized, super-patriots of today in their childlike fantasies, do the embattled colonists a great injustice, for they regard them as supermen with absolute wisdom, unaltered patience, and unanimous support in a pristine cause. But we understand the greatness of the founding fathers and Washington's farmer soldiers only when we understand that they persisted through years of their own mistakes, through treachery, corruption in high places, cynicism and cowardice among Americans all around them, as well as the bullets of the red-coated enemy.

We understand it all better when we understand that in its earlier phases the struggle was not even against British rule, but only against certain laws and acts by the fully accepted British Crown; that only later did it become an outright struggle for national independence and a new society; that during the fighting itself, at least one third of the two million colonial people were completely opposed to Washington's struggle; that never was he able to raise more than twenty thousand fighting men at one time; that thousands deserted, that financial support was often withdrawn, that hundreds of respectable businessmen made private fortunes in government contracts while the unconquerable few marched over frozen ground and left trails of blood from their unshod feet. We understand better why they could go on when we understand that Washington's personal strength lay not in his grasp of political philosophy, of which he had little, not in his powers of oratory, of which he had none, but in his elemental, rock-like power of personality and will.

4

We understand it better when we understand that the revolution was a part and a pawn in the general movements of world politics and power; it was won as much by powdered colonial diplomats at the European courts as by the ragged men at Valley Forge, for it was when the American revolt became part of a world-wide conflict between French and English imperialisms that its success became certain. Intervention of the French fleet was the final, decisive military act, but even then, at Yorktown, nearly half the foot soldiers under Washington's command were Frenchmen.

And perhaps there is a lesson for today in this American story; perhaps it means that we were never isolationist at all, that America and her fate have been involved in the general affairs of other men and nations from our very beginning; the American Republic did not spring full-grown from Jason's seeds; it was born from the intercourse of nations, in their normal ambitions, ideals, and their greeds, and though today it has become the biggest and strongest offspring, it remains a member of the world family still.

A FORWARD LOOK FROM
THE REAR

[September 7, 1951]

Every once in a while when befuddled by the complexities of modern politics, we find ourself yearning for simpler, more sentimental days when a French cabinet minister could fall over the way a picture was hung or an

5

Austrian government collapse because of the way a song was sung. We had hopes there for a while when Washington split into warring camps over the President's new balcony on the White House, but the Republican party campaigners sadly let us down on that one. Happy days are here again, however. This Capital City is in the midst of a fine squabble about the four immense gilded horse statues now flanking the approaches to the serene and lovely Lincoln Memorial; the real connoisseurs of sculpture are having at each other in a fine fury mostly in the letter columns of the *Washington Star;* and we are rubbing our hands at the prospect of Harry Truman and Bob Taft next year flinging out at every whistle stop such phrases as "neoclassicism," and "subconscious archaeologicalism," hoping that both candidates pronounce and comprehend these words better than we do.

If Harry Truman can't show that the opponents of these forward-looking gold beasts are reactionary mossbacks; if Bob Taft can't show the threat of dictatorship and bankruptcy inherent in this romanesque display—why, we don't know our men. The President knows more about horses than Taft, but Taft knows more about the gold standard, so we can expect an evenly matched struggle. How they will do arguing the merits of the undraped females sculptured beside the horses, we wouldn't care to guess.

The present argument, however, really concerns the horses, not the females; to be exact, it concerns the western portions of the horses, which happen to face to the east. More exactly, the western portions of those two horses at the end of Memorial Bridge, which leads to the Memorial from the Virginia side of the Potomac. The first impression received by motorists crossing from Virginia toward the Memorial is that a pair of enormous brass doorknobs have

6

been attached to the white Lincoln temple. People should not have been surprised by all this, because the statuary was included in the original designs for the bridge, long ago. It is true, of course, that the figures were originally supposed to be made of granite. But as the thing developed over the years, those responsible seemed to have been seized of the idea that when in Washington, do as the Romans do; because the figures are not only gilt, but gilded with an imperishable gilt made according to an ancient Roman formula; it is designed to survive fiddling, fire, and the centuries and may even be here when the Republicans take over.

So far, it's mostly the connoisseurs who are squabbling, but we could get a North-South fight out of this yet. The old South may be offended by the juxtaposition of those horses; to which the north will probably reply that, after all, the statue of the Confederate soldier standing across the river at Alexandria has his back to the north.

Compromisers have been suggesting that the statuary, beautiful by itself ought to be set up somewhere else, to soothe the feelings of those who think the Lincoln Memorial was beautiful by itself. A pro-statuary citizen suggested the Memorial be moved. Neither suggestion seems very practical, so the harassed editors of the *Star* today propose a solution designed to make everybody happy. "Let the horses," they say, "be placed on revolving pedestals. During the morning rush hour when traffic is moving across the bridge toward the Lincoln Memorial, the incoming traveler could at least look these gift horses in the mouth. In the afternoon, when the traffic is headed in the other direction, the horses can be turned around. People will thus feel," says the *Star*, "that they are learning art appreciation from the most pleasant approach."

7

A MASTER'S MECHANIC

[December 24, 1951]

For anyone who deals with the temporal affairs of men, it is always a little hard to speak publicly on Christmas Eve; there is nothing we could add to understanding of the spirit of this particular holiday; one either believes in the brotherhood of all men, in the possibility of a good and happy life for even the most wretched, or one does not believe it.

But we thought we might speak a few words about a man who did so believe and who was exceptional among us, because he knew a way of helping to bring about the good life for others, using the tools and the techniques of the time in which he happened to live.

This man died two nights ago, in a plane that crashed in Persia. He was Dr. Henry Garland Bennett, the sixty-five-year-old director of the Point-Four program for the technical improvement of what is called, in the handy clichés of government, the underdeveloped areas of the earth. It is a matter of some regret that so few Americans—even so few right here in the capital—were exposed to Dr. Bennett, for he was something rare among us here, something very earthy and strong and simple, representative somehow of the enduring simplicities, the natural, positive hopes that still prevail on the farms and in the little towns across this country. . . . He came from that kind of life and he never left it; from Oklahoma he brought it with him into Washington and the impersonal halls of government. At first this elderly expert on soils and grasses and fertilizers and plows, this bulky little man with his rumpled suit and his sad expression—at first he seemed out of place; he didn't use the vocabulary of government agencies, words like *implementation* and *co-ordination* and *policy level* and *working committees;* his words were simple and old-fashioned; he talked like a modest prophet out of the testaments and gradually the urbane men and women who worked with him fell under his spell, and their curiosity turned to personal devotion.

This reporter's total acquaintance with Bennett amounted to one hour in his office, but we shall always remember that interview. He moved along his walls, pointing to this place and that on the maps of far-off countries. His stubby finger traced the lines of the Tigris and the Euphrates and he talked about what a green and pleasant land it had been, in Roman times, how it had all turned to desert and poverty through the centuries; he talked of dams and pumps and steel-pointed plows, how little it would take in men and money, how few years it would take to reverse the course of history and make these lands bloom again. He talked of the climate and soils of India, said that with a hundred county agents we could tremendously increase the food-production of those starving people; and one believed him implicitly, for he knew exactly how it could all be done. So he roamed, with his words and his pointing finger over the map of this suffering world; and you felt that here was the true voice and meaning of America to the world; *this* was the special mission of our country in this century; this was the way for America to pursue the cold war. You felt that propaganda and weapons were ephemeral forces compared to this; that *this* was the thing we could do as no other people could

9

do it, and the Communists would simply be lost in our dust.

That is the way old Dr. Bennett made people feel. This, one felt, was applied Christianity; this man in his rumpled suit was a mechanic of Christianity, so to speak, one who reduced it to everyday life and knew how to make it work.

His death is a great loss, for he had started something here, something fresh and wonderful, in a government where men and ideas have grown tired and worn. But it seems almost appropriate that he should die at Christmas time, out in the Middle East, in that arid, Biblical vale of tears where the idea of brotherhood was first made human. He knew that once there *had* been cedars in Lebanon; and he knew how to make them grow there again.

HOW TO BEAR WITNESS
AGAINST THY NEIGHBOR

[March 4, 1952]

A listener in Meridian, Mississippi, asks that we tell him briefly just what a Communist is. We are not sure we can, completely. We would suggest that a Communist is one who belongs to the party and/or subjects himself to its discipline, or one who clearly and consistently puts the interests of Soviet Russia ahead of his own country, or one who believes all the basic dogmas of Marxism. But beyond that, into the twilight zone of half or quarter Marxists, the misty zone of those who believe in some but not all the things Communists also believe in—into that murky region we timidly refuse to venture.

Some men, such as Senator Karl Mundt of South Dakota, have much more courage; and we would recommend to our Meridian listener, if he also is a man of courage, that he read the remarks of Senator Mundt in the *Congressional Record* appendix for January 24, 1952. Mr. Mundt skips over the obvious signs such as party membership or treasonable actions and says, I quote: "Your yardstick for measuring a suspect is his attitude on *issues of the day*." Mr. Mundt says it is your solemn duty as a citizen to measure, I quote, "your union boss, supervisor, next door neighbor, congressman, senator or anyone else you can observe, directly *or* indirectly."

But first you must accept Mr. Mundt's tidy premise that (I quote) "each issue has a pro- and an anti-Communist point of view." Mr. Mundt has marked his handy yardstick with a long list of current public issues. He warns that a suspect's view on a *single* issue is inconclusive; you must, he says, look for a pattern. How many black marks make a pattern? He doesn't say. Let's assume eight or ten and take them from the Mundt master list and look at them:

Communists want a federal deficit, he warns. Well, it is military spending, we should say, that causes the deficits. So if your suspect favors a big army, navy, and air force, keep your eye on him.

Communists *oppose* universal military training, Mundt says. So remember that, and forget all about Representative Powell of New York, who said on the House floor last Thursday that UMT was *conceived* by the Communists— this will only confuse you.

Communists, says Mundt, fight the Taft-Hartley Law

II

and are in favor of more public housing—so keep an eye on a large section of the Democratic Party. Communists, according to Mundt, favor federal funds for schools and colleges, the Missouri Valley Authority, and the St. Lawrence seaway, so put those things down on your check-list as you draw out your unsuspecting neighbor. Communists, says Mundt, favored David Lilienthal for the Atomic Commission and they took the President's side in the Truman-MacArthur issue, so you had better think hard about all those great newspapers—papers you always thought were conservative—which were wrong on both those matters. Also, by the way, look twice at any neighbor who thinks we *ought* to have higher taxes—that's part of the Communist line too, according to Mundt.

You see how it's done—the handy Mundt method for trapping your friends. You might jot the full list on your cuffs for quick reference during the bridge-game conversation. However, if you are the old-fashioned, lazy type of American who would rather leave such delicate matters to the FBI and others trained for them, and who finds it easier to trust than to suspect, then you might turn from Mr. Mundt to the editor of the *Saturday Review of Literature*. Mr. Cousins says, suppose there are a *million* American Communists and fellow travelers—an extremely high estimate. That would mean it's at least ninety-nine to one that your boss or your neighbor is just as loyal as you are. I quote Mr. Cousins:

"If each American cannot look at his neighbors or the leaders of his community without wondering whether any of them lead secret and subversive political lives, if he is to be torn with doubts about even his best friends, then we have shattered the articles of human faith on which a democracy must rest."

ANY RIGHT-HANDED AMERICAN
BOY MAY BE PRESIDENT

[April 23, 1952]

In case you didn't know it—one American President had an artificial jaw, one never voted in his life; Jefferson, not Washington, first warned about entangling alliances; Herbert Hoover did *not* say grass would grow in the streets if he was defeated, and Mrs. Andrew Jackson was the only First Lady who smoked a pipe. . . .

You probably didn't know some of these things—we didn't either, but today we have been leaving current politics to our betters in order to pick nuggets from a five-hundred-page gold mine entitled *A Book about American Politics;* it is written by that old hand at Washington correspondence, Mr. George Stimpson, and destined, we figure, to rescue a lot of columnists and commentators facing their deadlines on dull days.

Personally, we are fascinated to discover, via Mr. Stimpson's book, that we've had only one bald-headed President, John Quincy Adams, and only two city-born Presidents, Theodore Roosevelt and William Howard Taft. James Madison was the shortest President, five foot four, and Lincoln the tallest, six foot four; the only left-handed Presidents were Garfield and Truman. Eight Presidents never went to college, and only two, Buchanan and Cleveland, were bachelors. Taft, at three hundred and fifty-four pounds, was the heaviest President, and wits of the time

13

said a man was shooed away from a bathing-beach because Taft was using the Atlantic.

Garfield was the only President who saw himself nominated, Grant was the only Republican President to serve two full terms and we're a little surprised to learn that G.O.P.—that is, Grand Old Party—first applied to the Democratic Party, and that Herbert Hoover was the first President born west of the Mississippi River.

We won't tell you who was the first President *not* born a British subject, which President shot a man dead, and which First Lady never saw her husband while he occupied the White House—after all, Brother Stimpson has to sell his book and we can't give it all away; but we might go into a few other matters. Such as the fact that every President elected at twenty-year intervals beginning with 1840—that is, in 1860, 1880, and so on—every one of those Presidents died in office.

Where did we get our political words and phrases? Well, *candidate* comes from the Latin *candidus*, meaning "white." Romans seeking office would appear in the Forum dressed in a white toga. *Ticket* comes originally from the French word *étiquette*, which meant a label, a card, or a sign. *Ballot* comes from the Italian *ballotta*, meaning "little ball"; the ancients voted by tossing pebbles into an urn. *Dark horse*, English racing slang, was first applied politically to Rutherford Hayes; *bandwagon* wasn't used politically till the Bryan campaign of 1906; *Old Guard* was first applied to standpat Republicans in 1880 at the Chicago convention, when Senator Conkling spoke for Grant, with the words: "Pull no skulkers from under the ammunition wagon; take the tried and true old hero, with the Old Guard behind him." *Hat in the ring* came from Western sporting slang, was popularized by Teddy Roosevelt when he said to Cleveland reporters: "My hat's in the ring; the fight is on and I'm stripped to the buff."

An AP story first used "smoke-filled room" in 1920, meaning suite 804 and 5 in Chicago's Blackstone Hotel, where the leaders decided on Harding.

The labels *conservative* and *liberal* go 'way back, of course. In recent years somebody unknown defined a liberal as a person who has both feet firmly planted in the air; Elbert Hubbard said a conservative was a man too cowardly to fight and too fat to run—and Winston Churchill had his own definition of *reactionary* when he was called one during a debate on Greece: "An armed Communist advances upon you, and you react against him. Therefore," said Churchill, "you are a reactionary."

THUS FAR AND NO FARTHER, BUREAUCRACY

[April 25, 1952]

The news from the north is dire and dark. Authorities in Minneapolis, the very heart of transplanted Scandinavia, are trying to abolish the smörgåsbord; claim it's unhealthful to leave food sitting out exposed; what madness! This is no letter-to-your-congressman affair; there are times when men must *fight* and we expect the next wind from the north will bring to our ears that awesome cry from the city streets: "Smörgåsbord-lovers of America, arise! You have nothing to lose but your appetites."

Who be these authorities of blind and arrogant power?

How comes it that they have crept into the seats of office while honest *spēke pölse* eaters were sleeping in their beds, trusting life, comfortable in conscience and digestion? Thus is honesty betrayed and meekness scorned. In good faith, we of Norwegian, Swedish, Danish descent accepted the promise of America; we are all Americans now, our fathers said; and they did not combine, by race, as did the Italians and Jews in their great cities, to seek the places of power; they did not, on St. Olaf's Day, jam the streets, stop the traffic, and demand that all wear a bit of color as do the Irish on St. Patrick's Day. They did not throw their weight around at all; they asked but one thing to keep— their smörgåsbord.

But we are men of reason, we Norsks and Svenskas; let us make one last appeal to sweet reason's ear. A menace to health, the fragrant and lavish smörgåsbord? The facts speak otherwise. What is the life expectancy of a child born to the eaters of bean and cod in Massachusetts? About sixty-four years. One born mid the corn pone and fritters of Mississippi? About sixty-three years. One born amid the raw-meat-eaters of Texas, where men allegedly are men? About sixty-two. And in Minnesota, Iowa, the Dakotas, where the smörgåsbord counters feed and bless all who are able to walk? About sixty-*seven*.

And why this happy state of collective health? Because the smörgåsbord lies open, unashamed, in all its natural colors and odors; thus human juices are caused to flow in keen anticipation, and digestion is thereby properly accomplished. And then the exercise—the seven or eight walks between the courses. Primitive man hunted, dug, pulled, and sniffed before he ate, and as science knows, the farther from our natural habits we regress, the sooner we decay.

If logic fails, then consider the crime portended here

against form and beauty. Who would encase in pallid glass the brisling sardine, still irridescent from the sea? Who would wrap in frivolous Cellophane the solid and faithful forms of sweitzer ost? Do they propose the Pilsener be served in wretched cans and taste of tin? The acquavit drip lifeless from some plastic faucet? And, crime of crimes, do they intend to cover and hide the röke laks, the cool and glowing salmon, the very ambrosia of the finny depths, its pink and shimmering gold the fleshly embodiment of the borealis, this supremest gift to man, direct from the hand of Tor and the Hall of the Kings?

It cannot be. So far, we say, and no farther. We threaten not, we of the rocks and northern seas, but we would remind ye from Ireland and England that once, as Vikings, we commanded your grassy soil; ye of sunny Italy and sandy Israel that once we took your women and your soggy foods and there was lamentation in your houses.

Tempt not history to repeat its bloody self.

Pending this, we shall gather in the market places of Minneapolis and send up one mighty shout:

"Til hèlvete ned regjeringen!" [1]

This is Eric Söevareid in Washington.

IN THE BEGINNING

WAS THE WORD

[*May 14, 1952*]

In our own disorganized manner, we found ourself spending the morning with politicians concerned with *people*, and the afternoon with a poet concerned with *persons*. The first were obsessed with the problems of collective

---

[1] "To h— with the government."

power, the second with the problems of the individual heart; both were talking about the Presidency and the leadership of this immense and various American Society. In the morning, we felt certain that what the country needs is men of action; in the afternoon, we were equally certain that what is needed in the White House is a poet or philosopher. This is a sad commentary on our own decisiveness, and we ended up in a foggy state of hankering after a combination of the two qualities, in one individual; we got to thinking about the present candidates and were not sure at all that any one of them qualifies.

The really great men are those who *do* combine these qualities; we have had such men before. There seemed so many of them in the history books—the Jeffersons, the Lincolns, the Robert E. Lee's; men who could pull the levers of power, and yet remain intimately, painfully aware every moment of what they were doing thereby to the hearts and hopes of lonely and lost individuals whom they would never know, save in that acquaintance with which the power of imagination blesses and curses all men of good will. We know we have had such men on occasion in the leadership, because we know it by their *words;* the exalted and wonderful words of a Lincoln, for one. Give us the man who can write or speak, even if only once in a while, in the noble cadences of the magnificent English language—give us such a man, every time, because whatever common faults and failings he may have, there is a certain nobility in him, somewhere; otherwise, he couldn't do it. You cannot dissemble for long with the English tongue; sooner or later it reveals your limits.

But it's not good form, any more, so it seems, to speak in exalted or passionate language about the hopes and fears and visions of the human creature; it is unsophisticated,

18

embarrassing for others, to speak unashamed about the beauties of this land and the great simple goodness of its deepest instincts and desires for this world of men. The great simplicities have gone out of our novels, most of the poetry is merely skillful, and the political leaders armor themselves in "statements" of what are known as "policies."

But men do not live by policies alone; it is when there is no *vision* that the people perish, and visions cannot be expressed in terms of policies; they can only be expressed in visionary terms, and that requires the use of words that modern leaders shy away from. Words like *love* and *kindliness, compassion* and *goodness; brotherhood* and *happiness.* . . . The politicians do not use them any more; they only use words like *security, strength,* and *standard of living.* They don't even use the word *God* any more, save when the ghostwriter puts it in the last sentence of the speech, just to be safe. Lincoln used it quite often, because it was on his mind a lot.

And maybe that gives us the clue to what has happened. Politics after all has profoundly to do with religion; the very political principles by which we live grew out of religious principles, in a confused struggle that took hundreds of years. But practically every leader now seems to have forgotten that, if he ever knew it.

Maybe Eisenhower is an exception; once we heard him talk about this, privately. He was arguing that Voltaire could not have been both an atheist and a believer in democracy. Personally, we had to do an awful lot of reading before we understood that the whole idea of democracy— that is, the dignity of the individual—grew directly from the religious concept of man's perfectibility, in the image of God. Eisenhower seemed to understand that, just by instinct. Anyway, he seems to know these great, simple words; somebody has got to say them; because we have an idea that's what everybody in this worried world is waiting to hear.

HOW TO EXPLOIT YOUR OWN
CHILDREN

[May 21, 1952]

The greatest show on earth is in town this week. We had expected to do a personal reconaissance under the big top and give you a considered analysis of any new developments in the ancient spectacle of organized bedlam. We found, however, that several hours of travel in a pitching DC-3 left us too light of head and faint of spirit to face three hours of Mr. Ringling's three rings. But we will give you a report on the 1952 circus, just the same: the eyewitness report of our two twelve-year-old sons, delivered both consecutively and concurrently during the dinner hour. As closely as we can recapitulate, their report, in part, goes like this:

"Well, the finger man wasn't there today, but this guy with the cups and saucers—you know, the finger man, Unus, he stands on one finger, and after he got all the cups and saucers up on his—like this, see—then, whoosh, he threw up a teakettle, but that Spanish lady, oh boy, oh boy, that's what I liked; gee, you never saw anybody swing a trapeze back and forth, I mean, it was so *purty* and then she just *jumped* straight up in the air and came down, and there she was, hanging by her heels—like this. . . ."

While the narrator of the above extricated himself from his upset chair and sped to the kitchen for a mop-up rag, the second narrator was demonstrating how one clown had swung on another clown; at least he *started* to demonstrate that, but it appeared that also he was demonstrating his new outcurve as performed at the school ball game earlier in the day. By the time we had this all sorted out, the narrator of the first part had returned, in full, bitter cry that it was not *either* the same clown as last year that had the windshield-wipers on his spectacles, and you couldn't either make a million pup tents out of that canvas even if it was the biggest canvas in the world, you couldn't make moren' about a *half* million and he was a tenderfoot scout and ought to know and his brother wasn't, so *there*.

Our mental notes of the report pick up about as follows: "Well, they had that same airport car, just *wallowing* around full of those clowns, and they all came out and there were about sixty-seven of them and they had cannibals this time and it was just a little, teeny dog in the end and that fashion show with the elephants, I didn't like that so much, it was awful *boring*, but we didn't sit so near the band this time and there was that *hideous* singer, so you could hear yourself think a little this time; anyway it didn't absolutely *bust* your eardrums, but, oh boy, this guy with the palomino horse, it was a Percheron, you know, but a palomino. Well, it just *lay* there on its back, just *still*, with its head on one side like *this*—ouch!" (Again we are obliged to interpolate an explanation—the nose of this narrator had come up against the coffeepot.)

It seems that twelve-year-old eyes begin to perceive the small deceits and shams of men that underlie the glamour and the gold. "Well, Pop, that dancing horse, you know that horse that dances—I thought they were abso-

lutely *crool* with all those checkreins—well, that horse
wasn't dancing in time with the music, they just kept the
music in time with the *horse*, because you could *see* it, because they didn't get the music stopped as quick as the
horse stopped; and those clowns were working men, too,
because when he came back, this man I mean, and pulled
on the ropes, he was still wiping off his clown paint, so I
don't know if he was a worker or a clown or which, but it
was the *same* man! "And those people over there in the
expensiver seats, why, they couldn't see any better than we
could and I thought I'd just save up my appetite till I got
home where the things are free, I just *borrowed* a little
of Mike's peanuts and pop, and think of all the people they
need to pick up peanut shells. I wonder what would happen if they went on strike and the President went on the
radio to tell everybody. But Mommy wouldn't let us go
over to the horse tent afterward; anyway I can ride as
good as some of those guys, they just *bounced*—what have
we got for dessert?"

This concludes our second-hand report on the 1952
circus; a report, we think, about as logical, ordered, and
clear as the circus itself.

WE TAKE UNEASILY TO SORROW

[May 30, 1952]

It is hard to speak public words on Memorial Day, harder
perhaps than on any other special day in the national
life and calendar. To institutionalize a sentiment, whether
of joy or sadness, is not a natural thing; All of us feel a

certain constraint on Memorial day, because all of us sense that it is those individuals and families with the most to say, who are the most inclined to silence. So sometimes all of us must feel that the greatest tribute to those now gone and to whom we owe our freedom would be, simply, silence.

That is done, sometimes, in certain countries, on such days of regret and memory as this; in Latin countries in particular, where all life is intermingled with a brooding sense of death and where the instinct to mourn goes always hand in hand with the instinct to rejoice. But we are not yet like that, here in our country, where it is the *future* that always seems close at hand, not the past. Other national communities will accept a full day of silence; but we are the nation of the one-minute silence; and somehow this seems right and good, for us.

Whatever our faults of national failure and our spurts of worry, *fatalism* is not yet a part of the American national spirit; it is good for our own health as a country and, we think, good for all of this uncertain world that this is so; and this is the deepest of all the reasons perhaps why we make this day of regretful memory and solemn ceremony also a day of picnic and party; this is why you see a few flags today at half-staff, and the others flying as usual, bravely at the top. We behave on our Memorial Day as we do because, almost unconsciously, we are making certain assumptions. We are assuming, as we think of past wars, that wars really cannot happen to us again; we are assuming, as we think of a brother or a neighbor who died in battle, that our present neighbors and brothers will never share that fate.

Our friends in older and sadder countries are always a little disturbed about this characteristic of our nature, a little distrustful, feeling there is dangerous unwisdom

23

somewhere in this; but they are feeling a kind of envy, too, as a man of heavy years feels as he watches youth. He knows it is heading for pitfalls and pain, but he also knows that without this irrepressible belief in life and safety there would be no life or safety, for him or anyone else, and that everything would come apart. From similar impulse, older and sadder nations instinctively cling to us, not only from their belief in our power, but because of our power of belief. Inarticulate and unformulated though it may be, this belief remains the ultimate wisdom.

And so, perhaps, we need not worry quite as much as we do about all the complaints that we do not really carry the message of America to foreign lands, do not really formulate and express what we call the "American way of life." One has a feeling that should it be neatly formulated, that will be a warning sign, a sign that it is no longer in our bones, but only in our minds, a sign that its essence and strength are gone.

Even on Memorial Day, consecrated to tragedy, our flag flies at the top of the staff, and that, after all, is the truest expression and formulation of the American spirit. The tragic view of life is not yet ours, and if it should ever be, *there* would lie the only real tragedy.

So perhaps it would not be in bad taste to suggest to those among us with intense and private cause for grief on this day, to think a little of our curious holiday behavior in that light; to see the picnics and the parties, not as an affront to them, but as sign and symbol of reassurance, for us *all*.

I'M GLAD YOU ASKED THAT
QUESTION

[June 16, 1952]

The dog days are with us again, meteorologically and *politically* speaking. At this season, every four years, all news commentators with a high sense of duty come to the aid of their listeners; they realize that the normal voter is too limp from the effort of hearing or reading what the various candidates are saying to spare any extra energy in figuring out what the candidates *mean* by what they are saying. This is where the news-analyst comes in; so if you will just lie back with a cool drink in your hand and a cold cloth over your brow, we will proceed to translate the political gobbledygook (which itself is translated, by the way, to mean baffle-gab).

We will give you first the familiar statement made by the candidate—*any* candidate—and then the translation. We have time here for only a few of the more chronic and painful examples, but will be glad to accept any further translation problems you may care to send in; satisfaction guaranteed, or your canceled postage stamp cheerfully refunded.

Now then, what does a candidate mean when he says: "I'm glad you asked that question"? He means: "Oh, oh, give me a moment to think."

"We must get the *facts*." This means: "I'm damned if I know."

25

"My candidate is a man of the people." If this *has* any meaning, it means that his candidate was also born in a hospital.

"Under no circumstances would I accept the *vice*-presidential nomination." Translation: "I gotta keep my presidential bandwagon rolling until after the first ballot."

"I'm in this fight to the finish." Translation: "The law sets the election day and I can't do a thing about it."

"We must have spartan economy in government." Translation: "This goes for *everything*, except, of course, grants to veterans, farm subsidies, old-age pensions, the new Air Force, and the projects for slum clearance, public housing, harbor improvements, and flood-control in my own state, plus, of course, that little Asiatic trip in a military plane that a few of us boys on the subcommittee got set up for next fall."

"I intend to hew to the line, let the chips fall where they may." What the candidate really means by this is that he intends to put his shoulder to the wheel and let his voice be heard.

"I intend to be the president of *all* the people." Translation: "The Constitution has fixed it so that *nobody* can escape."

"The primary result was a great moral victory for our candidate." Translation: "They beat our pants off."

"My opponent is trying to debauch the electorate by the unconscionable use of *money*." Translation: "*I* can't get the fat boys to kick in because they think I haven't got a chance." The same translation will do for the line: "I'm for the people and against the special interests."

"A vote for me is a vote for the American way of life." Translation: "I ain't running in Southern Rhodesia."

"If I fail of nomination, I shall wholeheartedly support

whomever my party may choose." Translation: "Maybe I can get a Cabinet job, at that."

"I can't tell you what a pleasure it is to return to your wonderful city." Translation: he can't, either.

"It's mighty fine to get back home with you folks and away from that great Tower of Babel on the Potomac." Translation: "If I get licked, I can always open a law office in Washington."

"We must return to the principles of our forefathers." Translation: "Things *must* have been simpler in those days."

And when a candidate for office replies to a question by saying: "I don't know," it means—he doesn't know.

He is the candidate you should vote for.

SEVAREID'S FOUR-WHEELED LAW

[*June 19, 1952*]

The people of New York City seem upset because they now have to pay an extra tax for the privilege of owning an automobile. They think this is the deliberate work of men and blame city officials. If they will just relax and take the historical view, they will realize it's merely another manifestation of the Malthusian law, as applied to automobiles. The Malthusian law says that people outgrow their food supplies in numbers, whereupon starvation and disease cut populations down to manageable size again.

There are now fifty million cars in this country; the

Malthusian principle as applied to cars, which we shall call, for convenience, Sevareid's law, is now coming into operation, and judging by the sheaf of parking tickets in our wallet, it's high time. If you will just be patient for, say, thirty years, the whole thing will be back in balance. Other manifestations of the law are the new auto liability insurance rates—going up about twenty per cent almost everywhere—the thirty-per-cent increase in damage *claims*, due, among other things, to the fancy fenders, radiator jewelry, and collapsible, tinplate bumpers; and, of course, the disappearance of the geographical frontier in terms of parking places.

The last, in fact, might be designated as sub-rule A. It has a captivating simplicity about it; you can produce more and more cars every week, but you cannot increase the square footage of the United States; it is amusing to watch mortals struggle against sub-rule A. San Francisco began the panicky rush by building a huge garage underground. Chicago is now trying the same thing at Grant Park; Los Angeles and Dallas, peopled by officials used to the great open spaces, suffer from claustrophobia, so they are going in the other direction and building garages *upwards*, in high buildings.

It can't work; sub-rule A can't be outrun, for a lot of reasons. Despite the traffic-accident rate, the population is growing fast, every new baby born with a driving license in his chubby fist. In addition to that, cars are being made so simple to drive that whole new categories of customers —eighty-year-old widows, college professors, old-guard Republicans, and others—are getting behind the wheel now. Furthermore, big cities are getting so crowded, housing-wise, that millions of people are moving into the far suburbs where they *have* to have cars, so they can drive back into the city to their jobs, where there is no place to put their cars.

Our natural law is working all right, and in occasional unguarded moments of optimism we think we might live to see the ratio right itself again. There are many other cheerful signs of this all around. Not only are the license, inspection, driving, and insurance charges getting encouragingly higher every year, but the red tape involved in these payments is becoming most hopefully complicated. In addition to this, the absence of downtown parking places means that city centers will soon be deserted by stores and shops; in Detroit itself, for example, gross merchandising business in the central district dropped two hundred million in ten years. Amusingly enough, the big stores in many cities are moving out to the suburbs; where they find that the postwar housing boom was built along the existing small roads, so that while there may be parking space, the traffic moves at only two miles an hour, and nobody can get to the new store before closing time.

Another amusing effort to defeat the natural law is the building of all these midget cars; can't work, because people are getting bigger, with longer legs every generation, and they soon won't be able to get *in* those cars.

When our natural law reaches its apex, cars, like people under the Malthusian law, will be choked, beaten, stabbed, and pushed into rivers by a panic-stricken populace.

There's only one possible way out: that is to go back to the old Herbert Hoover goal of two cars in every garage—and *leave* them there.

DOUBLE-THINK REDOUBLED

[July 2, 1952]

One of the evils of Communist rule is that the rulers re-interpret past history to suit their present needs. Thanks to George Orwell's book, this weird process is now called "double-think." And as Hitler predicted, the methods of totalitarian society force imitation of those methods in free societies. It seems to us that a perfect example of this occurred in the United States Senate today; the most powerful single individual there, McCarran of Nevada, reported on his long investigation of the private, international research group called the Institute of Pacific Relations. This group was composed of scholars, diplomats, professional and business people of various countries. Undoubtedly it contained some Reds, some pro-Reds, some fuzzy thinkers; undoubtedly also, the great majority of the Americans in it were perfectly loyal and patriotic men and women.

It is hard to weigh with accuracy the influence of the Reds and pro-Reds on the organization itself; even harder to weigh the influence the organization had on American government policy toward China; and it is *extremely* hard to decide just what effect American official policy had toward the conquest of China by the Reds. But not for Senator McCarran. For him it is all very simple.

This is the categoric statement he made today: "I am convinced, from the evidence developed in this inquiry, that but for the machinations of the small group that controlled and activated the IPR, China today would be free. . . ."

This, surely, is double-think on a scale to make one's reason totter. The boiling force of a profound revolution involving hundreds of millions of desperate Asiatics, nine or ten years of struggle with Japanese invaders, vast famines and floods, the endless movements of great armies over enormous distances, the power strokes of the Soviet Empire, the successes and mistakes of the United States and allied nations—wild epidemics of inflation, the hopes, the fears, the hatreds, the apathy of the most populous country on earth—the *outcome* of all these surging forces and conflicts, we are asked to believe, was produced by the work of a small group of men, most academic in temperament, who mostly thought and wrote in settings thousands of miles away from the scene.

This is Hollywood history in glorious technicolor; this is dime-store history in who-done-it form; this is strongly similar to the methods of Stalin's commissars, purging deviationist intellectuals; this is double-think redoubled.

Not a word in McCarran's speech about the material conditions of China during and after the war. No reference to the facts that the Chinese Reds, for years and years, controlled ninety million people with a powerful, disciplined army; that Chiang's China was never unified, but an uneasy, shifting coalition of local warlords; that inflation ruined his economy, that his soldiers were ragged slaves in vast numbers, that his generals again and again refused battle with the Reds, even to defend the Yangtze; that his troops deserted to the Reds on first contact over and over again.

Not a word about the long, dreadful American struggle to strengthen his armies—the hundreds of American kids who died in the green jungle hell building the Ledo road to free China; the innumerable smoking wrecks of planes across the Hump, where Americans died trying to reinforce Chiang; no mention of the hundreds of millions in loans and grants to Chiang, the bridge of ships carrying postwar supplies, the mass flights of American planes carrying Chiang's troops into position against the Reds and Russia.

All this, and more, is simply stricken from the record as if it never happened; much neater, much easier, to ascribe the fate of teeming, sorrowing China to a handful of American intellectuals, scribbling at their library desks.

How simple history would be to understand if such things were so!

HOT RODS ARE HOLY

[*August 13, 1952*]

We haven't a thing to offer tonight on high policy, because we haven't been able to get our mind off the case of Marine Corporal Frank Farkás. The case of Corporal Farkás may not involve high *policy;* but we can't help feeling it does involve high *principle*—namely, the right of a citizen to holler bloody murder when he gets done in the eye.

Years ago the District of Columbia passed a police regulation saying that nobody can put signs or symbols on his car for advertising purposes—save, of course, a simple business label. Well, around about '49 an infuriated local gent painted the words: "This is a lemon" on *his* car, and parked it right in front of the agency he bought it from. The agency screamed, and the gent was found guilty of violating that regulation, though we can't quite see what he was advertising, except unbranded citrus fruits. Anyway, the Auto Dealers Association here thought there ought to be a law, so the District commissioners rared up and passed a law—a new police rule saying, so help us Hannibal, that no person can drive or park any vehicle painted or adorned in such a manner as to cast reflection, scorn, or ridicule upon any make or type of vehicle. For two years this charming article four in section twenty has been on the police book of rules. Enter Corporal Farkás. *He* painted the word *lemon* on *his* car; also painted a couple of bright yellow lemons on it and drove it around. He was promptly arrested, told he wouldn't be prosecuted if he'd wipe off the offending paint—but the corporal's common sense told him the Constitution and general sanity were being violated, so he refused and was found guilty. This young Marine now declares he'll take this case to the Supreme Court or the Halls of Montezuma if necessary.

We're bursting with questions we'd like to ask, on the specifics, on the principles involved. Was the corporal libeling the *type* of car? Or was he just criticizing the one particular copy that he happened to get off the assembly line? Seems to us that's all he was doing. There are about ten million copies of the same car around; has he injured those ten million owners? We think not. How can you libel a machine, in the first place? If he's libeled the manufacturer, suppose he can *prove* the car is a lemon? Truth is supposed to be some defense for libel in this country. What have the police got to do with libel, anyway? We always thought civil suits took care of that.

Whose property has he ridiculed except his own? Does he own it outright or does the manufacturer still have an interest in it? There were no such conditions in his bill of sale. He can tar and feather his own car if he wants to; why can't he paint it up with any non-obscenity he wishes? We just don't get it. Suppose it was a palomino horse, not a car, and he hung a sign around its neck saying: "This horse is a stumblebum"; who's been libeled, the horse, the breeders of palominos, the horse's father and mother, or who?

We think this is a pretty serious matter, in this era of gadgets upon which all of us must depend. We can call people—politicians, the neighbors, broadcasters—to account, and publicly; a senator can smear a human being, but apparently an ordinary citizen can't criticize a heap of metal, even if he can prove his charges. The car-manufacturers have the right to yell at us from every billboard that their Hot Rod super-Seven is the finest thing on wheels, but you and I have no right of public rebuttal. Would any newspaper accept an ad or a letter from you or me saying the Hot Rod is a super stinker? Of course not. How, then, does a citizen exercise his right of dissent?

Well, we always knew that modern gadgets were becoming the masters of us humans, but we never knew till now that the gadgets had the law on their side.

Let us lift up our eyes unto the hills, brethren, and then *head* for them, fast.

THE COUGH HEARD ROUND
THE WORLD

[August 26, 1952]

A columnist in the public prints describes Eisenhower as looking grimmer and grimmer during his speech yesterday to the American Legion; the columnist attributed the general's pain to the audience reaction. But down in the fine print of another story we learned that his teleprompter wasn't working properly; and we're personally convinced that was the real cause of his suffering. As you may know, the teleprompter is the gadget that rolls up the lines of the speech, in enlarged type, so the speaker doesn't have to look down at a script. Ike's teleprompter either went too fast or too slow—at any rate, the lines weren't in sight when his tongue was ready for them and he had to improvise quite a bit.

Gadgets do just about everything else for us, these days, so we see no reason why they won't end up electing—or defeating—our Presidents. In a state of serene pessimism, we confidently await the day when a teleprompter will substitute an Eisenhower speech for a Stevenson speech or vice versa, causing the CIO to vote for the general and the Union League for the Governor, after which a great uprising of the people will smash *all* gadgets, in the manner of the ancients pulling down their idols, just before darkness and general madness settle over the land.

We have foreseen this since the time, years ago, when

35

we made a speech from the high-school stage in Pontiac, Michigan. From the antics of the audience, we had the impression that a plague of seven-year itch had suddenly invaded the hall; what had happened was that a microphone in the principal's office, also connected with the loud-speaker system, was also open; between the lines of our solemn discourse on the menace of Hitler, the audience was also getting the dialogue of two janitors making explicit comments on one another's ancestry. Of course there *were* those who said that it improved our speech out of all knowledge.

But we do want to warn the candidates about these things, especially when they work in radio studios; every gadget in the place is a Communist gremlin, just waiting to do you down. Hardly a radio announcer alive has not had the experience of the lights suddenly going out or the chair collapsing under him or the record on the turntable whirling merrily around, but giving forth no sound whatever.

Some broadcasting tables are equipped with what we call a "cough button"—a little button the speaker presses when he's about to cough, that cuts off his mike; when the spasm has passed he presses *another* little button to bring the mike alive again. This comes under the heading of mechanical *over*-protection against human frailties; because one news-broadcaster we know got the two buttons mixed up. For fifteen minutes his fascinated audience received absolute silence, interspersed at intervals by a fit of coughing.

Once in Paris, back in '39, we were on the air and a shutter blew open just as the air-raid siren went off. Got a lot of angry mail accusing us of trying to propagandize the American people into declaring war. Another time some receiving gadget in New York went wrong and our whole broadcast from Europe was carried over a competing network. Don't think they ever paid us.

Let animals loose among the gadgets and you really have a time. Many years ago, in Kalamazoo, colleague Bill Shadell had a lady singer on the air. She started backing away from the mike; there was a mouse in the studio. For the duration of the song Shadell, with a portable mike in hand, followed the white-faced singer around and around the studio.

We fear and distrust microphones; but some speakers are just depressed by the gadget's mute lack of response. This characteristic caused one announcer's mind to crack. For ten years he had poured his golden voice into microphones; one night he finished his earnest, mellifluous eulogy to somebody's soap flakes. He stared at the mike, suddenly struck it with his fist, shouting: "Why don't you *say* something?"

He rushed out of the studio and we never saw him again.

THE QUID PRO QUID

[September 3, 1952]

General Eisenhower made it clear today that by *mess* he does not mean (a) a military meal or (b) milk given by one cow at one milking; he said he means "muddle" or "botch"—and we are glad he's cleared that up quickly, because we were having enough trouble with President Truman. At Parkersburg yesterday the President let fling at Republican snollygosters. We repaired to our dictionaries

37

at once, but an immediate difficulty arose. Had the President really meant snolly*gas*ter? Now, a snolly*gas*ter is a strange wild creature, seen but never confirmed, like the Loch Ness monster. The last one seen around here, according to the *Washington Post*, was four feet high, weighing about a quarter ton, covered with brown silky hair and with fourteen toes, unevenly divided among four large feet.

Nobody could immediately call to mind any Republican who looked *exactly* like that; and, anyway, a check we made with the White House today confirmed that the President *did* mean snolly*gos*ter. A snollygoster is a fellow who seeks office regardless of party, platform, or principles—who gets there, according to one authority, by sheer force of monumental talknophical assumacy. So *that's* clear.

The whole matter set us to messing (that is, botching or muddling) with our dictionaries; and we thought you might want a seasonal refreshening (to use a Stevenson word) on famous American political epithets. They break down generally into two categories, those used to designate groups and those used to designate individuals. In the first category, among the most famous were these:

"Sons of the wild jackasses"—not from the Bible, as many think, but from a speech by Senator Moses of New Hampshire in '29. He meant a group of Republican senators opposing higher tariffs.

"Lunatic fringe"—from a letter by Theodore Roosevelt in which he said there is a lunatic fringe to every reform movement.

The "scalawags" were white Southerners after the Civil War who joined up with Republican carpetbaggers, and you know who *they* were. The "bloody shirts" were post-

Small Sounds in the Night

Civil War Northern demagogues who perpetuated the bitterness for political advantage.

The "boondogglers," of course, were the leaf-rakers, et cetera, on Roosevelt's WPA rolls, but the word was once legitimate enough, meaning a hand-made article of pioneer days. "Bourbons" were the same as "economic royalists," who were the same as the "malefactors of great wealth," who were the same as the standpatters, sit-tighters, the dyed-in-the-wool, the rock-ribbed, and the die-hards, all of them pretty well defined in the phrase that they had learned nothing and forgotten nothing. We'll skip the hunkers, copperheads, and locofocos and get into epithets intended for *individuals*.

The dead mackerel in the moonlight which both shone and stunk was Randolph's description of Jackson's Secretary of State Livingston; the labor-baiting, poker-playing, whisky-drinking, evil old man was Vice President Garner, as described by John L. Lewis. The "peacock of politics, all fuss and feathers and fireworks," was General Winfield Scott, otherwise known as the military dabbler in politics and Old Granny. It was President McKinley who was alleged to have a backbone of chocolate éclair. "That man" was Roosevelt, all right, but originally it was Thomas Jefferson. The modern trick of sliding two words together was most famously used with "globaloney," meaning the theories of Henry Wallace, and was spoken by Clare Boothe Luce.

Political epithetry of course is quite different from gobbledygook or bafflegab, which means bureaucratic lingo; we are keeping our pulse on bafflegab, too, but have time here only to report *one* new addition: *quid pro quid*. When an ally is given American aid in return for the firm promise to accept more aid later, that is the *quid pro quid*.

BEIZBOL IS BRUTAL

[*September 16, 1952*]

We got to reading that story from Moscow informing the world that "beizbol," the American national sport, is really a brutal, murderous enterprise in which men are maimed and killed, players bought and sold as slaves, and eventually cast out to die of starvation. We were a bit puzzled as to what kind of sports information the Russian people are getting from here. So, with the permission of the FBI, we have invited to this broadcast the well-known Washington correspondent for *Izvestia*, Arch MacDonaldovsky.

You can stop clicking your heels, MacDonaldovsky; just sit there across from me and explain how baseball looks through Marxist eyes.

MAC: Every day in Boston, New York, Chicago, is slaughter, stealing, men dying on bases, pitchers on hooks, men running scared for home, murder every day, sometimes two times a day, with searchlights—but in Brooklyn is something different. Is *moider*. What is difference, please?

SEV: Well—it's a rather subtle difference. Brooklyn is an unenlightened, deviationist, counterrevolutionary minority element. But obviously you've been reading the sports pages closely, and I'm afraid sports-page English has confused you.

MAC: Not confused. Is all clear. Every day is blowing up

pitchers, you are scorching people with line drives, you are putting men in cages for batting them and sending them into pens with bulls.

Sev: Oh, come now, MacDonaldovsky, you don't understand.

Mac: Soviet peoples understand everything. Beizbol not even *fair*. Is like all capitalism, is encouragement of cheating. Batter hits fair ball and is put out, batter hits foul ball and is given more chance.

Sev: Well, *sometimes* he's put out on a foul ball.

Mac: Is unfair, with discrimination for political opinions. Look at Reds of Cincinnati, all the time pushed down into cellars to die.

Sev: Not *always*, MacDonaldovsky, and anyway, those are *anti*-Communist Reds.

Mac: You mean Trotskyists? Betrayers of the fatherland? Hokay, let them die in cellars, is justice.

Sev: I'm glad you don't find it *all* bad. But, after all, we have umpires there to see that the game *is* played fair.

Mac: Umpires have no hope. Will be killed by bloodthirsty mob, maybe today, maybe tomorrow. This is why dressing in black, no? I explain in *Izvestia* last week how umpire-killing is device of profit-hungry, Wall Street imperialist butchers.

Sev: Now you've got me. What's Wall Street got to do with it?

Mac: Is simple. Masses are encouraged to throw bottles at umpires, so Wall Street imperialists sell more bottles to masses, to throw more bottles at umpires, so Wall Street imperialists sell more—

Sev: All right, all right. I get it; you mean it's proof of the fatal, cyclical nature of the capitalist economy?

Mac: Exactle.

41

Sev: Well, at least you'll admit the masses enjoy a nice holiday at baseball games.

Mac: Nize! Is savage, brutal way for holiday. Beizbol parks full of people celebrating death of grandmothers. In Union of Soviet Socialist Republics all people *honor* grandmothers. In 1926 observance of all-union grandmothers' day, great leader Stalin, he said—

Sev: Oh, let's leave Stalin out of this. One last question: at least you can't maintain that silly claim that Russia *invented* baseball. Everybody knows it was invented by an American named Abner Doubleday.

Mac: *Nyet, nyet*—is confusion again. Beizbol was invented by beloved commissar of Soviet sport named Treepleday.

THAT WAS NO LADY, THAT WAS CLARE BOOTHE LUCE

[October 29, 1952]

W e've noticed that things haven't been quite the same around Washington since Clare Boothe Luce gave up statesmanship, or rather stateswomanship, and left the Congress. But every election year she swoops gracefully over the political scene like some dazzling bird of paradise casting a radiance of originality that makes one curse the commonness of one's own clay.

This year Clare Luce's ultra-high-frequency antennas have caught something in the political ether undetected by those of us who plod along with our clumsy dowsing-rods. She has picked up delicate short-wave signals from the women of the country and now tells us they are going to vote for Eisenhower, and the reason is this: Eisenhower, she says, "exemplifies what the fair sex looks for—a combination of father, husband and son." She proceeds further with her analysis by type-casting and states that President Truman reminds women of an uncle, while Governor Stevenson reminds them of a brother-in-law.

Our first thought was that European critics are quite wrong, that family life in America is here to stay; but going beyond that, we floundered. The whole idea of Ike's being a triple-threat man with the women seems a little unfair to Democrats, to say nothing of Mamie. And anyway *which* women was Mrs. Luce talking about? Ike is sixty-two; certainly women in their eighties and nineties can think of him as a son, if they want to, but if all those college girls we observe yelling for Ike think of him as a son or even as a husband, something is out of gear somewhere. We have to conclude that Mrs. Luce really means Ike gets all female age groups with all three of his personalities—but separately, group by group, not in combination, as she said. He's father for the young women, husband for the middle-aged, and son for the elderly women; and it's all right for election purposes—Democrats may claim Ike is all things to all men, but they would have no right to criticize him for being all things to all women, because he can't help that.

We've also had some trouble with Mrs. Luce's other categories. Stevenson quite obviously is not a brother-in-law—he's a cousin; he has cousins everywhere and says himself that if only his cousins will all vote for him, he's in. And President Truman may be an uncle to Mrs. Luce, but it hardly seems likely. As any good type-caster knows, uncles are kindly fellows who bring presents, or they are very rich bachelors whose will is constantly discussed in the family, or the uncle is that fellow who ran off to Jamaica with the chorus girl long ago and is no longer discussed at all. Truman doesn't fit.

To get a clearer picture, we turned the whole thing around. Which prominent *women* look like *what* to *men*? We took a couple of the women who appeared in the Madison Square Garden political show last night. Mrs. Roosevelt is certainly too old to be a male voter's daughter; she won't pass as a sister-in-law because we don't think she crochets, and for the typical male, that poodle haircut sort of rules her out as a *mother*. We can only put her down as an institution, and institutions fortunately have no relatives.

Then there was Lauren Bacall, the actress. We have no patience with the idea that she reminds men of a mother, or a sister-in-law; *wife* is getting closer to it, but that rough-looking Humphrey Bogart gets in the line of vision. Finally we came back to Clare Luce herself. Too chic for bobby sox, so she's no daughter of ours; too confounded *smart* to be a wife, and until she's photographed baking a pie, we won't take her as mother.

So we have abandoned the whole business, in something of the bitter mood of that wartime first mate who came on board our ship after a fight with his girl and announced: "If there were three sexes, women wouldn't have a chance."

POLITICS, J. P., IS DIFFERENT

[*December 16, 1952*]

The newest appointments for the Treasury pretty well demonstrate that men of big business will dominate the new Republican administration. This only partially represents payment for campaign services rendered; more importantly it represents the scale of instinctive personal values possessed by the President-elect. Those who know the general well have always known that in his private hall of heroes successful men of business rank below none except one or two of his military demigods such as General Marshall. This comes, perhaps, from his boyhood in the Midwest, a place and a time in which financial success equated with leadership and respectability. Long before such things as new deals were heard of.

This may be an important test of the widespread idea that what we really need in government is more businesslike methods; these men will come into departments, some of which are now bigger, more complex than the biggest corporations. If they do well, it will go a long way toward laying the ghosts about business leadership, toward lifting the inferiority complex of businessmen, still lingering since the depression.

If government has grown and changed, so has American business, in these years; and a new type of business leader has developed, men of the tough ability required for leading a great modern corporation, yet with a far more acute

45

sense of public responsibility than their predecessors. There is no department of government that cannot be made more efficient and economical, but in the process of trying it, the new men will learn that running the public's business is considerably tougher than running their private business. They will find a congressional committee quite different from a stockholders' meeting; they will have to justify their budgets to a hundred powerful outsiders, not just to a board of directors with a common interest. They will find that they can't quietly conceal a mistake in their judgment of an employee or a problem; instead, opposition congressmen will be demanding their files, and a score of reporters will be demanding explanations for the public. Some of them, perhaps, will enter office with the normal businessman's scorn for the politician, and end up with a sense of awe for the complex arts of politics and the wish that they themselves had been trained in the political mill. Some will enter office with a preconceived scorn for the so-called bureaucrat and will find themselves relying on bureaucrats who know three times as much about the department as they will ever learn. They may not come to agree with Mr. Cyrus Ching, who left a successful industrial career for government and concluded that the level of ability was higher in government than in industry, but they will revise their notions considerably, just the same.

And they, and Eisenhower, will probably find that they cannot really operate as a "team," fond as Ike is of that conception. They will find that the cabinet is no longer a policy-making central body but a weekly forum for brief reports; they will find themselves separate administrators of quite separate departments, men enormously overburdened with details, with very little time for long-range, reflective thinking, singly or collectively.

And Ike will find, if he does not already know it, that he can take only his minor cues from his Cabinet team or his White House staff; that, in truth, they must take all major cues from him; that he must lay down the philosophy, the policy, the long-range programs, into which their day-to-day acts and statements must fit; that otherwise there is no effective government, however businesslike may be its organization and procedures. Which may or may not have something to do with the interesting fact that this country, which has exalted the businessman more than all other countries, has never yet chosen a businessman for the biggest job of all, the Presidency itself.

HISTORY KNOWS HARRY
WAS AROUND

[January 7, 1953]

Harry Truman sent to Congress today the last State-of-the-Union message it will receive from him; a Presidential message, containing no specific recommendations for the future, since the future is for his successor, but giving a wide-ranging, panoramic picture of where we have been, where we are, and in general terms where we must try to go. It is a valedictory, a statement of faith in what he has done, and an act of counsel for those who now take up the burden, written in the tones of an elder statesman wishing his successors and his countrymen steady sailing in the days ahead. In scope and phraseology this is perhaps the best and loftiest statement to come from the White House in Mr. Truman's tenure; there is not a quarrelsome note in the document, and it should help to clear the air in Washington, to quiet the petty recriminations and boastings in both parties which still poison the atmosphere, despite the fading of election day and the imminence of inauguration.

Truman does not maintain, as he has sometimes seemed to do, that he is handing over a country and a free world in excellent shape, with its major problems already behind. He points out in clear and rather memorable language the prodigious size of the problems and dangers ahead, and one suspects that there will be many occasions in the future when the new leaders will refer to this brief from opposing counsel to illustrate the enormity of the problems they will be struggling with. All retiring Presidents are more conscious of their successes than their failures, and Mr. Truman, it seems to us, has made the very best defense of his record possible. He ignores the vast welter of secondary faults, the petty corruption, the inefficiencies, the examples of subversion which became, by sheer accumulation, a major matter. On such things he was slow and astigmatic; but it can be argued that on great and pressing world matters where the very survival of free nations was at hazard, he was, more often than not, quick and clear—and immensely courageous. And it is on these matters, of course, that he dwells in his statement today.

The great world tragedies in his Presidency were the Communist conquest of east Europe, of China, and the invasion of South Korea. There is no convincing argument that any American President or policy could have prevented the first two losses, though there *is* a strong case for the thesis that we could have prevented the Korean invasion.

Truman is surely entitled to remind his successors that

we *did* win the big war, we did save west Europe from outright economic collapse, and Italy and France from Communist control, we did rescue Greece and fortify Turkey, and helped make it possible for Yugoslavia to break from Moscow's control; we did save the United Nations from disintegration over Korea; we did, with the UN, help usher small nations like Indonesia into sovereignty, did help prevent war between India and Pakistan, did get the Palestine war settled, and did save one third of Persia from Russia in '46. The United States did rearm, and it did help Europe lay the foundation for a single market, political federation, and a common army. It did save half of Berlin from blockade and Communism and it did get Japan started toward democracy and solvency. This is no mean record; indeed, the foreign-policy history of no single nation shows any kind of a parallel.

Tremendous as these accomplishments have been, they amount, in essence, only to giving the free world another chance; whether it takes that chance and makes it good will depend on the new American leaders as much as upon anyone else, or more. The resources, knowledge, and energy required are present. But there is point, we think, in Truman's warning that one great menace capable of spoiling the chance is our own fear, the present corrosive distrust turning citizen against citizen, ally against ally.

If the new leadership can dispel this fear, it will surely have won a precious new foothold in the long struggle for peace in liberty that has only just begun.

THE DAY THAT MINKS
RAN IN CIRCLES

[January 9, 1953]

The municipal press has been telling us about the thousands of businessmen, society ladies, lawyers, would-be appointees and lobbyists about to descend on this capital city for the inauguration—so many people with those debased dollars to spend that every limousine is already rented, every drive-yourself car, and it appears that all nine thousand Washington taxicabs will be in operation. It's quite clear that hundreds will escape injury and death only by the skin of their mink.

The more we've thought about these innocent citizens throwing themselves into the maelstrom of the Washington streets, the broodier we've become; and it occurred to us, as an upstanding public servant, that we ought to offer what advice we can, in advance. Of course, we have a secret, selfish motive too—ever since we read the Horatio Alger books, we've dreamed of snatching a corporation chairman out of the path of a runaway streetcar, receiving a summons from his office next day, with the offer of a vice-presidency and his daughter's hand.

The local chamber of commerce is issuing free city maps for the visitors, and our first piece of advice is to throw them away. A map of Washington will show you where something *is;* it won't give you the faintest notion of how to *get* there. Washington is built on the circle system. And the logical result is that you drive in circles. The streets have a way of leading *into* a circle, but not leading *out*. We knew a fellow once who got dizzy in Scott Circle and around seven in the morning ended up there having a bag of peanuts for breakfast on a park bench with Bernard Baruch, who had taken the wrong street toward Lafayette Park and missed it altogether.

We ourself—though we are only quoting the wife here —once missed a dinner party because we got caught in the pentagonal axes connecting Dupont Circle with Washington, Thomas, Scott, and Logan circles, and simply caromed off one into another. Not only missed the party but had to take the car to a garage to get the wheels straightened. All those executives coming to Washington with the reputation of men who drive straight at their objectives—they'll have an awful letdown. Things just aren't *done* that way around here. And we do mean *around*.

If, by some stroke of fortune, you do get off a circle, you will find yourself in a one-way street. These streets will take you either to the Potomac River or to Baltimore. Best thing to do in that situation is to stop your car and leave it, like a former French Prime Minister we knew, who left his, with a note on the windshield saying: "Mr. policeman, I am very sorry."

Now about Washington taxicabs. They are small, low-ceiling cars. You'll have to hold your top hat; if you're subject to colds, better wear a beanie. If it's snowing or raining, don't even look for a taxi; trudge. Of course this is just when people *need* taxis, but they all go home in bad weather. Don't get into arguments with the taxi-driver, either. If you are a Republican, he'll be a Democrat; if you are a Democrat, he'll be Republican. And if he suspects you are a former pedestrian, have relatives who are pedestrians, or once joined an organization with pedestrians in it, just get out of the cab at the first stop light. But you better make it to the curb, fast.

If there are two or more of you in the taxi, watch what you say. Not that the drivers are enemy agents or anything like that; they're just *interested*. There is a famous story around the press club here about a dignified radio commentator who once drove in a taxi up to the White House gate with a foreign dignitary on his first visit to this country. The commentator said to his guest: "You see, in America even the 'umble cabman may approach to the very portals of the mighty." When they got out, the cabby handed the commentator his change, looked him in the eye, and said: "Listen, mister, I ain't so humble, see?"

"A" FOR ACHESON

[*January 14, 1953*]

This twilight week of the long Democratic Party rule is wearing to its end. The old, familiar figures are cleaning out their desks, saying their farewells, each in his personal way. The President, as he sees individual reporters, fixes his thoughts on the high points of his career in office, and spares few of his personal enemies, such as General MacArthur; Mr. Averell Harriman argues for the foreign-aid program, with the absorbed attention to detail characteristic of his mental workings; Secretary Acheson presides over his final news conference with grace and urbanity, strong feeling encased in a subtlety of phrase almost too subtle, so that reporters are put to it to be sure they have caught the full flavor of what he is saying.

These men, and others like them now departing, share something in common these days, perhaps worthy of comment. They are, obviously, *happy*. None of them seems to wear the slightest attitude of *defeat*. The lines in Truman's face are still there, but his face is ruddy with the kind of new-found health that comes from within. Harriman's slight deafness suddenly seems to have disappeared; he exhibits a humor that has not been his characteristic in the recent past, and happily complains that he seems to be gaining about a pound a day. The Acheson mustache points don't seem to be bristling any more, and he's back in the hilarious storytelling mood unknown to those enemies who regard him as stiff and stuffy. The prospect of *entering* public office may excite the spirits of some men, but for those who have had it, the longest and the roughest, the prospect of *leaving* office seems to be a prospect of purest joy.

There is little doubt that even Mr. Acheson, target of the most uninhibited guerrilla attack in modern American times, is leaving office with no outward signs of bitterness, reasonably serene in his conviction that whatever the verdict of his present enemies, the verdict of history will be on his side. This was the implication, in a sense, of much that he said today, in taking his leave of the Washington correspondents, among whom his admirers are considerably more numerous than they are on Capitol Hill.

When he said to the reporters: "Do not think too ill of my successor if sometimes there is a reminiscent note," he seemed to be saying that his successor will be uttering many things that he has uttered, taking stands that he has taken, defending the time-honored foreign service as he

53

has defended it; because, he seemed to imply, there are certain bastions of continuing human knowledge and effort that will and must survive the fevers of the moment; because the foreign conduct of a great nation in the world is never entered upon lightly or for the passing hour, but instead creates of itself wide avenues of world event and purpose while closing off others, so the great avenues of policy *must* be followed, whatever the encumbrance or the fears, until their final courses have been run.

And when Acheson was asked today about the new events in France and Germany which have checked the progress toward a common European army, toward the damming up of that Continental source-spring of Western wars—when he was asked about this new disappointment, he tried to put this, too, into historical perspective. This cloud in Europe, he said, is nothing compared to the clouds of real disaster that existed there in '47, prior to the Marshall Plan; yet there is more concern and public discussion now, about this new difficulty, than there was then about imminent collapse; and that in itself is a measure of the progress made. The basic force, he believes, is still toward unity, from strength to strength, for the whole free, Western world; pessimism, he believes, is a mistake, in simple fact.

If the history books *do* record a future Atlantic community, in peace and strength, certain names and certain acts must be listed in causal connection; and in that case, the name and the acts of Dean Acheson are not likely to appear at the bottom of the list.

HARRY PLANTS A TIME BOMB

[January 15, 1953]

Harry S. Truman, President of these United States for the last eight years, conducted his farewell conference with the Washington news corps today; and our last view of him as President was a view of Harry Truman at his best; wise, witty, generous in spirit—and to the very last a masterful political tactician, slipping a few time bombs into the opposition's pocket even as he embraced it with words of Godspeed for its voyage into power.

Reporters gathered early in the ornate, gilt and marble room of the old State Building across from the White House, some of them wondering aloud what this room would be used for in the future. What they meant by that was, simply, whether the new President would or would not continue these free and open question-and-answer sessions with the news corps. The press-club joke of the day made the rounds of the packed room; to wit: the train wreck, explosion, and busted Pentagon water main in Washington today were all part of the departing Democrats' scorched-earth policy. Then everyone moved around in single file to shake the smiling President's hand before the session began.

No one even had to ask about the future of the news conference. Mr. Truman himself was all primed, with a written statement that he read aloud. He urged the reporters to continue to dig out the facts of government for the people; he thought the free and open informal

55

White House news conference ought to continue; maybe there could be some improvements and safeguards, but he hoped that this direct line of communication to the people would never be cut. As for himself, why, he *liked* this kind of rough-and-tumble, give-and-take; if he couldn't take care of himself, as President, why, that was his own fault, not the reporters'. It ought to be a regularly scheduled conference; there were, to be sure, risks and embarrassments, but the advantages far outweighed the disadvantages; furthermore, when he was a private citizen he wanted to be able to know what was going on in government.

There was no doubt the President sincerely meant everything he said, but there was no doubt, either, that with these words he was planting a time bomb on his successor that Eisenhower can hardly afford to ignore. The general happens to have personal doubts about holding regular, ad lib news meetings. Knowing this, Truman was throwing him a challenge and implanting an idea in the public mind—the idea that if Eisenhower does not carry on with these meetings, it will mean that the public is being deprived of its rightful information, and/or that Eisenhower personally can't handle the journalists. Truman was cutting one more bench mark for his opposition party to measure the new leaders against, sometime in the future. Just as he has seemed to do by handing the new, business-minded administration the anti-trust suits against big business, just as he is about to do by reserving the off-shore oil for the Navy in the name of national defense; whether you agree with all this or not, it is quite a performance. The determined gentleman from Missouri will give up the great game of politics the day he dies and not before.

But if he was doing sleight of hand today with sticks of

political dynamite, he did it with consummate grace and skill. No, he would not answer a question concerning his election-campaign criticism of generals; he wanted, he said, everything to be sweetness and light for the inauguration; yes, the general had kindly offered the special Presidential car for his return to Missouri and he had gratefully accepted. No, he would not accept any directorships in corporations, because that would amount to exploiting the high office of the Presidency; yes, ex-Presidents *could* still serve their country; look how Herbert Hoover had served it in his marvelous recent work on government reorganization.

And that was it. The press and radio men gave him an ovation as he finished. Almost the last public, official words of Harry Truman, a profoundly partisan man, remorseless foe of his political enemies, were words of praise for Herbert Hoover; whom Harry Truman now joins, in the illuminated wings, off stage.

NONE BUT THE HONEST
AND WISE

[January 19, 1953]

Tomorrow the thirty-fourth President of these United States steps into the long line of succession dating back one hundred and sixty years. Citizens will note and remark the events of tomorrow according to their natures; for this reporter the wonder of the inaugural event lies in its *continuity;* in the reminder that as a continuing, unbroken re-

57

public we are an *old* nation; raw and immature we may be in aspects of our culture; in our political culture, we are mellowed, mature, and *wise*.

This change of command does not wait upon a ruler's death, nor wars and uprisings; through even the most terrible of civil wars the change has occurred, always at its appointed time, always by the process agreed upon, and never once by fraud or violence. In the light of the history of modern nations, this is a remarkable demonstration of a people's ultimate devotion to principle above party and to laws above men. The world today thinks of American influence in terms of *power;* in a sense, our real influence is in terms of political *steadiness*.

In one detail American inaugurals have never varied since Washington's. And that is the oath the new President swears; those words remain intact. In other respects inaugurals have widely varied. When Jefferson was sworn in the first time, he simply walked back to his boarding house on New Jersey Avenue, lived there the first two weeks of his Presidency. At his second he authorized an inaugural parade down Pennsylvania Avenue, and we have had the parade ever since. The most anxious inaugural was Lincoln's first; civil war was in the air, and the Army posted loaded cannon in every street leading to the Capitol Plaza, sharpshooters in every window down the avenue. The worst inaugural weather came on the March day that William Howard Taft was sworn into office; the city was buried under a snowstorm, cutting the telegraph wires to the rest of the country. At Grant's second inaugural it turned so cold the champagne was frozen at the inaugural ball, and the valves in the musician's horns froze shut.

Eisenhower's inaugural speech will run to about two thousand words. Washington's second, the shortest on

58

record, ran to just a hundred and thirty-four; the longest, eight thousand words, was given by Harrison in 1841; William Henry Harrison delivered it bareheaded in a cold rain; he then reviewed a long parade, danced at three inaugural balls, and died one month later from the exposure.

No law says the inauguration must take place at the Capitol, though most of them have done so; the only one held at the White House was Franklin Roosevelt's fourth. The most lavish inaugural festivities took place at Theodore Roosevelt's inauguration in 1905, with everybody parading, from Civil War vets to cowboys and Indian chiefs.

Warren Harding was the first President to travel up to the Capitol ceremony by automobile; Wilson's inauguration was the first recorded by motion picture; Harding's was the first to be broadcast by radio, and Truman's, in '48, the first ever televised.

President Eisenhower will find the White House ready and in perfect order tomorrow; but when Franklin Pierce spent his first night there, he found dirty dishes, muddy carpets, no lights, and sleeping, indifferent servants.

The White House has been called the President's house, the great house, the castle, the people's house, the executive mansion—and Theodore Roosevelt made "White House" the formal and official name. Some Presidents have loved the building; Truman has called it a prison; Lincoln called it "this damned old house."

But all of them would have agreed, as all of us tonight would agree, with the words spoken by the first President to live there, John Adams. He said: "I pray to heaven to bestow the best of blessings on this house and all that shall hereafter inhabit it. May none but honest and wise men ever rule under this roof."

CONTINUITY'S CONQUEST

[*January 20, 1953*]

This old Capital City, witness to many public transactions, reached the heights of excitement today, and at this hour tonight has reached the depths of weariness, save for those hardy souls still on their feet, dancing and singing at the inaugural parties. The eye and the ear could not take it all in; for sheer size, the parade today has probably never been equaled in this city; nor have the other festivities been so charged with electric pleasure for the participants, at least since Cleveland's inaugural in the eighties, when the Democrats broke twenty-four years of Republican rule. The Republicans today had waited a long, long time for this, and they came from every corner of the country to make the most of it.

But, as with all memorable American inaugurals, the partisan pleasures and triumphs were kept to the fringes of the event; in its center and heart, at its high moment of solemnity at the Capitol Plaza, this was a day and occasion for all members of the American race, whatever their political beliefs, secondary to their belief in their country, their pride in its famous story, and their faith in its days to come. When all is said and done, more than partisan feelings lay behind the country's choice of this man to be its leader; there was also, deeply felt, if haltingly expressed, a yearning among millions for a renewal of the sense of national unity; *force* does not hold this diverse American federation together, laws do not really do it; it is done by an *idea*, deep in the consciousness: the idea that this is a special portion of earth, with a special destiny; all of us, however unconsciously, want to feel this, to see it clearly, if only for a brief moment, at intervals of time. By symbolism this is done; by the hand on the open Bible, by the cadences of the marching feet and the rank upon rank of rippling flag and pennant; by the look in one face before us all, the sound of the same words in all our ears in the same instant of time. By these devices, the unity of common identity and common fate is made alive again; however brief the moment and the glimpse, they resurrect the American vision; this event, most surely, is requisite to the well-being of us all, individuals in America, and to America in this world.

The inaugural address itself was clearly designed to re-create the American idea, to state it clearly, to give us all a sense of our identity; it was from beginning to end a definition of the basic American idea, which is moral in its nature. Implicit in it was recognition that if this moral conception is ever lost as the American base, we shall not only be without meaning in the world, but we shall be powerless to hold the free world together in freedom and in peace.

It is a short time, in years, from the inauguration of the first Republican President, Lincoln, to this taking of the oath today; but it is a very long time in the terms of what has happened. Lincoln and a generation of succeeding Presidents gave thought and words to the preservation of America only; this President, and all his successors, must think and speak about the preservation of half the earth; and that is the measure, not only of our expanded duty, but of the prodigiously expanded burden upon the man who takes the oath. A wisely conceived Constitution has meant that the powers of this office have been expandable, as its obligations have expanded; but this has made the office no less difficult; what it has done is to make it an imperative that none but the very greatest men shall be handed this burden; made it certain that none but the greatest can even approach complete success in his performance of the office; made it axiomatic that the limits of any one man's strength and wisdom will be quickly reached and revealed —and made it, therefore, the part of all of *us*, in the name of peace and our children, to witness the continuing performance in all possible understanding. For to no avail is any president wiser than the people.

THE BUSINESS OF AMERICA
IS NOT BUSINESS

[January 23, 1953]

We have been trying, recently, in some of these pieces, to think out loud on this matter of the federal administration returning to the control of businessmen: to estimate how they will do and what this turn of the cycle may imply for the national course. We have tried to anticipate the strengths of this body of men—so different from the big businessmen of the Hoover era—and what their weaknesses in political life will be. We find, happily, that this job of analysis is done this week far more exactly than we could do it by Mr. Adolf Berle, in the current issue of the *Reporter*. Mr. Berle is long experienced in government and diplomacy and is one of the sharpest students of

American corporate structure and psychology. We thought it would be a contribution to understanding of the new Washington regime if we passed on to you, though in over-abbreviated form, some of the Berle observations.

His first point is that the big businessmen Eisenhower has picked represent a totally new business generation; they are a different breed from the men in the Hoover regime and there is no great reason to think this regime will be a repetition of Hoover's. As Berle puts it, in Hoover's time these men represented property and ownership; now they represent power and management. They are salaried *administrators*, not owners; products of the managerial revolution. This new generation have been business *politicians*, though they would not put it that way. They have had to deal constantly, for business purposes, with public opinion, in a way a Morgan or a Mellon never dreamed of doing. They have had to deal not only with public opinion, but constantly and most intimately with government, as an essential factor in their own business. More and more, American capitalism is a system of joint government-industry planning; and this is not going to change; government, after all, is the biggest customer of big business. The folklore, the clichés and propaganda of business may still denounce all economic planning as socialistic; but that is only because the talk of business has not yet caught up with the reality of business action. The vast oil industry, for example, operates on the Interstate Oil Compact, a price stabilization plan. It is much the same with the steel industry, beginning under the voluntary allocation act.

Business may talk about private enterprise, but *big* business today is public enterprise, irrevocably intermeshed with the welfare of community, region, and nation; less and less can it behave with exclusively private interests in

63

mind. Big businessmen may argue that individuals or labor unions are too much concerned with security, yet because of its very position in society, big business itself must constantly seek security of markets and prices and insurance against all possible risk; it may criticize unemployment insurance, but for its own protection it must seek fair-trade laws to allow price fixing and higher tariffs, and it fights anti-trust legislation. It's publicity opposes the idea of government in business, but in time of business trouble it must seek government help at once.

This is *one* handicap some big businessmen will carry into government. Their social thinking is far behind their own social practice and inconsistent with it. Then, too, they are, by nature, practical, rational men; they limit their thinking to the common-sense answer, and, as Berle says, that is right and proper—for *business* leadership. But they will find that leadership of a *nation* is a different thing. Men, in the mass, never have sacrificed or died in the name of common sense, and never will; only for ideas, hopes, and dreams will they do that. So Berle believes the brilliant business executives now taking over have a profound lesson to learn if they are to succeed as the leaders, the spokesmen, of our common destiny.

A mighty and bitter lesson; and, he writes, from the splendor and bitterness of its learning will be distilled the next phase of American life.

READY—SET—RELAX

[*January 30, 1953*]

The uneasy interregnum between the election and the inauguration has been followed by the uneasy interregnum between inauguration and the State-of-the-Union message—the concrete program—scheduled for next week. In the meantime, like a squad leader waiting for the signal, administration chiefs are pacing about, checking a chin strap here and a belt buckle there. We notice that White House secretaries are being warned about loitering and smoking in the anterooms, while the Attorney General, the Secretaries of Interior, Agriculture, and maybe others are issuing orders to their workers about getting in on time, keeping the lunch hour down to the legal limit, and fighting the in and out baskets right down to the five-o'clock bell.

This sounds brisk and businesslike, and it's pretty hard for a taxpayer to find any fault with it. It will undoubtedly confirm and soothe the emotions of those critics who picture government as a great mass of overfed bureaucrats dawdling through the day as the world goes to pot; but it would seem to play hob with those *other* critics of government who picture Washington as a vast babel of hectic, confusing activity—mimeograph machines drowning us with reports, studies, releases; papers stamped and re-stamped, bucks passed and re-passed; it just goes to show that *every* government order, no matter how minor, is bound to annoy somebody.

65

As a natural-born loiterer, who can easily make five trips to the water-cooler in the course of one paragraph, we find ourself, after a brief struggle with our taxpayer's instincts, slipping to the side of those forces that represent feet on the desk, a chat with the guy in the next office, and the over-time bull session at the lunch table, complete with penciled diagrams on the tablecloth. We are partial to such institutions because we have observed that *ideas* come out of them; you can speed up a mimeograph machine or a messenger—maybe even the digestive process—but we've never noticed yet that you can speed up the process of human *thought*; everybody's trying to speed up the machinery around here, and while we notice tables of organization carefully providing for specific *action* on every official's part, we don't see any such chart specifically setting aside a man or a group of men to do nothing but *think*, to think about the *kind* of action and the *direction* of all the movement.

Modern government is probably a little too complex to adopt the rule of the Ancient Greeks who insisted that philosophers be allowed to run the state, but we seem to be approaching a condition where men of ideas, long-range *thinkers* are actually disbarred from participation. We notice only men of *affairs*, not men of ideas, on the White House staff; and with the exception of Mr. Dulles, this also seems true of the Cabinet. What has happened to those rare specimens, like Henry Stimson, who could both conduct affairs and ponder their conduct is a sudden mystery. Superefficiency has meant that nobody has time any more to be more than one thing—an administrative machine *or* a thinker, and in the present American atmosphere to be a thinker is to be an intellectual, an egghead, or in the scoffing words of Senator Mundt about Dr. Conant, a "bookish" creature—in other words, a suspect character.

Speed with the in and out baskets didn't produce the Bill of Rights or the Monroe Doctrine; Lincoln's administration was horribly inefficient, but the Emancipation Proclamation came out of it, and a lot of bull sessions in the easy chair preceded Wilson's Fourteen Points. The strange thing is that Eisenhower himself knows and has often remarked, that the great presidencies were not the businesslike regimes, but the regimes of the dreamers, the thinkers.

So we make bold to suggest what his first executive order should be—a directive to all officials: pull the plug on the electric duplicator and drag in the footstool.

We will feel more comfortable, too.

THE PUBLICITY SAINTS

[*February 5, 1953*]

It could be just an attack of premature spring fever—we notice a faint breath of color on the Potomac willows, and a neighbor found some forsythia budding out. Anyway, this was one of those days when we couldn't ponder up a single idea about government that somebody else hadn't already treated better than we could. Whenever we find ourself devoid of nice, clean-cut American thoughts for civic betterment, we get to brooding around in murky corners among a lot of ghostly shapes of impressions, enthusiasms, and resentments that no pillar of society ought to waste any time on. Today we got to thinking about the late Gertrude Stein and something she said to us once, and wondering what she would say about it now if she could see the way it's all turned out.

This was about fourteen years ago, and Gertrude was remarking that something new had appeared in the world, people whom she called "publicity saints." She was fascinated with this phenomenon. She thought the Duchess of Windsor was one example, and maybe Eleanor Roosevelt was another. We remember suggesting to Gertrude that maybe she was a publicity saint herself, and the idea delighted her; she agreed that she was, but, she said, only of a minor order.

A publicity saint is a person who doesn't have to *do*, or create, but just has to *be*, to exist, and by the simple fact of his being, the modern substitute for worship—that is, publicity—continues to wrap the person in a halo, an aura of mortal sainthood. Now, usually, some event, some act, is required to start the individual off, but once well started, he or she never has to do or create another blessed thing. Publicity does the rest and the publicity saint evermore floats above the ground, with no visible means of contact, defying all previously known laws of gravitation. This has nothing to do with *fame* in the true sense of that precious word. An artist or a writer or a soldier may achieve true fame, but he has to paint, or write, or win battles, because that's where his fame comes from. *He* can't float at all. He can fly, but that's because he's got wings and strains to use them; only the publicity saints can float, without effort.

Now, an intertwining part of this mysterious development, is the alteration, the corruption of *news*. Half of the daily news has become mere publicity. It used to be news only if a person did or said something that changed something in one way or another. Not any more. Take Mr.

68

Bernard Baruch, an eighteen-carat publicity saint. He hasn't said or done anything that changed anything, for years. But look at the pictures and the news: Baruch sits on park bench, Baruch meets boat; Baruch blows nose. Gertrude would have loved Baruch.

But the thing that would have staggered Gertrude is the multiplying of the middle and lower orders. And the most amazing thing of all is that it is the lower orders who get the most passionate worship. Not many people will gather and salaam for Thomas Mann, a great writer, or for Charles Chaplin, a great actor; but, brother, duck for the nearest exit and avoid the stampede if Walter Winchell or Dagmar floats by. Or Arthur Godfrey. When Arthur had the next office to us here, he used to worry about his feet. Not any more. He floats now.

We don't know the exact protocol positions of all the new publicity saints; maybe Faye Emerson ranks above Grover Whalen; maybe Mike Romanoff outranks George Allen, the friend of presidents, or Perle Mesta, the friend of friends of presidents. It's hard to tell. We wish they'd decide and issue themselves numbers. It would be a help.

And Lord knows we need straightening out about Zsa-Zsa Gabor. We know she's a publicity saint; her portrait adorns all the news stands, each one more brilliantly varicolored than stained-glass windows. With effort, we expect to learn to pronounce her name; but we'll never understand *what* she is, just *that* she is.

With Dagmar it's a *little* different. She not only *is*, she *has*.

ERIC SEVAREID

HOW TO BE BIG IN
WASHINGTON

[*February 9, 1953*]

We've noticed, in various countries, that wars, revolutions, and even political crusades fail to change many things, including the folk-habits of salon society. And that's quite all right with us; get too far away from the rule book on etiquette and protocol and you get into trouble. Our colleagues in this trade once assigned us to arrange the seating for a dinner with the President and government leaders; just before everybody filed in, a protocol expert, ashen white, rushed in and rearranged everything, accusing us, between gasps, of trying to overthrow the government.

The protocol never changes, it seems, but crusades and other upheavals *can* create new problems for protocol. The dispatches from Rome today, for example, inform us that while diplomatic society in that capital is not exactly agog about the appointment of Clare Luce as the American Ambassador, still it is somewhat a-sweat. No *woman* ever held a job like that in Italy. Consider a few of the problems. As the newest Ambassador there, she would normally be at the foot of the table at formal diplomatic dinners. But she's a woman and as the most distinguished *woman* at any diplomatic dinner, she also ought to be at the host's right hand. We suppose they could solve this by using round tables, but, as we said, salon habits are hard to break

70

and they probably won't do it. Then what do they do *after* dinner? Does Ambassador Luce retire with the other ladies while the male diplomats hang around for their cigars and brandy? If she's expected to, won't she be offended? If she stays with the men, won't the other ladies be offended? It's a dilemma. When that Italian director ran off with Ingrid Bergman, we were all for breaking relations with Italy, but not now; we'd like to see how the Luce problem is worked out.

Here in Washington, the etiquette experts are enjoying quite a rush of business. Not that the upheaval here has changed the protocol, it's just changed the people. Cloth coats and businesslike efficiency seem to be for *daytime* uses only. The new people are trying to change the old Washington methods, but they're trying to *learn* the old Washington *manners*. We called up a couple of the little schools here that teach salon and dining-room deportment, and they report a large crop of new students—government lawyers, congressmen, agency heads, and their wives. One course—one night of study a week for three months, a hundred dollars—teaches them how to find their dinner partner at a big embassy affair, not to leave before the ranking guest has left, and so on. Another course—four afternoons a week for six weeks, three hundred dollars—gives you the works, including, we quote, "the creation and maintenance of a social position in Washington."

None of the schools seems to use those hundred and ten "Rules of Civility and Decent Behavior in company and conversation" that George Washington wrote out for himself at the age of sixteen. Lewis Glaser of New Haven has just reprinted them in an exquisite little book. Among other things, young George wrote down: "In the presence of others sing not to yourself with a humming noise, nor drum with your fingers or feet . . . spit not in the fire, nor set your feet upon the fire especially if there be meat before it . . . cleanse not your teeth with the table cloth, napkin, fork or knife. . . ."

Well, the only advice we would offer the new congressmen and others about society here is not to try to change their *speech*. They might get their come-uppance. We recall a gathering that included a minor State Department official of the old, stilted, and stuffy school who garnished his conversation with French words and phrases whenever possible. Mr. Paul Porter, then head of the FCC, grew a bit weary with this, and when the gentleman said he'd been having trouble with his liver, Porter said: "Liver? Surely, you mean your *pâté de foie gras?*"

A NEW WRIGGLE IN
WASHINGTON

[February 12, 1953]

President Eisenhower went over to the Lincoln Memorial this gray, damp morning and paid his respects to the memory of the first Republican President, whose birthday this is. Like most American soldiers, Eisenhower has long felt a special fascination in the terrible drama of the Civil War; and one may wonder, as the White House burdens lay down the inevitable furrows in his face, whether he, like other recent presidents, will find himself turning again and again to the personal story of Lincoln, the Chief Executive. All manner of men have found help and sustenance in that story—now almost a religion—of Lincoln's incredible strength and patience under the most appalling cares and dangers.

There are certain limited parallels between the first White House days of this latest Republican President and the first days of Lincoln. Sparks in the national air then could set off civil war, as sparks in the international air now could set off an even more terrible world war. But Eisenhower has some elbow room, sometimes, for maneuver; Lincoln had almost none. There was stalemate, in a sense, at Fort Sumter then, as there is stalemate in Korea now; hot talk then of blockading the Confederacy as there now is talk of blockading China. There is a certain air of tension in Washington today, three weeks after the inaugural, but there was unbearable tension in the Washington air three weeks after Lincoln's inaugural; and General Winfield Scott was saying: "A dog fight now might cause the gutters to run with blood."

The auspices of election were vastly different between the first Republican President and the latest; Lincoln's election was a rocket, signaling certain violence and disunion; Eisenhower's election was a national expression of a deep-seated desire for unity and political peace. The new Chief Executive is enjoying a considerable political honeymoon, at least with his own party; Lincoln enjoyed none at all; *his* Cabinet was put together for political reasons, Eisenhower's for administrative reasons. The members of Eisenhower's Cabinet are still anxious to follow his smallest wish, Lincoln faced conniving and a power struggle from the very first day; and within a month of his inaugural, his Secretary of State was complaining that Lincoln had no policy and proposing in almost so many words that he, Seward, take over from behind the scenes. Three weeks after inauguration, Lincoln was trying to see everybody

73

who wished to see him, trying to do everything himself; Eisenhower, three weeks later, stringently rations his visitors and his time and from training and instinct delegates everything that can be turned over to others.

As now, appointments were then a Presidential headache. Regional demands were, and are, a plague to the President. Eisenhower is known to be tired of New Yorker's claims; Lincoln, after sending a Massachusetts Adams to London and a Massachusetts Motley to Vienna, said to Senator Sumner: "now . . . I hope you will give me a little time before I hear from Massachusetts again."

There was a big sweep-out of Democrats then as there is right now. The office-seekers wore the new paper collars then, as symbol of status, as they wear the homburg now. But office-seeking is a quiet, efficient matter of telephoning and secret conference now; then it was a shameful, public shambles; the very White House grounds, halls, stairways, and closets were filled with place-seekers, and Lincoln sometimes had a physical struggle to reach his diningroom. In Willard's Hotel, bars, barbershop, halls, staircases, and porch bore a heaving sea of the hopeful. Once Lincoln exclaimed: "If our American society and the government are demoralized and overthrown, it will come from the voracious desire for office, this wriggle to live without toil."

But some things have changed. If it was a struggle then to keep men *out* of government, it is now, very often, a considerable struggle to get the best men *into* government. Eisenhower will struggle against *that* current, as Lincoln struggled against its opposite. And who is to say that the new-fashioned reluctance may not be as serious a threat to government as the old-fashioned eagerness and ambition.

74

DROP THE DIRTY WORD

[February 24, 1953]

This was one of those calm, pleasant days around Washington—government doing nicely, trees beginning to bud, Vishinsky still quiet—one of those days when a commentator sees the night approach with the awful feeling that he won't be able to scare up a single disaster or threat to the human race or the American way of life. We had just about thrown in the sponge today when our eye, ever-alert to anything that might even have the makings of disaster, fell upon a little item in the *Wall Street Journal;* we seized upon it in the joyful conviction that here was a cloud, not yet larger than a man's hand—in fact, weighing only two and a half pounds—but containing within it future storm and havoc.

This cloud is in the form of a tiny sound-recorder, manufactured in Germany. It is so small, you can stick it in your pocket, and it's microphone is inside what looks like a wrist watch. A thin wire runs from the wrist-watch microphone to the recorder itself. But that's thirty-five dollars extra; for the regular price you get a microphone that is worn in your lapel, which you can neatly cover with a blossom, fresh or artificial.

With this you are a fully equipped, up-to-date, electronics-style eavesdropper, and, brother, the fun you can have, the people you can ruin. No longer does a neighbor lady have to ask the other neighbor lady to take her word about what a *third* neighbor lady said about her hat or her

75

kids; no longer does an ex-government employee have to run the risk of denials that his former boss once said he had a Russian ruble in his coin collection. If it's now true that *denial* has become one of the dirtiest words in the language, it won't be true long; we can soon drop the word from the language, altogether.

The *Wall Street Journal* tells us how the tiny gadget was used at the General Motors auto show in New York. Twelve gentlemen wearing them circulated among the visitors, asked a few leading questions here, just eavesdropped there, and they have sent back to GM executives miles of frank, unguarded comment about their new cars. Now the *intention* here, obviously, is proper enough—they just want to know what people *really* think about their cars, in order to please the public better with the next model; but we still have a small, sneaking feeling that the practice is not quite cricket, and that what is strictly business in the hands of one group can easily become monkey business in the hands of other groups.

Of course, it's a great boon for those with the suicidal desire to lose their illusions. The boss can have *his* secretary wear one of the gadgets in the washroom and he'll know exactly how the other girls in the office feel about him and his waistline. The hostess can have her maid wear one in the powder room and she'll never have another illusion about her own parties. She can save money, too, because maybe she'll never have another party. It's dandy for car pools. You could record what one member says about an absent member of the pool and then use it to blackmail the first member into moving out of the neighborhood, in case his dog is tearing up your vegetable garden. It will be a perfectly grand thing to take along to the office convention in the big city; you could keep the wire for years, and play it back for P. J.'s wife, any time P. J. refuses the raise you deserve.

When everybody has one of the gadgets the country will be secure, at last. Because it will put an end to casual, uncalculated conversation; an end to all thinking out loud, all verbal groping for ideas. It will stop this silly business of talking politics with strangers on streetcars, of talking back to policemen, of unburdening your soul about your boss, your senator, or your mother-in-law.

It will save the country because it will end common trust; and, as many congressional investigators have taught us, common trust is dangerously un-American.

ON CORPORATE INSULTABILITY

[March 9, 1953]

If your resistance is not too low, at this late hour, we do wish you would help us worry about a thing going on in New York City. There's a play up there called *Mid-Summer*. In the play is the character of a chambermaid, a sloppy person who dabs at the dust and gives advice to the guests about their personal lives. So what happens? The Hotel and Club Employees Union, Local Six, A.F. of L., is picketing the theater, claiming the maid in the play is a slander on the chambermaiding business and all therein.

There's another play in New York called *The Crucible*, about the Salem witch trials of long ago. It shows some cruel and ignorant judges, a piece of history as it pretty much was. What happens? The American Bar Association writes a letter to the playwright, Arthur Miller, asking him

77

to cut out the offending lines. Why? Well, says the Association, it's not only a reflection on the lawyer business and all therein, but it breaks down respect for law and justice.

There must be a phrase somewhere to cover this kind of creeping confusion. The institutionalizing of the individual, perhaps. It's a fast creep, too. The other week some congressional committee was discussing a distinguished book that characterized some Texans as rough, tough, Mexican-hating, women-beating individuals. Immediately a Senator declared in righteous indignation that this was a slur on the great state of Texas. The other week an Oklahoma girl was accused of plagiarism in a national essay contest. Was the case treated on its merits, the girl as an individual? No, the state congressional delegation rallied round, for this, they said in effect, was a slur on the great state of Oklahoma. So we have now got to the point where, if you aren't careful, you can slander a piece of geography.

Playwright Miller answered the offended Bar Association and refused—hurray—to cut out those lines. He recalled that when he wrote *Death of a Salesman*, sales organizations flew to arms. Miller said that the logical end of all this would be that he would have to write about people with no occupation whatever. But, he added, if he did that, café society would probably feel put upon. The only safe thing for a writer to do, he indicated, would be to write only about people who aren't born yet.

Well, we've always been the greatest country in the world for organizations and groups; and now we seem to be happily handing over our personal individuality to our groups; they're now endowed with living, breathing, pleaseable, or insultable personality.

Institutions now feel happy or sad, have headaches and hangovers, and, obviously, gastric ulcers. It's a fascinating

78

and sort of disturbing spectacle. Any night now we expect a nightmare in which the Stock Exchange Building walks over and embraces the Union League Club, or the *Chicago Tribune* tower stalks across the country and falls angrily upon the UN Building in a great crashing of glass and gargoyles.

If we can't lick this development, we may as well join it. We wear slouch hats and get up late. We're just waiting for the first movie with a bad-guy character in it who eats late breakfasts and wears sloppy headgear—and we're going to sue.

If the lawyers can claim that those stage characters will tear down law and order, we know just what we will do when we see the next magazine cartoon showing a radio broadcaster as a dope. We'll claim that this not only threatens free speech, the Bill of Rights, and the Constitution—it also tends to depress the electronics industry, which could lead to an American depression, the collapse of our allies' economies, the loss of Europe to Communism —and then, of course, world war and the destruction of civilization.

We won't exactly picket the magazine—we get sore feet too easily—but with a nice little boycott, chain letter, and black list, we can put it out of business. After all, civilizations are hard to come by, and no effort is too great to save the one we've got.

BACK TO THAT GOD-AWFUL
NORMALCY

[*March 11, 1953*]

A lot of people take the passing of Stalin as a comforting sign that the world will get back to sanity; but, like any pundit worth his salt, or his commercials, we have been by-passing the obvious events, applying our eagle eye to the more subtle developments; and we are happy to report two events in the news, unnoticed by less acute observers, which are clearly harbingers of better times, firm evidence that Mr. Taft's philosophy is winning out and that the country is on the road back to normalcy. One sign was the photograph of the President wearing a five-gallon hat and the other sign—even more significant—was the announcement of a bunion derby.

This bunion derby will be staged by the Highway Sixty Association, a group of men dedicated to the welfare of good old sixty; *women* will make a walking race from California to the Virginia coast—on number sixty—and the winner—natch—will get a Hollywood contract. If you have forgotten about bunion derbies, then you have forgotten about the wonderful decade of the twenties; you have forgotten—let's face it—what normalcy *is*.

Normalcy was Florida real estate and Aimee Semple McPherson, who disappeared into the ocean and reappeared on the desert; normalcy was Father Coughlin thundering against political wickedness every Sunday aft-

80

ernoon. Normalcy was the great rash of flagpole sitting and the apotheosis of the noble Shipwreck Kelly, who outsat them all, until a lesser breed of men reduced the art to sitting in tree houses. Those were the sound, progressive days when an upstanding young man tried to emulate the Human Fly, on the barn roof, and trained in icy water like the Great Houdini. Those were the days of *action* when a young couple had spunk enough to shuffle around the floor of the dance marathon, days on end, instead of passively reclining before a television set.

Those were the days when the old American pioneer spirit flared up again and leading young men had the grit and spirit to conquer new heights, to be first in their line —the days of the first man to drive a car backwards across the United States, the first to fly a hundred loop-the-loops in succession, the first to swallow a whole school of goldfish, the first to walk up Pike's Peak on his hands . . . the glorious, exciting days of the pie-eating, coffee-drinking, Yo-yo-spinning contests that filled the front pages. The days when heroes had no clay feet, when adults cried over Rin Tin Tin, when this reporter shook hands with Jack Dempsey and refused to wash his right hand for a week thereafter. The sound, old normal days of Tex, King of Tramps, who painted his monogram on a thousand boxcars and privies from Maine to California; the days of honest passion when you could pop-bottle an umpire, lay a wager whether One-Eye Connally would crash the world series. When a Senate filibuster really *was* a filibuster, *à la* Huey Long, when a few words in a Kellogg-Briand Pact were proof that war could be dismissed from mind forever, when Roger Babson was proving that prosperity was permanent, and when Joseph Stalin was a distant character whose middle name seemed to be Trotsky.

The clean-cut days when a man was a man, and you could see a six-reel Western free of women and of what we scornfully called "love stuff"; when a movie star was *expected* to have a forty-room mansion, and two swimming pools, when March fifteenth was just another day in the calendar.

In the days of normalcy you didn't flabbily sit around waiting for government to help you, but repeated with Coué every morn: "Day by day in every way I'm getting better and better." Indecency was kept in its place in the days of normalcy—the dirty books had plain covers and were slipped from hand to hand—not gaudily posted, in color, on every news stand. The days when the true movie fan argued the respective incomes of Constance Bennett and Mary Pickford and not the respective measurements of Russell and Monroe.

No, we welcome the new bunion derby and Ike's Stetson hat as he steps in the right direction, back to the days of glory; and if the doc says the old ticker and the blood pressure will stand it, we're off to join the procession.

EAU DE COLOGNE AND A
USED STABLE

[*March 17, 1953*]

Since it is our daily duty to ponder matters currently agitating the public and governmental mind, we hereby consider the matter of chile con carne. The chile bowl has been elevated to the rank of "issue" because of my colleague Costello, CBS White House correspondent.

He made the mistake of giving President Eisenhower's personal recipe for chile over the electric radio; movement around this news office has been a bit difficult ever since because of the piles of letters requesting copies.

Our own interest, as befitting a pundit, lies in the politico-sociological implications of this matter; and it is quite apparent to any shrewd observer that this is a two-edged sword. As the greatest living authority on chile—a Texan, naturally—has put it in his basic work on the subject, *four* things temporal are held inviolate in Texas: women, states' rights, a cattle brand, and chile. While the President's passion for chile con carne may go a long way to hold the Lone Star State in the Republican fold, even should Ike *not* get them the off-shore oil, still there is political dynamite in Eisenhower's chile bowl. The criticisms of his recipe as so far expressed—that he should use tomatoes, that he should *not* use that flour-and-water paste—these criticisms are as nothing to what may be expected once the word gets around Texas that Eisenhower sometimes uses ground round steak in the pot. My aforementioned authority, Mr. Joe Cooper, author of the basic work entitled *With or Without Beans*, includes therein a full-page drawing with the caption, in heavy black lines: "Only barbarians and Yankees make it with ground meat."

Ike, however, has at least a small out; he can reassure Texans that he often does use chuck meat and on the lean side. And if he will casually let it be known that he tries to get the neck meat from an *old* critter, he may be able to hold Texas in the Union. For, as Mr. Palmer Hoyt of the *Denver Post* is quoted in the Cooper volume: "Not only will the old ox plow the straightest furrow, but he also will give you good chili meat."

Joe Cooper, Texas newspaperman, unfortunately died

three months ago, in Dallas, just after his book was published. And thus passed one of the leading members of the F.O.R.S.C.P.—Fellows of the Red Squeezings of the Chili Pod. But his work remains immortal and should go far to restore chile to the gastronomic position Texans believe God intended it to have. Books are very often the result of some deep emotional shock or trauma; and it was seeing a television commercial that showed a family eating chile with *forks* from a *plate* that drove Mr. Cooper to his typewriter.

There are Texans who have been known to take a ship to New York in order to avoid New Jersey because of what New Jersey does to chile; but Mr. Cooper rather inclines to the other view—that there is *no* bad chile and can never be. His treatise, we think, is fair and balanced; he does not claim *everything* for chile—for example, he says that it will not make water run uphill, but it *will* stoke a locomotive to the next coal bunker.

It was Dr. Jim Dan Hill who said: "When you exhale after the first bite—and you will—if you note a pale, blue smoke, somewhat darker than a dairyman's breath in a cold, Wisconsin dawn, think nothing of it. It is the normal, internal combustion of the supercharged Mexican red pepper."

Identification by *aroma* leaves a wide range. Mr. Cooper is willing to settle for the well-known Texas conclusion: "It's bouquet should be somewhere between eau de cologne and a long-used stable."

On one matter there is no possible argument: what you drink with chile. Mr. Cooper establishes conclusively that there is no reasonable accompaniment to chile save a pot of coffee with sufficient strength to float a handful of buckshot.

ROCK 'N ROLL, EGGHEAD
STYLE

[April 6, 1953]

The great thing about the news business, they used to tell us, is that you meet such interesting people. Take our boss, for example. He has developed to a fine point the art of keeping other personalities in balance, so to speak. Take today, for example. Just before he telephoned, we had opened a letter written on the beautifully embossed stationery of a college president. The letter was an invitation to address his June graduating class, and, quote, because of your ability to analyze and report a troubled world to itself, unquote, to receive an honorary doctorate.

We hadn't had time to glance through this letter more than seventeen or eighteen times and drop a casual word about it in more than six or seven adjoining offices when that interesting man telephoned from New York. He said: "Doing a show from the White House grounds at four thirty; want you on for two minutes analyzing the Easter egg-rolling."

We dropped the receiver as though it were a burning object. Egg-rolling! A man whose advice was impatiently awaited by a host of young minds about to confront the complex civilization of our times; a man who had great Churchillian periods already rolling through his head— well, this was intolerable. Egg-rolling indeed! He couldn't do this to us; we'd see him dead before we'd accept any such preposterous assignment.

85

Well, when we got into the White House grounds it was drizzling; there were a lot of people still milling around, but only the par players were still at the sport. At first glance, the game didn't seem to have any particular rules to it; we thought the wisest course was to sit on a bench under an ash tree and study up a bit on egg-rolling, hoping somebody would yell "fore" if we were going to be disturbed.

It seems that the egg-rolling custom dates back to the days before the Civil War; the Civil War, we surmised, interrupted it, just as did World War II, and this phantasmagoria before us was the first White House enterprise in egg propulsion since 1941. The real origin of the game, or custom, was the ancient Scottish ritual of rolling oat cakes down a hill at Easter time. It didn't seem to us that eggs were any particular improvement on oat cakes. Unless the ancient Scots made them with a steam press, it hardly seems likely that oat cakes would roll any better or worse than eggs, and the egg is not what we would call a natural roller.

Consulting another source book, tucked inside our raincoat, we learned that the small fry (there's a pun in that somewhere) used to roll their eggs on the grounds of the Capitol until 1878. On Easter morning of that year, Capitol police chased them away; but American children, unlike eggs, have a lot of bounce; they immediately organized themselves into a march on the White House. The Republican President Rutherford B. Hayes had faced a good many political audiences before his election and, so we read between the lines, he knew that an egg in the hand is worth two in the beard; he let the little angels into the grounds. And except for the recent war years, they have gathered there at Easter with their rolling equipment ever since and White House gardeners have voted Democratic.

As we sat there analyzing, it seemed to us that the White House grass could have been cut a bit shorter; we'd say it was more like a fairway than a green. Of course, that rug on the East Room floor is perfectly suitable for putting practice, but most men are weak in their approach shots and you do need space for those. A surprising amount of wild onion in the lawn. The combined odors of wild onion and egg mash reminded us pleasantly of a breakfast omelet they used to make at that little place on Third Avenue.

Well, it was almost dusk by the time we had the situation analyzed. As we left, ten truckloads of men with rakes and brooms came in the gate. We thought we overheard them muttering something about "cleaning up the mess," and we were hoping none of the President's speechwriters was within earshot.

GOD, CONGRESS, AND TIME

[*April 23, 1953*]

On Sunday most of the big cities of the land will go on daylight-saving time or, as variously known, fast time or summer time; but the District of Columbia will not, not for an additional week or so, and in the interim the District residents will be having a bad time. This is because of Congress, which runs this voteless community; somewhere deep in the recesses of the Capitol a congressional committee, working by kerosene lamps, one eye on

87

the hour glass, is scratching with goose-quill pens on the bill to give the capital city daylight saving.

This takes thought, and time—slow time—because Congressmen have not forgotten those immortal words, graven on many a sundial, spoken by Senator Overton of Louisiana. In 1948 he rose to address the Senate as follows: "Standard time is God's time, the time set from the very creation of the world. Mr. President," he shouted, "this bill is radical, irreligious, iconoclastic, infidelic, agnostic, blasphemous."

You can see the fix the lawmakers are in; any suggestion that one is anti-religious is as bad as any suggestion that one is pro-Communist, and this carries, ergo, the possibility that one may be fricasseed back home, come balloting day.

Still, the bill is designed to save something—to wit, time —and the folks back home are also passionate about economy; this explains why so many committeemen are going around looking pained; they have been sitting on the horns of a dilemma, and who wants to get up an hour earlier to do that? For congressmen from a purely farm district, however, both course and conscience are clear. As Senator Langer once said in the chamber, "The farmers of North Dakota are against daylight saving time in the District of Columbia."

Ever alert to the burdens upon our lawmakers, we have hit upon a scheme to solve their dilemma, especially for those congressmen from the circulation area of the *Chicago Tribune*. All they've got to do is switch from the devil to the British—it's easy, daylight-saving time is a British plot to mix up Americans and create national disunity. And we can prove it, right from their own propaganda, a large book called the Something-or-other *Britannica*, which you

88

will find right there in the Library of Congress, entirely overlooked by the Un-American Activities Committee.

The whole socialistic scheme originated in 1907 when an Englishman named William Willett campaigned for putting the clock ahead, or putting the clock "on" as the English say in their peculiar English. In 1909 Parliament sent the daylight-saving bill to a committee; this committee sat around moving clock hands back and forth and figuring on tablecloths, and seven years later daylight saving went into effect. It took World War I to do it, however; in fact, nearly every country in Europe did it, in order to save fuel for lighting and heating. But British farmers screamed bloody murder, or maybe just bloody, and like American farmers they have done so ever since. They claimed milkers had to get up an hour earlier and work in the dark and that farm labor just stooged around for an hour in the morning, on management's time, waiting for the dew to dry on the hay and corn harvests.

In 1917 the plot took hold in the United States; Congress passed a law for national daylight-saving time, but you've got to get up even earlier in the morning to catch the farmers out, so in 1919 the law was repealed over President Wilson's veto. Since then it's been spotty around the country, some states and cities using it, some not. This is a messy situation, and nothing gets more messed up than network radio and television programming; that is why, at this season, you see so many station managers going around with the colors all chewed off their hand-painted ties.

For a while, until this town, Congress willing, joins the others, we will be broadcasting, we think, at ten p.m., which is eleven in certain Eastern cities, but still ten in others, we guess, and of course nine in the Midwest cities with no daylight savings, but apparently ten where there is. Anyway, just tune in at the usual time and if you hear what sounds like subdued screaming, you've got us.

PETS ARE UNFAIR

[May 1, 1953]

An AP story from New Mexico today makes it clear that the human being not only is standing at the crossroads but has Armageddon just behind him, the eight ball just in front of him, and the sword of Damocles hanging over his head, which, of course, is bloody but unbowed. It's high time all right-thinking citizens take time by the forelock, the bull by the horns, put their shoulder to the wheel, and do something.

This story quotes a veterinarian to the effect that people are making neurotics out of dogs. Dogs are getting peptic ulcers, just like radio vice-presidents, only it is people who give the ulcers to dogs, not advertising agencies. This vet, who ought to be prosecuted by the society for the prevention of cruelty to people, claims that dogs get nervous because their masters are nervous. He goes on to say, if the owner jumps and rushes to the door when the bell rings, then the dog will probably do the same thing.

This is preposterous; this is the current insanity of rewriting history, applied to the animal world. We can only conclude that this vet is getting in training to run for the Senate, where, no doubt, he will move the appointment of a committee of animals to investigate people. His thinking is upside down; or at any rate circular. Suppose for the sake of argument that pets are catching neuroses from people; who made people neurotic in the first place? Pets. Why, after all, is the man running to the door when the bell rings? If our own experience is any guide—and who ever heard of a commentator who disbelieved his own experiences?—he is running in order to get there ahead of his beast and prevent him from chawing another chunk out of the doorsill or the mailman.

We are contemplating writing an authoritative treatise to be entitled *Pets That have Made Me Neurotic*. It all began with a giant St. Bernard that sprawled on the sidewalk on our direct route home from school. Try to walk by him and he growled. For months we had to sneak home, round about through Perkins Woods. We are convinced that our tendency toward the parenthetical phrase can be traced right back to that.

The more we think about this New Mexico vet, the more we think he ought to be quarantined. People wake up in a startled sweat; dogs do not. This is because no dog has a traumatic history of people jumping on his chest while he is still deep in dreams.

We happen to own two horses, one canary, and a goat—though there is always some question when the feed bills arrive as to who owns whom. All these creatures are obviously paranoiac, with schizoid characteristics, but it's their own fault. They make each other neurotic. The white canary used to sing beautifully as long as he was around people. The moment we put a female canary in the next cage, he shut his mouth and has kept it shut ever since. The chestnut gelding is nervous because the bay mare bites him; this produces screams of mortal agony at night; but try to put the bay mare in another pasture next morning; the chestnut goes mad with loneliness and begs the mare to come back. He's simply a masochist and it's not our fault.

If the American family is in danger of dissolution, it's the doing of pets. Pets take sides; they usually take the side of wives and children and against the breadwinner, or, as he is rapidly becoming, the feedwinner. Take the goat. A goat will case a joint very quickly and discover who's who. If he gets loose in the house and chews up slippers, pipes, and felt hats, he knows he will get a lambasting; whereas if he eats a comic-book collection and rips up an evening dress he will get the love-and-affection treatment to make him see the error of his ways. This is why he goes on chewing up slippers, pipes, and felt hats.

Far be it from us to decide which creature wears the crown in the animal kingdom, but we know darn well who wears the cap and bells. The awful thing is we're getting used to them. But we'll make one last desperate lunge toward freedom. Anybody want to buy a goat? All right, we'll swap him for your old strait jacket.

ON PULLING RANK JUSTICE

[*May 4, 1953*]

At Valley Forge Army Hospital that small group of returned war prisoners described by official but mysterious sources as suspected converts to Communism have finally had a chance to speak their minds about the treatment they have received at home. Their opportunity was long overdue; what many persons here thought earlier is proving to be correct—that a gross injustice has been done to these soldiers by one of the most extravagant cases of low-level thinking in high-level places that we've observed in quite a long time. A group of some twenty-three returning prisoners were barred from reporters in Tokyo and flown secretly to the United States. The secrecy, of course, did what it generally does: produced intense curiosity, heightened suspicions, and a flood of conjectural stories to the effect that these young men had undergone "brain-washing"—whatever that is—at the hands of their Communist captors. One gathered from the stories that they would have to be rewashed behind closed doors before being allowed to associate with the rest of us pure and right-thinking citizenry, in whose interest, of course, they had suffered unimaginable hardships.

Some of these men in that hospital are today described as bitter beyond speech, and it seems obvious on the surface of things that few American fighting men ever had more cause to be bitter. They fought, they were captured, and they suffered, month after endless month; they had done their duty, and a lot more besides, far more than ninety-nine per cent of us are ever called upon to do. Then at last to come home and to receive not the profound gratitude of their superiors and their fellow Americans, but suspicion, to be locked up in a secret airplane, denied contact with normal American life for days; handled as though they were disloyal to the country they had just been suffering for—what a piece of business this affair has been! What a way to instill loyalty to country in any doubtful case; what a way to remove whatever psychological scars the prison life may have left upon their young minds! Surely the scar of this treatment by their own service and superiors is likely to heal as slowly as any they received

93

from their relentless Communist captors. Little wonder that the psychiatrists at Valley Forge Hospital are deeply disturbed over the handling these youngsters have received.

It is the testimony of the reporters who have now been allowed to question these men that they appear no different from the other returned men of the camps. They are at Valley Forge because of their physical illness and their bodily wounds. For some, psychological help may be required, but not one of them, we are told, is primarily a psychiatric case, and what emotional and nervous disturbance a few may show has no relation to any political opinions.

Some of these men like many others were subject to constant Communist lectures and other forms of mental and emotional pressures. One of them said he had signed a so-called "confession" that the UN was using germ warfare. At the time he signed it he was under morphine and recovering from the shock of amputation of his arm. Under coercion and threats several signed the famous Stockholm peace appeal; well, so did thousands of American civilians at home, some of them perfectly reputable people, who didn't know or didn't take the trouble to find out that it was a Communist device. The war prisoners, of course, had no means to find out anything, to hear any other news, month after month, but the one-sided versions they got from their captors. Some of them inserted praise of their prison treatment in their letters home because they were told that if they did, their letters would really be delivered. Which of us, weighing the alternatives these boys forcibly faced day after day, can know that he would not have performed these meaningless gestures?

From such evidence as this came the preposterous conclusions about "brain-washing" and suspected disloyalty.

94

It seems obvious that somebody in a high place could use a little brain-washing himself, if those who do the scrubbing can find enough material to work on.

THEY WENT THAT-A-WAVE
LENGTH

[*May 26, 1953*]

It doesn't happen very often, thank goodness, but every now and then the run of news in Washington fails to turn up a single item a pundit can deplore, view with alarm, or fashion into a what's-the-world-coming-to commentary. For some reason, entirely beyond us, when Washington fails in this, it is the state of Texas that comes through, nine times out of ten; and it is Texas that has saved us in the nick of time today, with a development that is clearly number-three category—what's-the-world-coming to.

You can't keep a good industry down, as they say over in the Chamber of Commerce, and when we read the other day that transit radio—in busses and streetcars—was declining around the country, we were confident it would pop up in some other form. Sure enough, thanks to Texas, it has. It is about to rescue the last victim of quiet and the subversive forces of solitude—the lonesome cowboy; hereafter, if he wishes, radio music, news, and drama will accompany him down the trail, be it Santa Fe, Oregon, or Lonesome Pine. He can have, so help us Harry Carey, a portable radio built into his saddle.

In case you think we are pulling your leg, chaps, boots,

spurs, and all, we refer you to that favorite light reading of corral and bunkhouse, the *Wall Street Journal*. There it is in bold, eight-point type, a dispatch from San Angelo, Texas, which says the Leddy Boot and Saddle Shop is offering the new Cadillac-type saddle for sale, with a built-in Motorola. The control panel is made of tooled leather, with dial and volume numbers stamped in. As for the batteries, they go in matching saddle pockets, one on each side, of the horse, that is, and the antenna is looped and sewn under the saddle skirts; price, three hundred twenty smoleros, as they used to say in Texas, when Hopalong was only in book form. However, if you happen to be a cowboy who owns a little ol' tidelands oil well on the side, you can have a silver-embellished model for five hundred ninety-five.

Well, there it is; it does, of course, raise certain images in one's mind, which amount to problems we suspect were unforeseen by the manufacturer. Where, for example, does the cowhand pack his extra sacks of Bull Durham, to say nothing of his canvas roll of beans and hardtack? Not that we want to press this question too far; we're afraid further inquiry will reveal a neat vacuum pack compartment back of the control panel for stowing bottles of caviar and light Burgundies, for quick, one-handed snacks during the heat and excitement of the roundup. And it's certainly going to put an end to the third-reel scene where Buck dashes into the corral, slams his saddle on Old Pal, and takes the gate in a jump. By the time he gives the batteries a quick shot of the old Ad-X2 brand, extricates the antenna from the lariat and adjusts the dial for the short-wave set in the sheriff's Fort Worth penthouse, why, them rustlers would be gone so far that-a-way it would take radar to track them down.

However, we can see at least one advantage. If you've ever heard a genuine cowhand sing "Bury Me Not," which we doubt, you will realize that the canned version supplied by a remote disk jockey will be a considerable improvement on the night sounds of the lone prairie. In fact, we can see a lot of advantages the manufacturers probably haven't thought of. With a little co-operation from the nearest radio station, the cowhand, before turning in, could set the radio to produce the sound effects of pistol shots at intervals, to scare the wolves away from the calves. Or he could arrange for whinnying sounds at dawn, to bring the horse to the saddle, instead of vice versa.

One perplexing thought: how do you take a Hooper rating? You know how many cars are on the roads with radios, but how do you check the number of horses carrying your favorite daytime serial? What do horses think about daytime serials, anyway? We entirely fail to see how even a veterinarian, let alone George Gallup, could ever find out, given the well-known fact that the horse, unlike most animals, possesses no stomach muscles permitting regurgitation.

THE CAREFUL SCRAWL OF CHAOS

[June 9, 1953]

Even here in the Eastern seaboard states the word *tornado* has taken the big type in the headlines away from the word *truce;* and in the upper Midwest where this reporter has spent the last two days, nobody talks about

97

very much else. It is the excited query of the children, the ice-breaker between strangers in plane or day coach, and the vein of reminiscence among the old. A cool, pleasant springlike June lies upon that rolling land; the corn in Iowa is ankle-high and green, and its serried rows as far as the eye can follow appear like narrow ribbing holding the curving side of the world together. The Midwest never looked more beautiful or bountiful, but the evil presence is everywhere. From the train you see the little knots of men standing before the village bank and you know instinctively how their conversation runs. No land in the world is safer from man-made troubles than this Mississippi Valley; and nature is nearly always friendly, as witness the opulent natural richness everywhere. There are the occasional blizzards, but men are used to those, know what to do, and there is generally good warning. The tornado gives no real alarm in advance, follows no predictable course, and, unlike the blizzard, will take the child in his crib as easily as the father hunting the cattle in the field.

Midwesterners are sure this is a record freakish year; despite the disclaimers of the meteorologists, much street-corner and front-porch conversation firmly puts the blame upon the atomic tests out West. Many will never believe anything else. Tornadoes grow out of otherwise normal storms. One struck Sunday night in the quiet Iowa college town where this reporter was sleeping in a great many-gabled, old-fashioned house. And to one long absent from the region, the ferocity of the Midwestern summer storm is a stunning revelation. The house quavers and groans, shutters crack like pistol shots, and a whole room is drenched before one can leap out of bed. The thunder rolls and echoes across the dark prairies, and through the lashing of the rain you hear the distant sound of the locomotive whistle like a foghorn in a raging sea. Suddenly all is quiet and the nightbirds, mysteriously alive, are immediately in song. In the morning you find the sun hot, the grass already dry; the whole sky is an innocent blue, and only the men with the trucks methodically heaving up enormous, splintered branches of oak are there as evidence that it was not all a dream.

No real tornado there. But the kitchen workers have been listening to the early morning broadcasts; the Anderson farm up the country road, they got it and their barn is gone; at another farm a truck hurled right into the parlor; the breakfast talk in Midwest homes, this month of June.

On the plane from Chicago this afternoon the pilot, well trained in what is called "public relations," even at ten thousand feet, knew what his passengers had in their minds. He descended to five thousand, veered at an angle, and obligingly advised us to look just to the left. The Ohio land looked serene, well ordered, and it took a moment to detect the traces. Then beside a road you noticed a kind of tan-colored smear, circled now by cars. The smear was the spot where a farmhouse had stood a few hours before. Then the green mass of the near-by forest; where the funnel had moved through, you saw the path of fallen trunks; then the funnel had moved across a wide green pasture; there you saw the precise pattern of the wind, white scarifications, circular, in perfect proportion, a chain of even, careful whorls or loops, as if a child, using white ink on green paper, had been practicing an old-fashioned lesson in penmanship, Palmer method.

THE GOPHERS AND THE GOP

[*June 11, 1953*]

The President was talking things over last night with North Dakota Republicans in the town of Minot, the Magic City. It would have pleasured this reporter to have been present at the meeting in the Leland Hotel on Main Street, if only to see if the kid selling the *Daily News* on that corner does any better than I did there at the age of twelve or so. But chiefly to see if the President has figured out North Dakota Republicans. They take a little figuring. They frequently vote Democratic and without a qualm; they keep a Republican like Senator Langer a lifetime, though he still often votes and talks like a New Dealer. They are Republicans because they are instinctively conservative, like to work for themselves, not others; because they are predominantly middle-class, have few tycoons, and very little working proletariat, so called. They want to be conservative Republican, but have a long history of third-party rebellions; for a number of years now they have been getting rich, but they still bear a slight resentment against the "big interests," so called. The reason for this strange pattern is simply that while they are rugged individualists, they have also been very ragged individualists and the memories have not yet died.

The President today stood beside the immense new Garrison Dam on the Missouri and told the crowd that the federal government must build such things in partnership with local government. It was a wise line to take; it would have been a mistake for him to deride such things as federal boondoggling to attack the New Deal. For a whole history of reasons.

Bismarck was dedicated as the state capitol in '89; a crowd of wind-burned farmers—the immigrants solicited in northern Europe by the railroads in order to make the roads pay—stood in their buggies and buckboards. The railroad men had picked Bismarck for the capital and they made most of the speeches. Nobody paid much attention to a bearded man who made a halting wet-blanket kind of speech. He was a government geologist who had been poking about in the soil and fossils of the region. He told them not to lay out the townships in simple squares as the railroad and other interests had done, but to plan along the streams; grain farming would do well in the eastern portion, he said; it would be hazardous in the center, and the buffalo grass must be left intact for cattle-raising in the western portion; for he knew from the fossils that there would be years of rain, then years of terrible drought. But no one paid attention. He was just a crackpot scientist; a long-hair.

Like a gold rush the Dakota wheat rush was on. There were some years of farmers' revolts against railroad rate-fixing, against crooked grain-elevator companies and the eastern flour mills, establishing a political tradition of rebellion; but on the whole, things went well. Then in the twenties the prophecy of the fossils came true; crops curled and died, the sun was like brass, the buffalo grass had been plowed under and the hot winds simply blew the soil away; year after year the land turned gray and only thistles and locusts survived in the ditches. Farms by thousands were left to the weeds, and exhausted men grew old as you watched, and died of broken hearts and hopes. No help came from Washington or anywhere else. Until

101

WEST BEND PUBLIC LIBRARY

the New Deal. Federal money and projects were poured into this desert and there was a time when more than half the state lived on federal work relief; but it pulled them through; then came the great new federal dams, the tree belts, the new seed and soil techniques and, partly as a result of these things, the rains came back. North Dakota is today green and lush, and its farmers drive big shiny sedans.

Maybe theirs is a very special case; but those terrible years left a scar in every man's memory. And that is why political oratory must be carefully considered in North Dakota. The old clichés, like boondoggling, creeping socialism, do-goodism, aren't so effective in those little towns. Men can forget quite a lot, behind the wheel of a brand-new sedan; but not everything.

IT WAS ONLY A LITTLE BITTY HOLOCAUST

[June 16, 1953]

Back in the thirties the gifted American novelist John Steinbeck published his unforgettable *Grapes of Wrath*, about the tattered Okie invasion of California. The indignant city fathers in one large California community held a public burning of the two or three copies they could find in the bookstores. Did this action save the city from dangerous thoughts? It did not. In fact, within a week the publishers in New York had a couple of hundred orders for the novel from that California community, a good many requesting it be mailed in a plain wrapper.

The moral of the story is that if you want to suppress

something, don't advertise it, and particularly don't advertise it with a bonfire. The gaudiest neon sign can't compete with naked flames for drawing-power.

Now, this is not a particularly high-minded reason for opposing book-burning—there are much higher ones—but it is one of the reasons why book-burning doesn't even serve the purpose of the burners, to say nothing of everybody who likes to read and believes in his own power to close the book before the book closes his mind.

This Capital City right now is engaged in one of its periodic scenes of high comedy as everybody rushes around asking everybody else: "Who dood it?" meaning: whom was the President talking about in his attack on "book-burners"? Yesterday McCarthy sounded as if he was sure the President meant McCarthy; today he says the President couldn't have meant him. Democrats gleefully point out that what conspicuous book-burning has gone on recently was done by the President's own State Department; the head of the State Department, Mr. Dulles, looks solemn and says in effect it was just a little fire; only eleven books in the Department's overseas libraries were actually burned after all. Mr. Dulles apparently would rather have all those printed words on the Department index buried in dank cellars or maybe eaten, if not by the writers, then by the librarians.

This whole business of suppressing so called "controversial" books in government libraries has now reached the hysterical or laughing-while-crying stage. It appears that some of his minions have now jerked one of Mr. Dulles's own books from the shelves, as a contaminated vessel, and among Washington reporters the current cause for hilarity is the suppression of a book called *Washington Witch Hunt*, written years ago by the highly conservative Bert

Andrews, who helped put Alger Hiss in jail. Another of the authors is Mr. Edgar Snow, who is now in the remarkable position of being blacklisted by both free America and Communist Russia. Mr. Snow's material in book form is suppressed while the same material in the arch-conservative *Saturday Evening Post* is allowed to circulate freely in the libraries. And Snow points out that if his writings on China must be suppressed, then so must the State Department's official White Paper, and the official U.S. Army history of the China war theater, which are even rougher on Chiang Kai-shek than he was.

There's no particular reason why taxpayer's money should be used to buy and circulate books by definite, proved Communist party members, but once you go past that definable limit, you're in a free-for-all, where any number can play, there are no rules, no umpire, and all is wild, wild confusion. That's where we are now. We are also in the position where our much vaunted moral leadership in the free world is collapsing around our blushing ears as half the free world laughs at our behavior; and as the Germans, who identify book-burning with Hitler, get scared and contemptuous and suddenly aren't impressed any more with our years of effort to teach them democracy and individual liberty.

The President said something else in that Dartmouth speech. He advised the graduates to have fun in life. They'd better not seek it in American political life. The fun has gone out of that. The humor is gone. We doubt very much that the political satires of even Will Rogers would be published today. He'd be accused of undermining the parliamentary institution. The country is not in danger of government by fascists or communists; it's in danger of government by stuffed shirts.

WHY DID THEY FIGHT?

[July 27, 1953]

Those of us comfortably distant from the sweat and the muck and the fear of the battle zone are trying to cast up the long-range accounts of this bitter police-action war. The achievements of this war may be very great indeed, but they lie in the realm of what might have been had not we fought. That is comfort for governments, conscious of where the stream of history was flowing; but it is, no doubt, cold comfort for the families who now confront an empty chair at the dinner table. They too are conscious of what might have been.

There were many mysteries in this Korean war. To this reporter the greatest mystery is the human puzzle of what made American youngsters fight so hard, so long, and so well in this kind of war. There have been armies that fought well only for loot; there was none of that in Korea; armies that fought well only for glory and victory; there was little of that in Korea; armies that fought well only when their homeland was invaded; this was not true of the Korean war; armies that fought well when the national passion was aroused, when everyone was involved; this was not the case this time; and armies that fought as crusaders out of burning moral or religious zeal; but thousands who fought so well in Korea had only the dimmest conception of what United Nations and collective security are all about, and had therefore no compelling belief.

But they fought, they endured, they stayed to the bitter

end; they fought a war they did not particularly believe in, to the armistice they have little faith in; and they will fight again, automatically and instantly, if the armistice should fail. They have done all this without requiring the moral exhortations and whippings of any political commissars; they have bled and died in the mud and the stones of that bleak and incomprehensible land, in full knowledge that half their countrymen at home were too bored with it all to give the daily casualty lists a second glance; in full knowledge that while they were living the worst life they had ever known, millions of their countrymen, and from the same cause, were living the best, most prosperous life they had ever known. They saw the emaciated Korean children around them and, knowing their countrymen showed little interest in contributing, they gave millions from their own paltry pay-checks; they knew it was too much effort for many of their countrymen to walk to the nearest blood-donation center, so they gave their own blood to their wounded comrades. And they fought on in no particular bitterness that all this was so.

They fought right ahead at the time military men of great authority were publicly arguing that they were being handled tragically wrong; they fought right ahead while politicians divided their countrymen about the very purpose of their fight, telling them that their wounds and aches were all in vain. And they fought ahead knowing that while allied nations were cheering them on, allied soldiers were not coming to help them in any numbers.

Why have these youths behaved so magnificently? It was true, as many said, that rotation was a substitute for victory in this war. But that was not all the answer. The rest of it lies very deep in the heart and tissues of this American life, and none among us can unravel all the threads of it. It has to do with their parents and their teachers and their ministers; it has to do with their 4-H clubs, their scout troops, their neighborhood centers; it has to do with the sense of belonging to a team, with the honor of upholding it, the dishonor of letting it down . . . but it also has to do with their implicit, unreasoned belief in their country, and their natural belief in themselves as individual men upon the earth.

Whatever is responsible, their behavior in this undefinable, unrewarded war outmatches, it seems to me, the behavior of those Americans who fought the definable wars of certainty and victory. For this is a new thing in the American story; and for those of us who write the story, as they live it, this is a thing to be put down with respect and some humility.

DUNG—OUT

[*July 30, 1953*]

The reason people take vacations is to rest up from all the work involved getting ready to take a vacation. I don't know if this is true of congressmen, but it's true of me. My own system of logistics is just to let all the material, or stuff, pile up in the office, then back the car to the nearest window and shovel it out—the books, boots, new parts for the garden tractor, matting for the dock, sacks of nails, horse feed, fertilizer, grass seed—stuff like that. It doesn't look well in a business office, and I am glad Father is not around to see it. He was raised on a farm and has a great respect for offices, and I know perfectly well what he would say. He would say: "Son, when are you going to dung out?"

The main trouble is the paper. The newspapers, magazines, clippings, letters, hand-outs, congressional speeches, bank statements, invoices, memos, or meemos, and undecipherable scribbled notes to myself. The thing is, I am the roll-top, pigeon-hole type character living in the modern, flat-top era. I did try the in and out basket system once, but the baskets disappeared, and it wasn't till late spring, when somebody leaned on the pile, that we found them again. The whole thing is pretty discouraging and it's becoming clear that with habits like these, I shall never get to be a vice-president like John Charles Daly.

Well, anyway, here I am, going off Saturday for a month, and here are all these clippings and notes, every one of which must have some reason for being there. When they were stuck there, the reason was known to both God and me, but now only God knows. They all contained the germ of some idea, but I'm blessed if I know what to do with them now, except to gather them up and sort of spray them into the microphone. Then I can go off with a light heart, clear head, and tidied-up conscience.

Let's see; here's a note from a constituent urging me to bring the dictionary up to date with some new words to describe modern life, such as *bombophobia*, morbid fear of being atomized. I think I'll turn that over to the Alsop brothers; they were first in this field with *Megadeaths*, meaning ten million deaths from an atomic-bomb strike. Here's a letter from a woman asking if I was the man she screamed at in Palm Beach when she won ninety dollars gambling. Not possible. My career with gambling has concerned only pennies, from pitching to pinching.

An invitation to attend the moral-rearmament conference in Switzerland. I know why I saved that one. When I was a college student and knew everything, including economic determinism, I scoffed at the moral rearmament people as waffle-headed. Now that I don't know so much, their idea for saving the world seems as sensible as any other.

Here's a friendly letter from the counsel of the House subcommittee on military operations. He says I compounded an existing distortion in quoting somebody else's quotation of Congressman Riehlman on the army-overcoat case. And I did it in a broadcast criticizing the inaccuracies of others, to make it all the more embarrassing. Here's a handful of little items in the general categories of where the human race is headed and the inscrutable future of man. The Japanese are now manufacturing synthetic rice. Pepsi-Cola lets me know they are now selling ice-cold Pepsis to Eskimos. Selling like hot cakes. . . . there's a new engine for power bikes that will do three hundred miles on a gallon. . . . in the Southwest, farmers find geese eat the weeds out of the cotton fields and leave the cotton alone. There's only one unemployed bricklayer in Denmark, so all public construction projects are postponed . . . the auto-gadget people say that years after progressing beyond wire wheels, everybody wants to buy simulated wire wheels . . . the idea of the bumper was to take the blows; now people buy rubber bumpers so the blows won't show even on the bumper. A New York restaurant provides a dictating service with its meals, for busy executives who want to have their ulcers now and get it over with. Well, the time is up and there's a whole stack left. I can't bring myself to throw them away; maybe if I just leave them near the air-conditioner vent, something will happen.

ROBERT A. TAFT, MAN

[July 31, 1953]

It is a little hard to imagine the national capital without Robert Taft. The schoolmasterish figure in the steel-rimmed glasses and the careless gray suit was not only a forceful personality on this scene; he carried a special atmosphere with him, he was a kind of condition of life. Taft had become a symbol of a distinct segment of America.

He was a very large piece in the mirror of mosaic in which Americans look to see reflected their own image of the American meaning. Only great persons come to have such a meaning to millions of people, and Taft was a very great person.

There was a single-mindedness about Senator Taft, a wholeness; and it was this that made even his bitterest enemies say: "At least you know where he stands."

To many Taft seemed to symbolize a past America that was simple, good, orderly, and safe; a past that anyone who lived before the First World War can hardly help recalling with nostalgia and a vague, impossible yearning to know again. When families were large, front porches were spacious, habits were regular, property was safe, and progress was assumed as a force of nature.

Many people who disagreed with Taft's most basic policies still voted for him, out of an instinctive feeling that even for them it was important to have such a man in the Senate. The feeling, I think, was this: they saw govern-

ment grow vast and involve their lives deeply; they saw
their country plunging into new and strange enterprises
in a desperate attempt to control a world in revolutionary
turmoil. They did not really know how things could otherwise be done, but they were a little frightened, and to them
Senator Taft seemed a kind of safety device, a brake; and
intuitively they wanted him there as an anchor to wind-
ward.

His deepest concern and learning lay in the field of our
domestic, internal affairs; and because of his respect for
facts, this concern drove him into domestic positions that
were liberal and progressive in the highest sense of the
terms—often to the confusion of extreme conservatives,
who regarded him as one of their own.

Because he had not made foreign affairs the same deep
concern, because the compulsions of the outside world so
often interrupted the pursuit of domestic progress, he felt
alien to many grave questions of foreign affairs. He had,
one almost felt, a resentment about them, a wish that they
would go away, so that we could all get on with the business of life in America.

Robert Taft seemed almost the last of a valuable vanishing breed of politician—the men like Webster and Clay
who dedicated their lives to government itself, to whom
the art of politics was a high art, the conduct of government a social science, to be mastered as scholar and carried
on with a scientist's devotion. To him the Senate was a
temple, not to be entered merely to boost a law practice
or to enjoy the sound of one's voice. To him the oppor-
tunist approach to politics was almost a sacrilege.

In politics what separates the men from the boys is this:
the boys want merely to be a part of the life; the men
want power, the highest possible power, and not to be

111

something but to do something; to change the national life as they believe it should be changed. That is why a hush settled on the Senate today. A man had died.

There were two Robert Tafts. The public Taft was austere, insistent, humorless, and sometimes harsh. The private Taft was startlingly different. He was mellow, relaxed, kindly, inclined at times to laugh at himself; and his charm could melt his most guarded enemy. For many here the visual memory they will longest retain is the picture of Robert Taft carefully wheeling his invalid wife through the crowd at some social function. There was no showmanship in this; he was devoid of that. It was simply the picture of a husband caring for his wife in sickness as in health as he had pledged himself to do. In his public and personal life Robert Taft never lightly gave his word or his affection and never lightly took them away.

ANARCHIST RETURNED

[August 31, 1953]

This reporter resumes tonight his occupancy of these four minutes of eternal time after a month's vacation from audible thinking, high-, low-, or middle-brow. Custom demands that I open by saying I'm glad to be back, but that will have to wait a day or two. Any broadcaster who can make people believe he's glad to return to work in the city of Washington on the hottest day of the year is qualified to run for Congress and ought to do so. Personally, I think I'll aim for much higher office, the highest, in fact. I've discovered I have one qualification for the job, at least—a love of long vacations.

The President and I have had quite a lot in common these past weeks, though he's been several thousand feet up and I several hundred only; and he's been associating with rainbow trout in a Colorado river and I with bluegills in Carter's Run. We've both been making the same fundamental mistake, trying to combine a holiday with work. He's been spending a couple of hours every morning dealing with such matters as the Far East conference, the federal budget, the Russian H-bomb, then slipping off to golf course or trout stream. I have been spending a couple of hours every morning dealing with such matters as fertilizer-distribution, fireplace-cementing, and weed-spraying, then slipping into the one easy chair of the shack—unless the small fry beat me to it, that is. In the matter of our common afflictions, however, I was one up on the President. His bad elbow interfered with his golf and his fly-casting, whereas my bad back only interfered with my cementing, spraying, et cetera; it didn't bother my easy-chair sitting at all.

As a citizen and taxpayer I have been hoping our vacation parallel does not extend to the psychological effect of the quiet holiday among quiet hills and pleasant waters —because the White House should be the last place for any tendencies toward anarchy. My own tendency toward anarchy is pretty pronounced right now, but will wear off in a few days' immersion in the spouting fountains of government and politics. I will get back to normalcy as soon as I convince myself again that it's not abnormalcy I'm getting back to. (I go through this after every peaceful holiday and you'll just have to be patient.) My annual yen toward anarchy takes the form of an uncanny, maybe senseless, but strong wish that all governments would just stop governing, all politicians just stop politicking; a weird feeling that if they would, everything would be all right; my neighbor would still plow his corn, the big hickory would still creak in the night wind, the frogs still sing in the pond, and somehow the peace of back-country Virginia would enter into the minds of men and all would be well.

It has to do, I suppose, with a person's sense of reality. Eleven months of the year for me reality is the federal budget, the Korean conference, the Russian H-bomb; and it seems frightening, incomprehensible, that millions of Americans can just go about their corn-plowing apparently unconcerned that these realities are thundering down the track in their direction.

And then one month of the year I lean on the fence and watch the neighbor plow. The fat white clouds drift and the great buzzards wheel; the pastures grow green, then brown, the frogs sing, and the hickory creaks in the night. This is reality; and the radio news, the newspaper headlines, are queer signals from outer space, unrelated, having to do with some remote race and planet. I suppose such feelings should disturb me; the truth is they comfort. And I have a small suspicion they come to a President sometimes too and comfort him.

But of course many can plow and only one can be President. So I would wish him a drop or two of this narcotic, peace, but not too much. Anyway, every man knows his own limit, and I've reached mine for now.

THE WEARY WISDOM OF
DR. KINSEY

[September 2, 1953]

It was a little off our professional beat, but this noon we covered a luncheon lecture on the behavior of females by the noted Dr. Kinsey. Washington is empty of both President and Congress right now, politics is in the doldrums, which probably explains the enormous turnout for the Women's National Press Club presentation of the famous sex statistician. Probably, but with Kinseyian scientific caution we wouldn't call it a certainty.

We noticed Dr. Kinsey getting out of his taxi at the Mayflower; they had to hire the big ballroom, incidentally. He walks with a heavy, weary tread; it can't be the weight of years because he's only fifty-nine, so maybe it's the weight of knowledge he carries around. In any case, acquaintance with thousands of people's sex secrets hasn't left him with sprightly tread exactly.

Women were a bit slow filtering into the ballroom, but the few men present were a lot slower. Cornelia Otis Skinner sat up, bright and beautiful, at the head table, and a thought struck us: if this keeps up, she will be identified one day not as a superb actress but as the woman who admits she was interviewed by Kinsey and doesn't give a darn who knows it. But no doubt the theater's loss would be sociology's gain. The President's sister-in-law sat up there too, looking grave and semiofficial. Constance Bennett was present looking just like Constance Bennett.

Justice Holmes once made a cutting little remark, *sotto voce*, at a dinner party. He said: "Washington is full of great men, and the women they married when they were very young." But looking around that ballroom today, we had the cheerful feeling that the situation has changed a lot; maybe reversed, for that matter.

There were some editors present whose editorial columns had rather deplored the new Kinsey report, and whose news columns played up every last detail of it. We noticed almost everybody had a detached scientific look on his face, and after he had been hearing Kinsey for a while, the expression came natural. Statistically and scientifically, it may be possible to doubt the validity of his reports, but it was pretty hard to doubt the validity of the doctor's faith that what he is doing is right and necessary and good for our society. He made some references to Galileo, Newton, and Copernicus, and the ignorant, institutionalized opposition they ran into; some in the audience seemed to think Kinsey was comparing himself with those titans of science, but we gathered he was just comparing the phenomena. When Kinsey had finished, we still had two disturbing questions in our mind. What is the effect on immature teen-agers who read all this evidence of how their elders really behave? And since he admits his six thousand interviewees do not constitute a true cross-section of the female population, how can you draw from them valid conclusions and generalizations?

On one thing though, the thing that draws out the impassioned evangelist in Kinsey, he was convincing. And that is the futility—indeed, the ignorant cruelty—of innumerable state laws purporting to govern the private behavior of human individuals. On this matter Kinsey is surely biology's angry man, if not God's. It is something, after all, to realize that, strictly speaking, ninety-five per cent of all men and eighty-five per cent of all women could be sent to jail under one law or another for their natural human behavior. Something to realize that some of these laws were designed to protect customs going back to the ancient Hittites, which were based on nothing more than superstition then. Something to realize there are acts for which some states provide no penalty at all, but for which other states provide life imprisonment. You got the frightened feeling we're all living in a legal jungle in the midst of darkest America. Well, it was all pretty sobering, and enlightening, too. Still, we didn't feel quite ready to revise the old saying and make it read: "All I know about women I learned from him."

THE COMPLETE POLITICAL MAN

[September 29, 1953]

In the Europe now trying to find a new base for its ancient civilization, there have been four great men of the continent, these last few years: Adenauer and Reuter of Germany, de Gasperi of Italy, Monnet of France. Three remain; Ernst Reuter died today. It was my privilege two or three times to sit before this man, the Lord Mayor of Berlin, city without a country. It was only a week ago tonight that millions of Americans saw him on the *See It Now* television picture of Berlin; the bulky, shapeless man with the heavy, owlish face, clambering around the ruins of the old Reichstag, talking about his city, his people, the

Communists, and the future. Perhaps those millions caught, in that moment, something of the essence of this man—his complete serenity. Reuter had seen it all; suffered it all. All the wounds of twentieth-century Europe in torment he had felt on his body and in his mind; and he had no fear any more.

In this country we prize political consistency; Europe does not, for Europe has been convulsed with violent change too often. Here we penalize and shun any political figure who has ever been a Communist, even in his youth; in Europe this would be an absurdity, a wicked waste of talent, because so very many of the very finest were once revolutionaries.

Reuter had been through it all. He was, at the beginning, a scholar of the classics. He was first a Social Democrat, and his conservative parents cut him off from all aid; he was a young pacifist, but ended up in the Kaiser's army; he was wounded, he was captured by the Czar's soldiers, he was a slave worker in the coal mines of Russia; he welcomed the Bolshevik Revolution, knew both Lenin and Stalin, became later Secretary-General of the German Communist Party. Lenin had called Reuter "brilliant but strong-willed, a little too independent." He was indeed, and he soon rebelled against Moscow orders, quit the party, never to return; and when the great test of Berlin's endurance came, five years ago, it was his sure knowledge of the Russian mentality, as much as anything, that forced the Russians to their most dramatic postwar defeat and set in motion the train of events leading to the powerful Germany we see today rising before our eyes.

When Hitler came to power, Reuter spent two more years of his life in a concentration camp; the London City Council got him out, and he spent the years of the last war in Ankara, as adviser to the Turkish Government on its transportation system. In this work he became an expert, and it was his command of the practical problems of traffic and logistics that also made considerable difference when the test of Berlin began.

The test, of course, was the Russian blockade of '48 and '49, the last strong-arm move the Russians have tried in postwar Europe. The Russians did this, took this risk of possible war, for one supreme reason—to force the Americans, British, and French to abandon their move to form a West German government, which, the Russians feared, and with some clairvoyance, would become one day the hard fist of an alliance hostile to them. Reuter begged the Allies not to give in, and he found a natural ally in General Lucius Clay. Reuter had anticipated the blockade; he was ready with lists of supplies, quantity estimates, time schedules, and the skeleton of an operating plan for overcoming the blockade by airplane.

Two and a half million Berliners required at least four thousand tons of fuel and food a day to survive. It began with a hundred American C-47's a day and two hundred and fifty tons; in six months the daily haul was well beyond the four-thousand-ton minimum, by spring it reached thirteen thousand, far above the pre-blockade figures for rail and water transport, and the Russians gave up. The week the Russians quit, the Germans were ready with their new constitution; in that, too, Ernst Reuter had played a big part.

He is, in fact, inextricably bound up with the whole rise of the new, democratic Germany. Reuter was the complete political man; he supported his friends, he knew his enemy—and he was beyond fear.

SPYROS, HE SLEEPS GOOD

[*October 1, 1953*]

Did you ever get that sudden feeling you are stuck in an old-fashioned rut with the world passing you by? Well, I was reading a publicity release from the Twentieth-Century Fox movie studios today and I got the feeling. It was all about a movie called *The Robe* and Cinema-Scope. The picture opened in Washington tonight with all the glamorous folk they could round up from the suburbs and Embassy Row. Anyway, the release kept saying: "It does not require use of glasses," exclamation mark. It was right there I got that feeling, because I could have sworn that the last time I dropped into a movie Mary Pickford looked just as clear and bright in her pigtails, and I wasn't wearing any spectacles.

I had such a panicky feeling about this that I hurried right over to the Mayflower to have lunch with Mr. Spyros Skouras, who seems to have replaced Mr. Fox as head of those studios. There were a lot of people, chandeliers, flowers, food, and a tiny aging Frenchman with a goatee. He was Professor Chretien, who invented the lenses for the CinemaScope process and is the new idol of Hollywood, so to speak. The funny thing is that he invented it twenty-five years ago, which gave me the comforting thought that maybe other people are a little slow on the uptake, too. It said in the release that the depression, then the war, then the materials shortage, had delayed the use of his process; but I guess Mr. Skouras hadn't read the release, because from the way he put it, Hollywood didn't start chasing the professor until last year, when things got a bit desperate, what with television.

Mr. Skouras was a little late in arriving at the lunch; he didn't really arrive, he erupted. Maybe you've seen a bull charge into the bullring and stand there a moment, pawing and swinging his head. Mr. Skouras swung his head a moment, then uttered a great bellow and charged down upon the professor, embracing him so violently that the professor almost fainted. I suppose you could call Mr. Skouras's feeling love at second sight.

Then Mr. Skouras plowed a wide furrow through the rest of us, over to the food, and pretty soon we were all sitting around the table. Mr. Skouras said: "Nice and quiet in Washington, huh, no excitement?" A movie critic said there was plenty of excitement. Imagine, he said, appointing a California politician to be Chief Justice. This resulted in a violent argument between two movie critics about Governor Warren. Mr. Skouras looked puzzled. Finally he said: "I guess you don't believe in democracy, hah?" The first critic lit into Mr. Skouras about the movies. He said: "Why, anybody in the movies with any education is sunk; he's just a dope in Hollywood." Mr. Skouras looked puzzled again. "I don't get," he said. "Say that line again, please?" The critic said: "Now, take that picture *The Scoutmaster*. You think you made a good picture there?" Mr. Skouras gave a mournful answer and added: "Don't quote me, please, I lose my job." The critic said another Skouras picture, however, was good. Mr. Skouras leaped in his seat. "Good, you say! Was wonderful!" The critic said firmly: "You and I have different vocabularies."

Mr. Skouras got up and gave a moving little speech. He described how his technicians first told him about the

Chretien lenses. "Never in my life I sleep good," he said. "That night I sleep so happy and I dream such big dreams —in Technicolor." Then it turns out the British have an option on the invention and he doesn't sleep so good again. But then the British waive their option and he sleeps good some more. It was all very enlightening, but it stirred up a few vague thoughts. Maybe pretty soon families won't argue about what they'll see or hear, but about what kind: AM or FM radio, plain or color television, 3-D, Cinerama or CinemaScope movies. It occurred to me that perhaps this is the ultimate triumph of technique over substance, of matter over mind.

Anyway, just as soon as I've caught up with that new novel called *Gone with the Wind* I'm going to give it a little real thought.

THE COST ACCOUNTING OF COHN AND SCHINE

[*October 8, 1953*]

You will remember the fascinating story of Cohn and Schine, the travels thereof. The two investigators for Senator McCarthy, who did Europe in seventeen days last spring, investigating not only possible Communists, but "waste and mismanagement" in our government information services.

The sequel is now available, courtesy of the *Baltimore Sun*, which informs us that the two young gentlemen spent $2,540 of federal funds in Europe, exclusive of their transportation, which was furnished by military planes. This works out at $74 a day for each man, and the tab is being picked up by Mr. Stassen's foreign operations administration. Mr. Stassen's own employees, while traveling, are allowed only $6 to $12 a day; but what makes it doubly interesting is that, according to Mr. Cohn, he and Mr. Schine spent more of their own money than they spent of the taxpayers'. So, then, each of them, at a rock-bottom estimate, managed to spend $150 a day, exclusive of transportation.

Now, this is not unusual. I have seen men get through that much in a day. It takes planning, energy, and stamina, but it can be done. The real test of a man's genius, however, comes when he makes out his expense account. As Mr. Bob Casey of the *Chicago Daily News*, a traveler himself, writes in one of his books: "There is a neat balance in the properly prepared expense account. The fine judgment required to arrive at it is a gift that has never been promiscuously distributed."

If Cohn and Schine had read Mr. Casey's book—I have a copy only slightly charred they could have borrowed—or if they had listened to some foreign correspondents instead of talking to them, they could have picked up a few of the finer points and avoided this fuss. The first lesson is that the old standard item "miscellaneous" doesn't work any more. It has been replaced by dozens of substitutes. "Car hire and waiting time, share of," is preferred by some of the better expense-account reporters, though "payments, private informants" is also a favorite and would have suited the Cohn-Schine needs admirably. (It lends an air of mystery, and the home office doesn't expect you to provide the names.)

As with most courses of study, however, Cohn and

Schine really should start with the basic works on the subject. They could learn much from the career of Mr. Junius Wood, who used to report Russia. When the home-office auditors itemized his food bills, they said: "What makes you think we will pass a bill for caviar for breakfast?" and Mr. Wood simply answered: "Eggs is eggs."

There was a *Baltimore Sun* correspondent who knew how much he had spent, but even by the wildest contrivances his itemization left him far short. At dawn over his fifth pot of black coffee, he gave up and inserted: "Robbed on boat, $1,000."

The little things can add up. During the Wilkie campaign, reporters went with the candidate to a Will Rogers memorial service. Mr. Fred Pasley's expense account carried the item: "White gloves for service, $2.00."

Perhaps the classic lesson in the art of the expense account is the story of Mr. Gene Fowler's Alaskan expedition by dog team to find some lost fliers. Somehow his itemized account was short. He recalled that his lead dog, Pogo, had died in the traces. His home office read in his expense account: "Flowers for bereaved bitch, $60."

Maybe all these instructive precedents come too late for Cohn and Schine. In that case I recommend they adopt the attitude of Lord Northcliffe's reporter in Russia, who itemized "One fur coat." Later in London, Northcliffe demanded he surrender the coat as company property. He had to go buy one in Bond Street at a fearful cost. On his next trip home Northcliffe said: "Russian winters must be milder. I see you don't have a fur coat on your expense account this time." The reporter answered: "Sir, you may not see it, but it's there!"

BACKWARDS INTO THE FRAY

[*October 15, 1953*]

An organization in Colorado known as the Institute of Humanics—H-u-m-a-n-i-c-s—is offering a thousand-dollar reward, I quote, "to the individualist who will spend the money in the most novel and creative way." They warn that anybody thinking in terms of pleasing the institute or society in general cannot qualify.

This lets me in. My plan will outrage half of American society and appall the institute. To begin with, I will use the thousand dollars to start another institute. I realize this will shock the Colorada people because there is nothing less original in American life than another organization. I would do the whole job alone, but the money would run out too fast; so I will take the thousand to incorporate and get other members and other capital. My aim is simple. It is to reverse progress, before it destroys us. We will call it The American Institute of Unqualified Reaction. The motto will be: "I Refuse to be Improved."

The first people we go to work on are those who are trying to improve the language. We might start with the McCormick newspapers, which insist on spelling "night" n-i-t-e and thorough t-h-o-r-o. Or we might start with the Institute of Humanics itself, and force them to undo the ugly violence they have done to the word *humanity*. Then we move in on the advertising field, and here I predict thousands of volunteer workers will flock to our banner. (Incidentally, our banner will not say "Forward" but "Retreat!") We use the old-fashioned boycott method. We absolutely refuse to buy, use, or even mention any product that contains lanolin, chlorophyll, viratol, iridium, proto-pectins, or solinate, or any product that has been vitamin-ized, pressurized, homogenized, or hammerized. We won't even permit the authors of these terms to come clean and explain to the public what the terms mean. We fix the breakfast-food people for keeps. We buy up all existing surpluses of cereals that pop, tingle, crackle, or cackle or that jump, twitch, or quiver, or make any other kind of noise or movement. And we dump the whole load in the Atlantic Ocean, whatever the risks of underwater ex-plosion and tidal wave.

For the people who spell *heat* with two "e's," *cool* with a "K," and *stay* without the "y," there really ought to be some special form of public torture, but since our institute is against any more new gadgets in any way, shape, or form, we may have to pass up this pleasure. Generally, of course, we will not be punitive; we will use the carrot, not the stick to encourage reverse motion. We will offer prizes to encourage people to refuse. For example, to the first radio announcer who refuses to speak dramatically, we could give an album of records that produce the sweet sounds of silence. To the first auto worker to throw sand in the assembly lines where they produce the labor-saving gadgets like automatic shifts, window sprays, and dash-board clocks that consume our labor and our lives getting repaired—to such a pioneer we might award a good serviceable oxcart. To the first office efficiency expert who refuses to make any more time and motion studies of how many steps the stenographer takes going to the file cabinet or washroom, we might award an IBM-X-17 personality analyzer machine, with a sledge hammer and carte blanche.

126

We recognize that the human mind like the body cannot live on extracts, but requires bulk. We will start our own magazine, a reverse-digest, called *Expand*. It will lengthen short articles and put meat on their bones. The cover will show an old lady with her clothes on. Any hero in any detective story we print who gets himself seduced will be shot dead in the next paragraph.

Well, the field is wide; we are open to new members. Just write in, last name last, on a parchment or slate or any old thing, and we're off. As Herblock puts it, "Ankle to ankle, men, and backward into the fray!"

THE ACTION OF WORDS

[*October 16, 1953*]

B ritain's great old man of the sea, Sir Winston, has received Sweden's Nobel Prize for literature, which nobody will argue with, and which, among other things, ought to ensure the kind of audience for his forthcoming and last volume on the great war that these books should have among those who wish to understand this incredible generation.

This luminous mind of genius, Churchill, lives now and clings to political power now for only one reason: to set strong blocks of peace under our shaking world; and in a way, perhaps, it is a pity that the first international award given him should not have been the Nobel Prize for peace, with which to close the magnificent course of his life. But nobody will argue with this, and those who know Churchill know that this award for his writings will tickle the old man's vanity. For he has delighted all his life in demonstrating his genius in the odd and unexpected ways. He did not receive the classical education from which most great masters of English have arisen; he was educated to be a soldier, not a scholar. And it has been always a keen fillip to his satisfactions that he could show writers how to write, and many painters how to paint. He even took immense pleasure in his abilities as a bricklayer. Lord Halifax used to tell the story of how he sat upon Churchill's brick garden wall at Chartwell and said: "Are you sure it will hold?" Churchill was furious.

But only the uninformed about his life will think of Churchill as a politician and strategist who dabbled in writing. He never "dabbled" in anything he put his hand to. He mastered it; he made it his own. You cannot call a man who has written twenty-seven books, all excellent save his one foray into fiction, you cannot call such a man anything but a professional writer. In fact, he first came into the British consciousness, a very young man, as a writer, with his accounts of tribal battles and campaigns in India, where he served as a Lancer. He wanted to say his say, he wanted fame, and he wanted money. And he was completely ruthless in going about it in those early days. If he couldn't get to the Khyber Pass as a soldier, he got there as a correspondent; if he couldn't get to the battles of the Sudan as a correspondent, he got there as a soldier. Without scruple, he pulled wires through his mother, who pulled them through the War Ministry in London or the big publishers, and he generally got where he wanted to go, at whatever cost in popularity among his fellow officers.

The modern tradition of the glamorous war and foreign correspondent who produces books and lectures, at a fee, had its beginnings with Churchill as much as with anybody else. After his capture and escape in the Boer War, at the turn of the century, he was the golden boy of England, almost like Lindbergh here after his flight to Paris. And Churchill made the most of it. He turned out the books and the articles, he lectured his way across North America at the highest fees; he assembled his hard-won and sizable capital, and then, as he writes it, "I got married and lived happily ever after." But the prodigious life and works were just beginning.

No one can really explain genius or assign comparisons to it; but if Churchill is not the greatest writer of our time, as writer, certainly no writer has so made his words come alive in the hearts of human creatures in our time. No words have produced such action as Churchill's words. I was in France and England in 1940—those days of despair and defeat, when all that was good and decent in life seemed to lie dying in darkness; and I will always believe that it was the words of this one man, alone, that like a shower of invisible arrows caught Hitler at the final barricade; his words that sparked the ignition in the vast, cold, broken machinery of European hope and courage. Words do not exist only for themselves, but to act upon men's actions. As the *Times* puts it today, well and bravely spoken, and spoken timely, words are the most powerful thing in the world.

The library dust will never dim the shining words of Churchill. The Swedes have chosen well enough.

FRANCE, NAKED AND
ASHAMED

[*November 10, 1953*]

If I sound a little unnerved tonight, it's because I am. I stand in threat of having to abandon a personal prejudice, and a man can take just about anything easier than that. This threat is raised by a little news story hidden among the bulrushes on the inside pages of the *Herald Tribune*. It tells us that the French Government is going to cut away a lot of the traditional Gallic red tape that makes existence in France a charming hourly combat with legality.

A step like this, of course, could ruin France. Eliminate government red tape and about one out of four French breadwinners would be out of bread. Factories making scratchy pens, gummy ink, and dusty legal forms would close their doors. The French Army would be able to move, and France might even win a war, which would unsettle the whole European balance of power. Telegrams would get sent, rents and taxes would be paid, factories would start pouring out clothes and cars and gadgets; people would no longer spend all afternoon on the café terrace, because it would be possible to accomplish something with their time. It would only be a matter of time before France had comfort, convenience, efficiency, plus ulcers, heart trouble, overproduction, and suicides—in short, all the blessings of progress, and that, of course, would be the end of France as France.

The French Government sounds quite ruthless in its intention. It not only proposes to reduce the number of identity, birth, marriage, divorce, celibacy, and residential certificates a Frenchman must carry around, but proposes to eliminate the certificates of non-remarriage, non-divorce, and non-residence. They also intend to make a birth certificate extract permanently good, instead of for three months; mark you, this is tantamount to eliminating the certificate of rebirth. Personally, I doubt if any French cabinet can survive such a program; Frenchmen just won't stand for it; they would have to look in a man's eyes, instead of his papers to be sure he's alive; they would have to trust another Frenchman's word instead of documents, and a Frenchman without that fat wallet of papers in his coat pocket is going to feel naked and ashamed.

Americans in France will run out of dinnertime stories to tell about their experiences. An American's sense of accomplishment in France will be taken away from him. I recall my former colleague Leigh White, who got married in Paris after seventeen weeks of some fifty-two separate visits to the *mairie*, the police commissariat, the labor exchange, and the consulate. Marriages fashioned with such loving care as that are marriages that last; and the church leaders of France better give this whole proposal long and deep thought.

No, France will just not be France, deprived of such characters as the post-office clerks on the Riviera. Once before the war an American friend of mine in Juan-les-Pins wanted to send a telegram to his native village in Ireland. He filled out the form and handed it to the clerk, who said: "No! No such place exists." The American said it did exist. The clerk riffled through the international postal guide and did not find it. The American pleaded that he be allowed to look. After much arguing, much pointing by the clerk to the yellowed copy of the law of 1886, hanging on the wall, which forbids the public to handle the postal guide, after all this the clerk relented, and the American found the village name himself. A week later he was over in Cannes and had to send another telegram to the same village in Ireland. The clerk at Cannes also declared such a place could not exist. He also failed to find it in the international postal guide. He also pointed to the law of 1886 and argued that the American could not touch the guide himself. Finally my American friend cried out hysterically that the clerk over at Juan-les-Pins had let him handle the guide himself. So this clerk said: "Ah?"—Very well, "*Allez au Juan-les-Pins!*"

UNCOMMERCIAL COMMERCIALISM

[November 19, 1953]

G reat Britain is about ready to close its eyes, hold its patrician nose, and leap into the swirling waters of commercial television. When the British people fail to amaze and perplex you, consider yourself dead. The British were miles ahead of us on television, just as they were on jets, radar, and other gadgets. The first television show I ever saw—a superb performance of *Journey's End*—I saw in the London flat of a lean young man named Murrow. That was in the fall of 1937. When I tell my thirteen-year-old twins that I saw television three years before they were born, they exchange those covert glances which mean: "Just humor the old man."

Small Sounds in the Night

Anyway, sixteen years later the British are gingerly edging up to make the leap into advertising by electronics. As you know, they have never had commercials on their radio. At this rate, heaven knows when they will get to 3-D magazine advertisements that you cut out and look at through glasses; or perfume ads that give forth a sweet odor from scented ink. You have to realize that the British make a subtle distinction between the commercial life and commercialism. For two hundred years they were the greatest commercial nation the world ever saw and are still one of the greatest, but among proper Britons commercialism is considered vulgar. What I mean is, the world's greatest traders still insist that tradesmen come in at the kitchen door. What I mean is, it was all right for them to set the coronation at a time that would draw the most free-spending American tourists, and all right to sell window space by the square inch, but it was vulgar commercialism for American television to show the coronation along with advertisements.

So it's natural that such a scrupulous people would approach commercial television like a respectable, middle-aged lady buying a yellow convertible—yearning for it, but embarrassed at what the neighbors may think. From what I can gather, the British have decided to paint the gaudy thing a somber gray, to blend with the general fog, and have it driven by a chauffeur with gloves on, so people won't stare too much. What I mean is, they don't mind taking the money, but they'd like to have it passed under the counter in a plain wrapper.

They will set up another government corporation to own and operate the new TV stations. The corporation will sell time to other companies that will produce the programs, and then they sell smaller smidgins of time to still

133

other companies, the firms that want to advertise their wares on the little screen. One of the main ideas is to fix things so that the actual advertiser cannot control the content of programs; and the government corporation at the top, incidentally, will have the censorship power to put out of business any producing company that puts on TV shows in bad taste.

This whole apparatus, of course, would cause any forward-looking Madison Avenue account exec to hang himself with his solid-gold cufflinks, but the British will probably like it. It will make them feel—well, safe. After all, the British fear un-British things the way we fear un-American things. So for many months, the best brains in London have been working on this plan to guarantee that the commercial TV shows will not be un-British; that is to say, that they will be dull. The London press tells us there is a great public fear of TV on the American pattern. This is the British genius at work in its purest form, since not one per cent of the British public has ever seen American TV. It's like their fear of McCarthyism; if they would just take a look behind the screen and see the baling wire, chewing gum, and Scotch tape that holds the thing together, maybe they wouldn't be so scared.

Their ads they will slip in just before or just after a TV program. This they call "contiguity to suitable programmes." What they seem to mean is the "cowcatcher" and the "caboose." If they're going to get ahead in television, you'd think they would at least learn to use proper English.

THEY AIN'T GOT IT IN
THE LEGS

[November 20, 1953]

Nobody can be everywhere at once, except Eleanor
Roosevelt and Arthur Godfrey—so, what with having to settle such matters as spies and thirsty Texas steers,
nearly the whole football season has gone by without benefit of my advice and counsel. As an iron-man sixty-minute
type of advice-giver, I realize I have been subconsciously
brooding about the return of the one-platoon system. I
advocated this move once in a judicious paragraph, and it
was certainly gratifying to see so many colleges promptly
follow my recommendations. I felt as I imagine Colonel
Bertie McCormick felt when the Army followed his advice
and adopted the machine gun, the tank, logistics, and
morale.

I have been a little disturbed, however, to read the findings of the University of Virginia doctor who reports that
with the one-platoon system football injuries have jumped
by thirty per cent. This is a development that bodes no
good for anybody, except doctors, but it's a serious question whether the one-platoon system is the real cause of
this. If we went back to the two-platoon era, there
wouldn't be so many injuries, but if we went back still
farther, to the iron-man era, there wouldn't be so many
either. For if you read on in the doctor's lamentations, you
discover that college athletes are simply not as rugged as

were their prewar predecessors. So do we soften up football again, or do we toughen up the football-players?

What has caused this? Well, if you read the Churchill memoirs you will discover how astounded the British were to find that when the American Army invaded Anzio, for one typical example, it had one vehicle for every four pairs of legs. American men are losing their legs; the Army agrees with the Virginia doctor—this generation of soldiers, like this generation of athletes, just hasn't got it in the legs; it comes, says the doctor, from too much riding in vehicles. The Army may agree, but considering its own ratio of wheels to legs, the Army is probably just as much to blame as anybody else. Anyway, we paid an awful price for this on those Korean ridges, and we are paying it on the football field.

True to the journalistic principle of examining the facts on the scene, to see if there is any truth to what one has been writing, I actually went to a football game this fall, the Michigan-Minnesota affray, as we say on the sports page. I took along an elderly aunt to advise, disregarded the envious stares of other alumni admiring the texture of my raccoon coat. Well, the number of injured men carried off the field was truly astonishing. Moved by college memories of Bronko Nagurski, Biggie Munn, Pug Lund, and other iron men of my time, I leaped up frequently with cries of indignation and desisted only when that old Ping-pong injury in the back muscles began to act up.

I have to make one exception, however, in this general indictment. The exception is that Minnesota halfback named Paul Giel. They must have dug this boy out of the big woods where automobiles haven't yet penetrated. I couldn't get my aunt to watch anybody else. "Good gracious," she kept saying, "he dances around like a cat teasing a bunch of clumsy puppies." It kills me to admit it, but I must say this Giel is superior even to the afore-mentioned greats of my day; and if Red Barber doesn't agree that this is the finest running back of the century, he ought to switch to Arthur's program and learn a little humility.

Tell you something else: the bands have changed. They have a couple of hundred in these college bands now, and they don't march, they dance; it's like a vast field of precision Rockettes. When Bud Aagaard used to fling the baton over the crossbar and actually catch it, the whole stadium yelled; now all the drum majors throw the thing a hundred feet in the air and never miss. But . . . I don't know. There must be something wrong in all this. I can only conclude that the way we did those things was the mark of fun-loving scholars; the way these kids do it looks like the mark of a misspent life.

THE PROPHETS CONFOUNDED

[*November 25, 1953*]

The only changeless thing about human society is change, and this is pre-eminently true of the American society. Many basic assumptions about American life made just a few years ago are already battered beyond recognition. New facts about the country are at hand, and as they are fundamental to any understanding of what and where we are, some of them might bear recital here.

Twenty years ago sociologists thought the American race was doomed to vanish through lowering birth rates.

People said the restless spirit of the pioneers was gone. They said country and small-town life was the typical American life. They said we had grown cynical about learning and culture. They said marriage was a declining institution. Some said the American of the future would have a darker complexion from the prolific spread of the Negro population. And all these assumptions have turned out to be wrong. The new facts come from the continuing findings of the Census Bureau's 1950 check and have been digested by the efforts of the Population Reference Bureau. In 1933 the American birth rate reached its all-time low, and the prophets of disappearance had some cause for their gloom. But in the forties the population jumped by nearly twenty millions, the biggest ten-year increase our history has known.

Americans are still restless and the West remains golden. More than three per cent of our people move from one state to another every year; the geographic population center of the country, Parkersburg, West Virginia, a century ago, is now in eastern Illinois; the area west of the Rockies has almost tripled its share of the population in the last fifty years, and California is now the second most populous state.

The proportion of Negroes in the population has been cut in half since the first census in 1790, and that decline continues today. Whites have increased to nearly 90 per cent; Negroes have decreased to 10 per cent. At the time of the Civil War 92 per cent of the Negroes lived in the South, and mostly in the farming regions. Now only 68 per cent are in the South; they are moving to other regions, and they are mostly moving into the cities.

So are the rest of us tending to the cities. Fifty years ago 60 per cent of Americans were in farms and villages; now

138

60 per cent are in the towns and cities; and everywhere big city centers or "loops" are decaying as families move to the suburbs with commercial establishments in hot pursuit.

The proportion of Americans getting formal education has steadily increased, among Negroes most of all, and a higher percentage of city people are getting it than country people. But while the percentage of Americans finishing college has increased, their proportion to the population is only a bit over 2 per cent. Divorces have increased, but then so have marriages to a very marked extent. More men than women get the divorce, which seems hard on the women, and there are also three times as many widows in this country as widowers. Which may mean that more surviving husbands remarry than surviving wives, but definitely means the women are living longer than the men. A girl born today has a normal life expectancy of about 72½ years; a boy, one of 66½. Instead of marrying later and later in life as in some countries like Ireland, Americans marry younger and younger. The average marrying age for men is now a bit under 23, for a woman a bit over 20.

We are becoming an older people; and this aging trend is going to continue for two generations. Women outnumber men in America, not only because they live longer but because the immigration pattern has been reversed and more women than men now enter the country. If this disproportion makes competition tougher for the women, they have the consolation of knowing that through inheritance and other means they are getting more and more of the nation's wealth in their own hands, dishpan or Pond's.

THANKS FOR WHAT?

[*November 26, 1953*]

It has been a fitting ritual on this particular day of the year that those privileged to speak their own thoughts to their countrymen should try to define and state the particular blessing of living on the American land. But here the Thanksgiving Day is closing, and I have come up to this speaking hour with nothing to offer. It was not for want of trying. I did lay aside some papers and books last night—some of the early Pilgrims' prayers, some of the statements of Lincoln, and a few marked pages from Walt Whitman; somewhere in those lines I was sure I could find the essence of what it is we can give honest thanks for in our American life. But it was one of those distracting days. First of all, the bed was too comfortable and the early morning dreams too pleasant, and, you know how it is, that visceral recollection that it's a holiday steals through the bones and you drift back to sleep in utter relaxation. Then when I walked out in slippers for the morning paper, I did have something Lincoln said upon my mind, but it wouldn't stay. The frost lay so white and clean upon the pasture, I could hear the horses stomping in the stable and the sound of church bells from over the trees. It was as if the sounds and sights of childhood had been re-created in a glory all about me, and of course serious thought could only be postponed.

Then, you know how bothersome it is, trying to pick out the proper tie and shirt and suit for Aunt Rita's

Thanksgiving dinner from all those overstuffed drawers and closets. Then the business of inspecting the boys in their first grown-up suits and man's shoes, wondering if it was the cut of the clothes that made them seem bigger and straighter, laughing at the remark that pretty soon I'd be wearing their cast-off suits as "hand-me ups."

I thought I'd have an hour there to read some more and get at the core of Thanksgiving's meaning, but there seemed to be some left-over mail and of course the phone would ring. After all, you have to pay some attention when you learn that one brother is safely home after two years in the Korean theater of war and the second brother has reached there with his battalion, but too late, of course, to be in the fighting. And then there was the news that the woman next door with the three beautiful kids had come through her operation successfully and our worst fears could be put aside.

It was just one distraction after another and concentration wasn't helped any when we figured out that there was enough money in the bank to take the whole family to Bermuda next week. Things just seemed to go on like that all day. I did bring along some of those papers, hoping to make a few notes during the afternoon, but who can do any serious thinking with the men cheering the football game on the big, new television set, the women endlessly handing you trays of hors d'œuvres, the smallest children jumping in your lap or playing tag all over your feet. And of course a Thanksgiving dinner with turkey, wild rice, potatoes, beans, cranberries, wines, mince pie, cake, and various liqueurs is totally destructive of any kind of thought.

To make matters worse, it happened to be my birthday, too, by some quirk of the calendar; I thought I'd reached the age where one's birthday was casually accepted by others, but it was one gift, one burst of singing after another. Well, I finally got in the car determined to make one last effort; but there was a kind of splendor about the sunset you couldn't help watching, and then those garlands of lights springing up as I drove toward the city. I suppose it's a hangover from the war years in the dark and frightened cities of Europe, but there's something about a city calmly, automatically bursting into light that always makes me stop and watch.

So that's how it happened that I got here to the studio tonight, an empty man unprepared to define and discuss exactly what it is we are thankful for in this land we live in.

LOOSE THREADS FROM THE FRINGE

[*December 15, 1953*]

The twenty-two young American GI's bide their time in the Communist tents at Panmunjom, refusing even to listen to their countrymen—evidence, I should guess, not of their confidence in their adopted philosophy, but of their lack of confidence in themselves. There they stay as the deadline approaches, intent upon selling their birthright for the cruelest political illusion ever to appeal to the very young.

Should we fail to get them back, we will not only fail to save their own individual futures; we will also fail of learning the full truth of why they did it; and it is of importance to thoughtful and responsible Americans to know exactly why. We have all read their names, their home addresses, and seen their photographed faces; and no doubt many of us have read into this scanty evidence our own theories of their motivations.

Any positive theory would be dangerous, on so little evidence, whether approached from the psychologists' starting-point, their childhood homes and emotional complexes, or the sociologists' starting-point, their community. No one can generalize on this in a positive fashion, but at first glance, anyway, certain things of a negative nature do seem to stand out. Remembering that the raw mass of the Army includes Americans of every social, geographical, and educational status, what is it that these twenty-two are not?

In the first place, they are not educated men. They have not been led to Communism by any so-called "dangerous" textbooks or professors. It is probably safe to say none of them had ever been exposed to even theoretical Marxism as students or readers. Those on the current American scene who follow the fabulous reasoning that there are dangers in liberal education, that educated men are "eggheads" and therefore suspect—such persons will find no comfort for their theories and prejudices in the case of these twenty-two.

In the second place, these men are not bold and resolute young men, of the kind who might become conscious spies or front-line fighters on any Communist picket line. Nor are they reckless adventurers of a kind of crazy, pioneering type. Their faces, by and large, are the faces of weak and irresolute young men.

In the third place, they are not members of racial minorities, hurt in their pride, given a martyr's neurotic complex by the slights and stings of society. They are not sensitive young Jews, and there is only one Negro among them.

In the fourth place, they are not, by and large, members of the so-called industrial proletariat, in which, by Marxist theory, Communist movements are supposed to find their strength.

What are they, then? Do they fit into any kind of common pattern? Generalization, as I have said, is dangerous here, but I have at least a tentative notion that most of them do fit a pattern. As I recollect, most of them come from small-town or rural regions of America; from farms or the lower middle class. And since many of them were non-coms, they were not the stupid, the outcasts of their primitive schooling. They had a certain sense of pride and personal aspiration; and they must have felt a frustration in their opportunities, for American small-town and rural life is not quite the happy fulfilling experience our folklore has pictured.

They come, I would suspect, from that strata which combines a little property with a little learning; people who fiercely try to protect what they have, suspicious of strangers, the big city, who think of government as the distant, ominous "they," not as "theirs." People who go for quacks, for Huey Longs and Father Coughlins and magical, simple solutions for their resentments. In sum, what the cynics would call the "crack-pot" fringe.

But such are always a small minority in our American life. And after all, out of the many thousands captured, only these twenty-two fell mental victims to the Reds. We may take this fact, not as a matter of shame, but a source of pride.

LANDSCAPE LITTERED
WITH LOVE

[December 18, 1953]

Nothing is quite so disturbing to a devout advice-giver like me as to discover that another advice-giver has beaten me to the punch and handed out a piece of advice that I had been saving, along with some old check stubs and moldy caramels. There I was, all set, whenever the moon was right, to advise an impatient public about views; only to pick up a copy of *The New Yorker*—the one habit, besides talking to myself, that keeps me sane—and discover that *The New Yorker* has already advised about views. Not only that, it has presumed to advise the President himself, which practically amounts to infringement of copyright.

The President owns an old farm in Pennsylvania. The farmhouse faces away from the view. A contractor is re-jiggering this perfectly contented old Civil War house. *The New Yorker* writer warns the President to leave the view alone. He says, "The way you get to the view at our place is to walk through the kitchen, then through the woodshed to the barn, then through the barn to a small, cobwebby window in the rear, and there it is. That's where it belongs, too," he adds. "Nothing can be more paralyzing than living in constant touch with a view. A view is like a bottle of champagne; it should be held in reserve in the cellar, not piped into the living-room, where everyone is at its mercy, morning, noon and night."

All too true, as we say in the advising trade. A splendid view is like a drug; its effects are exalting, but bound to wear off; even on a short, forty-hour week, the human creature can't produce enough continuing splendor in himself to match a constant view. He can see his splendor, but only in glimpses of accidental surprise through the cobwebs that festoon us all; he cannot fix it behind plate glass. Of course, some of us try. We pick out one or another of the many marvelous features in our own internal landscape and then not only do we try to fix it behind glass, but we constantly point it out to visitors.

Take the President, for example. He has a fine internal landscape with many splendid features; but he keeps pointing out that peak in the foreground called "sincerity." I don't know why, because that's just the feature a visitor sees most quickly by himself. A visitor also notices some fascinating little gullies and patches of woods, but every time he asks about those to complete his understanding of the scene, the President points to that peak again. Pretty soon, unless he posts the property, he'll find trespassers slipping around by themselves to find out just what the heck those gullies are.

People like Joe McCarthy make the same mistake with the landscape feature we call "patriotism." Not only do they point it out to all visitors with a set speech, but they keep running around to everybody else's property for a look. If they don't see it right off, they call up the county assessor, and before you know it the value of your property has declined on the public market. These people forget that most folks don't keep that feature around in the form of a skyscraper. They keep it the way they keep the water in the old springhouse that came with the place. They hardly ever think about it, hidden and quiet the way it is down in the woods; but come a need for it—a drought or a war—and they've got it all right. Had it all the time.

With other people it's love. They love everybody, and loudly. Their whole landscape is littered with love. Even more than sincerity or patriotism, love simply must be kept in small bottles, tightly corked, for special occasions. Otherwise the stuff goes flat.

I was about to say that still other people make the same mistake with sex-appeal. But I got to thinking about Marilyn Monroe, and all of a sudden something seems wrong with my whole argument. Remind me to re-examine this part of the evidence when I'm about seventy-five.

THE CONSPIRACY OF GOODNESS

[December 24, 1953]

Presidents and prizefighters don't have to work on Christmas Eve; bus conductors and broadcasters do. I have been informed from time to time through the mails that listening to a broadcaster can also be work any day in the year. For tonight, however, I will cling to the conviction that this hurts me more than it does you.

A broadcaster can easily talk about a war, an assassination, or a riot with quite a few well-chosen words. Why it is so much harder to talk about peace and love and good will is a rather disturbing question; another sign, no doubt, of the general corruption of the time. The time, that is, represented by the other three hundred and sixty-four days of the year; but not tomorrow. Not tonight.

ERIC SEVAREID

Obviously, if Christmas didn't already exist, man would have had to invent it; there has to be at least one day in the year to remind us we're here for something else besides our general cussedness. But you'll notice that we pick out the shortest day in the year in which to endure this painful reminder. With advance clearance by the Attorney General's subversives-control division, I'd be willing to start a movement for having two Christmases a year. Of course, if the idea is rejected, I'll disclaim authorship and put the blame for this radical notion where it belongs—on my children; on yours, too, while I'm at it. Children are natural conspirators. They seem to have secret, sub-rosa channels, a kind of network all around the world, of conspiratorial cells. I've run into the children's ideology all the way from Chungking to Oklahoma; everywhere they worm their way into the confidence of others, relentlessly planting their propaganda on behalf of love and kindness, generosity, trust, sunshine, holidays, and fun. It's time all right-thinking citizens took notice of this conspiracy and realize that if the world children's revolution ever succeeds, we'll be face to face with the prospect of Christmas every day in the year, even if it's called by some other name, or by no name at all. The whole thing would just about put broadcasters out of business, with no wars, riots or assassinations to broadcast about; and I for one shall be on my guard. No more toddlers are going to put their damp little hands in mine without producing their credentials first.

But this is not the evening for dark thoughts. I think what I intended to write about, before the typewriter took over the subject matter, was this business of sending Christmas cards. This is one of the aspects of Christmas that are supposed to be commercialized, to have got out of hand. I used to think so, but I'm not so sure any more. In the

148

first place, the printing and engraving craft has become a fine art, and my mail desk is festooned with small squares of color, each one a lovely and happy thing. In the second place, the annual pile represents regathering of friendships, some almost lost and forgotten, renewed now from the ends of the earth. If the little machine-made, mass-produced card is a commercial thing, my materialistic spirit, at least, is grateful for it.

One such card lies beside the typewriter. It is not a clever card; the print is simple and the words are old— four centuries old, in fact, written in 1513 by Fra Giovanni. The words are these: "There is nothing I can give you which you have not; but there is much that, while I cannot give, you can take. No heaven can come to us unless our hearts find rest in it today. Take heaven. No peace lies in the future which is not hidden in this present instant. Take peace. The gloom of the world is but a shadow; behind it, yet within reach, is joy. Take joy. And so, at this Christmas time, I greet you with the prayer that for you, now and forever, the day breaks and the shadows flee away."

THE COLD PEACE

[*December 25, 1953*]

This Christmas Day of '53, now passing with the setting sun around the globe, somehow has been different from the Christmas days of the last six tortured years. Both the President of our own country and the Moscow radio said that the prospects for a peaceful world are better, and somehow these expressions do not sound like mere pious hopes, for the first time in years.

A columnist today quotes Sir Winston Churchill as saying that when Hitler's Germany seemed so hostile and aggressive, he knew in his bones a terrible war was coming. But that now, even in the face of a hostile, aggressive Russia, he does not feel in his bones that war is coming. And this is a kind of confirmation, from the most sensitive and accurate of human antennas, of what many other men are feeling whose minds are trained to dwell on the level of people and politics rather than persons and things. They feel in their bones that the tensions are wearing down, that a period of peace, of a sort, is slowly settling over the troubled earth. Among acute Europeans this has been the feeling for quite some time; it is only now spreading to the bones of Americans in number. It is not strange, perhaps, that Europeans should sense it first and most strongly; they carry, after all, an immense heredity of war and peace within their bones; their homes have been the ancient battleground; and they dwell now between the hostile Titans, America and Russia.

They have made a subtle, but probably realistic, distinction between the period of the cold war and what they now call the period of the cold peace. They define the periods this way: the cold war was the period when the great powers spoke and acted as if they were at war, but stopping short of declaring war. Cold peace is the period when the great powers speak and act as if they are at peace, but stopping short of negotiating a settlement. If the world is, indeed, coming into a new period, as so many wise men believe it is, this will serve to define the period as well as anything else.

If that is the definition of the new period, its nature is

an enforced peace, a balance-of-power peace; not the re-laxed peace of trust and friendship that men have sought since the dawn of nations and so rarely found. But a balance-of-power peace is far better than no peace at all. The unwrapping of the secret of the atom has meant that this time the precarious balance between the titans is cemented in place by mutual fear. An umbrella of fear broods over the vast world spectacle of hostility and revolutionary change, but it is better, perhaps, than no umbrella at all.

The free and the Communist worlds have stumbled and staggered through these postwar years of rearrangement into a crude balancing of their military forces and their geographical positions. The Communists have reached the place where they cannot, with impunity, physically advance in Asia. We have reached the place where we cannot easily cause any Asiatic nation to follow our lead; and the same is true for both of us in Europe. And behind all this is a balance of human psychology which was not the case in Hitler's time of glorifying war itself. This time the peoples and leaders of neither opposing power want world war. Hitler wanted war itself; the Kremlin may want the fruits of war, but not the war; America has never wanted either.

Within the balance of strength is also a balance of weakness. Russia's own economy and her satellite system are very shaky. On our side, India and Italy, for example, may go Communist, and a depression here, collapsing the free world's trading system, is not impossible. It may be that this period of the cold peace will be a contest of endurance; and our task then will be to make very sure that our own establishment, however shaky, does not crumble first.

DIAGRAMMATIC BLISS

[*December 30, 1953*]

This is going to be a little hard to do with voice alone; television could perform a greater public service with its visual charts. But there was a situation up here in New York that presented quite a challenge to an analyst, and since television seemed a little slow about it, there was nothing I could do but bow my head and lumber in to the public's rescue. Great black headlines have shouted out the words, "Babs," "Ruby," "Zsa-Zsa"—photographs all over of a man in striped pants, quite a lot of women smiling or scowling, and one woman wearing a black eye-patch, like that fellow in the shirt advertisements, and looking just as self-satisfied. If this wasn't a situation, then all my instincts acquired in twenty years of writing situationers have gone for naught, so to speak.

The action of the plot concerned a prospective wedding, a quiet, simple wedding, it said in one place, between the man in the striped trousers, Rubirosa, and the woman named Babs. All the other characters turned out, upon examination, to be subsidiary to the main action, but conditioning it in one way or another. They are friends and relatives, one woman who was either a jilter or a jiltee, but mostly ex-wives and ex-husbands. Breaking all this down into categories, I found that the friends and relatives fell into two easily separated groups: those who approved the marriage of Babs and Rubirosa (no relation, incidentally, to that singer, *La* Rosa) and those who did *not* approve. The ex-wives and ex-husbands also appeared to fall into these two categories of attitude, but I found it simpler to divide them according to nationality and social status. And pursuing this method, I found that the ex-wives of Rubirosa consisted of one American, one Frenchwoman, and one Dominican, while the ex-husbands of Babs consisted of one count, two princes, and one movie star. The woman in the eye patch did not seem to fit any of my pluralized categories, so I set her aside temporarily as the unknown factor, or factor X.

I then sat down to work out the problem, and the first thing I discovered was that while my categories were valid, my method was wrong. Lists, boxes, and circles, in the manner of a government reorganization chart, got me nowhere. This was an inorganic approach, and the problem clearly required the organic approach. Eventually I hit upon the scheme of using the double-wing back formation of the football diagram, which, of course, enabled me to follow the action, with solid lines for the central, and dotted lines for the secondary or blocking, actions.

Well, the final answer was easily found. Babs was Barbara Hutton, one of the richest women in the world; Rubirosa was the Dominican diplomat in quotation marks who used to be married to another of the richest women in the world, Doris Duke, who, said Ruby, was going to be very, very happy about this, but was also going to laugh. The action of the friends and relatives and the ex's consisted in rushing to telephones to tell reporters what they thought of the marriage or rushing away from telephones so they wouldn't have to tell what they thought of it. The girl in the eye-patch, Zsa-Zsa Gabor, turned out to be the jilter or the jiltee. Her action in the plot I can only describe as circular. She said she had jilted Ruby; he said nuts. She said he had thereupon hit her in the eye. He said: "Un-

153

ladylike publicity-hunting." She said Ruby still loves her, but at the same time she seemed sure Ruby and Babs would be happy because they are both "sveet, vunderful keeds."

Her circular action fouled up my solid lines, so finally I threw her the hell out of my diagram. This permitted the central action to go forward, and so Babs and Ruby were duly married this afternoon.

It was, as they said, a quiet wedding, but not exactly a simple one.

THE YEAR WHEN

[December 31, 1953]

It's a serious question if anybody is listening to the radio —or should be—at this hour, just before the new year is rung in. But there must be a few hardship cases around, people who were too tired to go to New Year's Eve parties (or maybe too wise) and other people driving around the block for the twentieth time looking for a parking space.

Somebody, with greater wit and wisdom than I, will doubtless define and describe this year that has passed and place it in its historical niche. Personally, I find that while I can add the year's events, I can't add them *up*. So the next three minutes will merely swarm with digits running around loose, with anybody who feels like it entitled to seek the final sum.

1953 was the year when the top hat began to give up the ghost in favor of the black homburg, and tornadoes and unseasonable drought convinced a lot of people—disappointed in flying saucers—that the atomic explosions have radically changed our weather. It was the year when the United States agreed to end a war short of military victory for the first time since 1814, and the year the piston engine went out, for the Air Force, replaced entirely by the jet.

It was the year Americans generally began to worry more about their jobs than about Communists, when businessmen rejoiced over a businessman's administration and immediately began to worry about business; when somebody marketed a new beer for women which doesn't taste so grossly beery, and called *that* progress, and when automobile salesmen suddenly discovered they had to get out and *sell* their cars. The year when the big American Cadillac began to appear all over Europe, and the small European car began to appear all over America; the year when many people got tired of hearing and reading about where mankind was heading, and took to escape novels and books on the individual human spirit and on how to build your own house without the roof falling in. It was the year the last assembly line manufacturing axle grease for buggies and wagons went out of business and the first Western saddle with a built-in radio was manufactured. The year a man named Spillane almost destroyed the fine art of the detective story; when motion pictures got fewer and better, traffic became totally impossible, the commercial centers of the big cities began to stagnate, and the female chest measurement became an instant, unquestioned passport to fame and fortune.

It was the year when a drink made of Russian vodka became very popular without a single senator demanding an investigation, when the American minister of justice broke the seals on secret police reports for political purposes, when Americans with some regard for the Bill of Rights got really sore, began to write letters and take to the soapbox themselves, and the year when the Government of the United States in all its august majesty burned some books for fear of words.

It was the year when the word *American* became intensely unpopular overseas and was instantly restored to popularity by a single Presidential speech offering the first workable way to do something about the ominous atom.

It was the year a President showed a First Lady how to fan a six-gun, color television got a real go-ahead, one-platoon football was restored to its rightful place, and the sex habits of women became public, scientific property along with lung cancer and the cigarette. It was the year a Secretary of State could propose secret talks with the Russians and not be denounced as subversive; a golfer won a match with an eighty-yard chip shot, and men were solemnly warned they must never, never wear white shirts before evening.

Quite a year, however you may add it up. For myself, I can only quote the words on the little card pinned over the doorway to this CBS newsroom. The words in would-be German dialect which say: "How is it ve get so soon old und yat so late schmardt?"

THE MEN WHO

[January 1, 1954]

They have the happy custom in England called the New Year Honors List. The sovereign gets the new year off to a cheerful start by announcing the names of men and women who have distinguished themselves in some way or other and who thereby receive a title or mark of merit. Royal honors do not exist in this country, but I thought I might encourage the government to start a reasonable facsimile some day by awarding a few individual honors right here. We might call them the annual eleven p.m. Monday-through-Friday-news-broadcast-over-this-station Honors List.

First, to the President for his speeches of April 16 and December 8, which reactivated the dormant human nerve that governs the instincts of hope and tolerance.

To Queen Elizabeth, who restored the sense of youth and glamour to tired, old, and slightly shabby Britain.

To Konrad Adenauer, who led a politically mass-minded people up the road toward individual freedom and democracy.

Jean Monnet, the first citizen of Europe, whose dream of a united Europe resulted in the first shipments of European-produced steel to the common European market.

The book-reviewers who had to read the *entire* Kinsey report on women.

Sir Winston Churchill, who again restored words to their lost dignity in this world of action by reminding us that thought produces action and that men think in words.

The Nobel Committee, for the common sense to award the peace prize to George Catlett Marshall.

To Hunt, Hilary, and Tensing, who conquered Everest and showed a flaccid civilization that personal adventure remains a noble calling.

To thousands of GI's in Korea who demonstrated that an American soldier does not require glory, loot, pay, or even victory to perform the duty he is asked to perform.

Our Order of Scientific Detachment goes to the Austrian who lived a whole year in a glass bottle and concluded that life inside a bottle isn't much different from life outside a bottle.

Our Order of Stupid Splendor goes to the American GI in Germany who didn't get the word to leave, and so stood guard over an empty boat for six days and nights.

An honor to Mr. Adlai Stevenson for knowing when a man should speak out and when he should hold his tongue.

An honor to Theodore H. White, the first journalist to make the crushingly complex and prosaic story of postwar economic Europe both understandable and exciting.

To Harry Truman for coming to rest at Independence, not the Waldorf Towers.

To Carl Sandburg for editing his six Lincoln volumes down to one.

To the Vice President for rebuilding himself by quiet and useful means and not by stunts.

To Ben Hogan for demonstrating the lost quality of steadiness, and Tony Trabert for giving new hope to diabetics.

General Bedell Smith, a tired and sick man, who has prevented the diplomatic service from being entirely emasculated by political hacks and hatchets. To Ambassador Bohlen and John Paton Davies for refusing to quit under the slings of slander.

Ireland's author Sean O'Faolain for writing the truth about his own countrymen. The papers and magazines that had the commercial courage to print the full story of cigarettes and cancer. To the advertising man who restored my sense of magic by describing the new car as smaller on the outside and bigger on the inside.

To Postmaster General Summerfield for actually starting to modernize that service.

The Order of Parental Consternation goes to my thirteen-year-old Mike for knocking down a quail at a hundred feet, through trees, on his first shot with *my* new gun; and the Royal Order of Astonishment to my thirteen-year-old Peter for making the eighth-grade honor roll.

Something ought to go to my wife for putting me up and putting up with me—and for myself, I'll take whatever medical science wants to award me for helping so many insomnia sufferers find oblivion at this late hour.

AS GOD INTENDED

[January 14, 1954]

This is a proper evening for analyzing the psychosociological relationship of modern transportation to old-fashioned weather. Actually it defies analysis; it also defies description. But, as my scout master used to tell us, leave us try. Let us consider the test case of a typical citizen traveling from New York to Washington. Take any day after a heavy snowfall; today for instance. Take any citizen; take me.

At two p.m. I climbed from the curb to the street in uptown New York. They have a system in New York. In order to let traffic move, snowplows push the snow from the middle of the street toward the sides. This barricades every car parked on the sides until the February thaw. It narrows the negotiable traffic lane to about eight feet, so that traffic cannot move anyway; in order, no doubt, to restore the whole situation to the *status quo* ante-snowfall, when horns and cusswords did the trick.

Cheating slightly by choosing the hood of a low-slung

MG, I climbed to the street and a taxi. From there to the Penn Station is a normal ten-minute, fifty-cent run; it required 38 minutes and $1.05. I made the club car of the train in an asthmatic forty-yard sprint.

By Elizabeth, New Jersey, I had recovered my breath, paid for Seat 11 in the parlor car, and put back on my overcoat, gloves, and hat; the conductor laughingly informed us the heat would be off until Philadelphia, where a new engine would take us over. It is an hour and a half to Philadelphia; it took us two hours and a quarter. Most of the time I stood in the smoking compartment; in there it was up to 40 degrees Fahrenheit. Two business types were arguing the virtues of snow removal via the shoveling-down-the-manhole system, versus the shoveling-up-into-a-truck system. I hunted up my parlor-car seat; it had also been sold to a large gentleman with a cauliflower ear.

In the club car the ranks of freedom-loving citizens looked like twin rows of mummies in mufflers. The train was stopped. We sipped hot toddies and brooded; outside, it began to snow again. Somebody said that his smart pals who had taken the plane were now probably grounded in Teeterboro, peering out the plane window and hoping Arthur Godfrey would not choose that moment to return for revenge. This produced a cracking effect on one or two faces, which could in a pinch be described as a kind of ghastly smile.

The train moved, stopped again; the porter gave us one of those toothy minstrel-show grins and said it appeared a rod or something was busted or something, somewhere. It wat at this stop, I think (we visited every ward in Philadelphia), that the British type came in. He was the British Rotarian-type type, red-faced, boomy of voice, and he informed us this was just like being back in good old England—no heat, train stalled, and so on. He laughed heartily and he laughed alone. We moved, stopped again. I figured we had by then lost our right of way and were sidetracked to allow a streamliner full of laughing millionaires go through on their way to Florida's sunny strand. Around this time a procession of overcoated people looking like fresh recruits, or replacements, began to move through the car; from rear to front, then from front to rear; various theories were offered: they were commuters on the wrong train; they were Wilmington people trying to get off and walk; or they were a delegation elected back in the coaches, seeking an audience with the engineer to present their views.

I must have passed out. Next thing I was conscious of was what I took to be dawn breaking over the Polar Cap; turned out to be the lights of Washington's Union Station. In the cab to this studio I thought for a while of giving up my membership in the train-lovers' association and throwing away my badge with the motto: "We travel by train as God intended man to travel."

But then I thought: no, God was probably just testing my faith.

COCKER-SPANIEL TOWN

[*January 20, 1954*]

From a column in the weekly *Observer* of London, I have been learning what life is like in the United States, and it seemed only fair that I should pass on my gleanings to other natives of that foreign and mysterious land. A lady writer named Ernestine Decie has been detailing, for British readers, the habits of the species Americanus, particularly the sect or tribe that inhabits Washington, D.C. She does this in the form of question and answer.

The first question is, "How does one get clothes dry cleaned in Washington?" Her answer: "One gets clothes dry cleaned in Washington by telephoning a dry cleaner." Next question.

"What personal contacts can a resident foreigner have with Washington individuals?" Ernestine should know there are no individuals in Washington, only Republicans and Democrats, but she goes on to say that contacts are easily available, except among the permanent residents of Washington. The true Washingtonian, she says, and I am quoting verbatim, so help me Horace Greeley, is called a "cave dweller" and is almost as difficult to know as a Muscovite. Now look, Ernestine, that dry cleaner who came to get your clothes, he is a permanent resident of Washington. What if he did hide his face in his fur collar, give you a pained look, and go off with the clothes at a run? Simply meant he had a toothache, and he knew perfectly well that if he missed his dental appointment he couldn't get another one for six months. And your taxi-driver—how in the world did you avoid knowing all about him, his heart symptoms, his chicken farm, and his views on pedestrians?

For getting to know Americans, Ernestine tells her London readers, children of "suitable ages" are an asset, though, I quote, "not as surefire as poodles for establishing immediate rapport." Well, could be, but it strikes me Washington is more of a cocker-spaniel town. Ernestine reports that political conversation in Washington is "fraught with peril" for a foreigner. And so, she says, "be-

162

hind a diplomatic façade, one can often detect a molar being ground to the gum." But that's only with newly arrived diplomats; the old hands already know about the dental-date problem and leave their molars alone; they suddenly remember a previous appointment or just get drunk.

Question three: can one travel in the country? Ernestine says yes, one can. The cheapest form of travel, she says, is by car, but it is also the most dangerous form. I quote, "on the sleek super highways, the pace is literally killing and the motto 'sauve qui peut.'" (Essayists in London papers love to drop in French or Latin phrases, in italics; they would use Greek, too, but it generally raises too much l'enfer in the composing room.) Well, "sauve qui peut," if you can get past my pronunciation, means, in this context, force the other guy in the ditch if you can and then step on the gas before he remembers to notice your license number.

"This compulsive haste," writes Ernestine, "forces a bonnet-to-rear bumper technique of progress" (*bonnet* is English for hood). Which produces the terrifying mass smash-ups. No passport or permits are needed, she informs her readers.

Question four is about hospital treatment. She seems pretty accurate on this one, but she could have pointed out that a room with bath in a modern American hospital now cost more than a suite at the Waldorf.

Question five: are there any fresh vegetables in America? Ernestine says yes, and adds some hard words. "Few buy anything but frozen orange juice; the squeezer gathers dust and the palate learns to distinguish between one brand of flavored water and another." I dread the time when Ernestine discovers Americans also buy frozen waffles to pop in the toaster; and I might say to her that when the time comes that this is done with the ancient and honorable

163

American pancake, I will consider the end of the Republic is nigh, take Ernestine's trembling little hand in mine, and migrate to London.

HOW TO QUIT NON-SMOKING

[*January 22, 1954*]

The current flap about smoking and lung cancer shows signs of settling down to some really broad-scale efforts to find out exactly what the story is. A dozen separate studies have been going on, here and in England, for several years. Then the cigarette-manufacturers launched their own inquiry; and today it was announced that the federal government is also getting into the act.

Up to now, as I read it, most of the private studies seem generally agreed that there is a definite and direct statistical relationship between cigarette-smoking and the rising incidence of lung cancer. Some of the researchers working on this are personally convinced the statistics point irrefutably to a causal relationship as well. But there has so far been no completely convincing scientific proof of this and still less has there been any final conclusion as to just what it is in cigarettes that may cause lung cancer and why and how. Clearly, an immense amount of work remains to be done.

The new effort by the government will also be a statistical study, but it will work in reverse from the previous studies. In those, figures were gathered on people who had already died of lung cancer or who had developed it. Then, the researchers worked backward into the life history of those people in terms of their smoking habits. The government researchers will start gathering the smoking-habit data of people now alive and well, then make their check as and when these people die. They are inclined to think that the previous system may have permitted a certain amount of bias to creep into the assessment. The guinea pigs for the government study will be a good cross-section, three hundred thousand veterans of World War I, who are now being asked to answer some searching questionnaires on their habits. Since these men hold government life-insurance policies, which come in as they die, the recheck will start at that point. Four to five thousand of these veterans die each year, so in about two or three years the government researchers will have a fair statistical base from which to discover a trend, if any.

This reporter is baffled by all statistics, but I consider myself an authority on giving up smoking and going back to smoking. Mark Twain used to start off a new pipe by having some man, somebody, he said, who was better off dead, break it in for him with an extra stem. Unfortunately there is no way to shift the painful burden of quitting smoking over to somebody else; I have tried all the systems, hereby listed:

1. Don't inhale. No comment on this one is required.

2. Take a cigarette only when the clock hand is on the hour. During this effort I broke my watch spring from constantly winding it too tight.

3. Smoke only after each meal. I found this caused too much domestic complaint about the empty icebox in the morning.

4. Do no smoking at all till after the lunch hour. I found myself staying up till four a.m. so I could sleep until noon, and the shame of it became just too much.

5. Carry around an unlit cigarette to suck on occasion-

ally. The late Chief Justice Vinson used to do this, but I think he quit it for the same reason I did—everybody offers you a light, and the explanation begins to sound silly.

6. Keep no cigarettes and smoke only what you can borrow. I lost some very good office friends that way.

I have just read of a new system. Dr. Alstead of Glasgow University says, stroke the tongue with a stick of silver nitrate after meals. The combined taste of that and tobacco is preposterous and unendurable. Dr. Alstead said he has recommended this to many friends; and without exception, he reports, they have given up silver nitrate.

I will admit that I quit smoking once for fifteen months. I woke up feeling wonderful, went to sleep feeling wonderful. My views on life, politics, and general human destiny began to change; I became an optimist, which meant that professional ruin as a commentator stared me in the face. So, with a great effort, I mastered my will power and went back to smoking.

THE JUMPING COFFEE BEANS

[January 28, 1954]

Well, all I know about coffee is that the way my wife makes it, you don't stir it, you crank it. She subscribes to the old Turkish proverb that says coffee should be strong as the devil, hot as Hades, black as death, and sweet as love. But at these prices I, like many of you, no doubt, am thinking of going to the opposite system of gently swishing one coffee bean in a cup of hot water.

A couple of centuries ago a commentator named Alex-

166

ander Pope, who probably had a side contract as public-relations man with the Brazilian lobby in London, wrote a handout saying: "Coffee . . . makes the politicians wise." So, instead of sending a letter to your congressman, you might ship him a pound or so of the stuff; unless he gets a pay raise, he can't afford to buy it himself, and he is going to need all the wisdom he can drum up before this coffee-price business is figured out. But he's going to have a shot at it, with both barrels. The American Congress, full of direct intellectual descendants of Noah, always believes in having two of everything, so we are going to be witnessing two investigations of coffee prices. One by the Federal Trade Commission on Presidential orders, and one by the Senate Banking Committee. The banking committee, naturally, because of the close relationship between a cup of coffee and a bank account.

You can have your choice of three different theories why coffee prices have leaped through the roof: the extensive crop damage in Brazil, where the bean, as well as the nut, comes from; speculation and sharp practices in the market; or the outmoded production techniques of growing coffee in the face of modern demand. The Brazilian Government says it's number one; the U.S. Department of Agriculture says it's number three; a few suspicious senators say it looks like number two—speculation—and all the speculators say "Unh-huh." Still, the very announcement of the President's investigation depressed both the speculators and the price of coffee futures.

It's not for me to charge anybody with un-Brazilian activities, but on the surface evidence, things don't seem quite far' and squar'. Somebody, or at least something, is flouting the law of supply and demand. Because in the last five years American civilian and military coffee-consumption has dropped by two hundred million pounds, but in that period the price of coffee here has doubled. And Senator Beall of Maryland points out that we get only fifty per cent of our coffee from crop-damaged Brazil. And only one fifth of Brazil's crop was damaged anyway. All told, Brazil's exports were reduced by damage only about one fourteenth. Nor have the inventories of American importers dropped very much. So something is missing somewhere—or, rather, something new has been added, and the senators and commissioners will now try to find out what it is.

In the meantime, coffee customers and retailers all around the country are thrashing about in their own gestures of protest. Consumers' boycotts develop here and there, but the history of consumer boycotts in this country is not one, exactly, of spectacular success. The spirit is willing, but the tongue goes dry and the flesh becomes weak. An operator of a hundred eating spots in New York City has new signs urging the customers to drink tea. In Philadelphia a big hotel attaches a nickel to the menu. If you don't order coffee, you keep the nickel. (Wait till my kids hear about that.) And in an Arkansas town a jeweler has put coffee in his show window, alongside the diamonds and pearls; he says sales are brisk.

We have no domestic tea lobby in this country, but the boys from the dairy states know a good thing when they see it; so Senator Aiken of Vermont earnestly advises everybody to drink more milk in place of coffee. Well, a pound of coffee gives you about forty cups; a pound of milk gives you two glasses. And a pound of coffee is only ten times more expensive than a pound of milk, not twenty times. The Senator's way may be the way to health, but, by my arithmetic, it is also the way to bankruptcy.

E. DAVIS, MAJOR MINORITY

[*January 29, 1954*]

It seemed to me that it would be a mistake, if not down-right un-American, to allow this evening to pass without saying a few words about a gentleman who happens to labor on another network, which shall be nameless here. I don't know how Macy's handles such a matter in relation to Gimbel's, but the problem does exist and somehow must be met. I am referring to that owlish gentleman with the horn-rimmed spectacles, the dry twang of a modern Mark Twain, the cool intellect of a Plato in tweeds, who has a passion for reason in his words, and in his heart the love of his country naturally come by in one who was an Indiana boy when the horizon was far, porches and families large, and hope was in the air.

Not that Elmer himself would ever torture the English language with a sentence as long-winded as that one.

It seems that Elmer Davis has abandoned the sea of nightly radio, but is reappearing, if not in the desert, at least on the wild waves of Sunday television. There was a large gathering in a Washington hotel tonight to meditate and mark these events in the life of E. Davis, on the quite natural assumption that an event in his life is an event in the life of the country. To deplore, no doubt, the effect his departure from audio may have on the nature of the nightly air, and to celebrate his reappearance in audio-video. This has been done in connection with the annual birthday dinners honoring the memory of Franklin Roosevelt, and it has been done appropriately enough because in a way Elmer is one of the legacies Roosevelt left behind when he departed this capital.

But if the breakers of wartime needs had not deposited E. Davis on the Washington shore, he would still have been around, and he would still have been heard. Of course, he has been in a rut, constantly offering the same commodity, day after day, common sense; by present fashions this marks him as a strange character indeed, but still there seem to be enough old-fashioned eccentrics around so that his wares find a market here and there.

You can describe Elmer Davis by two different standards; by one, rather prevalent today, he is a muddle-headed do-gooder because he believes three meals a day are fun for everybody; he is a soft-head, because he would rather hit a man in the nose than kick him in the spine when his back is turned; and he is an egghead because he can read without moving his lips.

But in the long run I suspect a different and older standard will apply; and by that one, Elmer is the whole man and the complete American. He is a man from Indiana, and he is also a classical scholar. And there is in him, therefore, a rare synthesis: an awareness of life's tragedy, of the bleak glory of man's ancient pilgrimage, and still, through it all, the warm and eager hope of the American dream.

An English commentator of the last century, William Hazlitt, once wrote a kind of political credo for himself. If Elmer ever wrote his own, the words would come out about the same. As follows:

"I am no politician and still less can I be said to be a party-man; but I have a hatred of tyranny and a contempt for its tools; and this feeling I have expressed as often and as strongly as I could. I cannot sit down quietly under the claims of barefaced power, and I have tried to expose the

little arts of sophistry by which they are defended. . . .
I deny that liberty and slavery are convertible terms, that
right and wrong, truth and falsehood, plenty and famine
. . . are matters of perfect indifference. That is all I know
of the matter; but on these points I am likely to remain
incorrigible. . . . It needs no sagacity to discover that two
and two make four; but to persist in maintaining this obvious position, if all the fashion, authority, hypocrisy and
venality of mankind were arrayed against it, would require
a considerable effort of personal courage, and would soon
leave a man in a very formidable minority."

All this could be said, I think, of Elmer Davis, a formidable—indeed, a major—minority.

ME AND MY GROUNDHOG

[February 2, 1954]

I don't know who started all this business about Groundhog Day; or why, or what he expected to prove by it;
but whoever is responsible I can only call a major champion of a minor issue; as a matter of fact, if we look at this
whole affair from the point of view of others besides the
groundhog, assuming the groundhog has a point of view
about anything except my dam and my new rye grass—if
we see it steadily and see it whole, as the poet said—why,
it seems like a miscarriage of justice. The groundhog
doesn't deserve a day dedicated to him. He doesn't deserve
an hour; all he deserves is the few seconds it takes to heave
a rock.

This whole idea about the groundhog is of extremely

171

doubtful veracity. I doubt very much if he comes out of his hole on February 2 to look for his shadow; in fact, I don't really believe he comes out of his hole at all around this time of year. He comes out earlier and he comes out later, when the new grass is small and tender and he can do the most damage to it; the rest of the winter he just sleeps and licks his chops like the pig that he is so appropriately named after.

Last February 2 I happened to be up at the cabin, so I made a point of investigating this thing. I know where his hole is, right under the logs behind my dam, so don't anybody tell me I was watching a rabbit hole or a fox hole; it's the hole my particular groundhog dashes into regularly. Anyway, he didn't come out of his hole at all last February 2, and all I learned from the investigation was that I had soaked my britches sitting on the moss behind the brush pile all day and had a cold coming on. Of course, there is the remote possibility that he didn't come out because he could see me and see I had a gun, but I have dismissed this possible factor on the basis of prior evidence that this particular groundhog knows all about what happens when I shoot at him—or, rather, what doesn't happen. He has developed an air of arrogance about my aim which is hard enough to stand when exhibited by the junior members of the household and utterly unendurable coming from a groundhog.

I don't think the groundhog cares what day it is; he isn't going to come out until he's good and ready, and that will be the week my new orchard grass comes up so fresh and tender and so easily uprooted.

Another thing—about that shadow. Did *you* ever see a groundhog's shadow? Did you ever know anybody who ever knew anybody who ever saw a groundhog's shadow?

Of course not, now that I pin you down. Well, the last time I saw my groundhog I made a point to look for his shadow. There was a bright morning sun shining on his ugly gray bristles, so if he had a shadow I would have seen it. I didn't see it, and I know why. *Nobody* sees a groundhog's shadow, and much as I hate to challenge tradition—the whole trouble with the world is that nobody respects traditions any more—still, I am forced to conclude that the groundhog himself couldn't see his own shadow, even if he has one. The reason is obvious. God did not build the groundhog with shadow-seeing in mind. He built the groundhog with practically no legs. There is almost no space between the belly of the groundhog and the ground, so he has a very tiny area in which to put his shadow; and that area is situated at such an angle from his piggy little eyes that he couldn't see it anyway—not unless he can see right through his own ribs; and if all groundhogs are as well provided for as I provide for my groundhog, their ribs are too well padded with fat to see through. So my own scientific deduction is that the whole thing about the groundhog and February 2 is a hoax, and I wish the newspapers would quit mentioning it. All it does is get me lying awake until February 3 wondering if the beast has succeeded in burrowing that hole clear through my dam, in which case I have no more pond.

The only thing that gets me back to sleep at dawn on February 3 is the thought that if he does burrow clear through, he is going to get drowned.

THE NOT QUITE
AND NOT QUITE NOT

[*February 5, 1954*]

I am in receipt of a communication from Mr. Georgie Jessel enclosing an elegantly engraved certificate of membership in the Society for the Prevention of Cruelty to Vice Presidents. Appreciative as I am of this unsolicited honor, I do not expect to develop overnight that quietly superior air worn by those who know that while many are called, only we few are chosen. Clearly Mr. Jessel has chosen every writer, broadcaster, and editor on the mailing list of any knowledgeable press agent, so he probably does not intend this to be a secret organization. Mr. Jessel was what used to be called a "luminary" of stage and screen and is now a vice president himself, of a pen company; and I would not be at all surprised if his field of executive responsibilities has something to do with public relations.

But Mr. Jessel is a vice president and obviously he has already begun to experience those vague vapors of unease that go with this peculiar rank and position, whose occupants, like a lieutenant colonel, are not quite, and yet are not quite not. Because of the special organizational suspension of all vice presidents, who have at least one foot planted firmly in mid-air, they have always been the objects of more ridicule and japery than pity or respect. Mr. Jessel is out to change this by the traditional American device of organizing his compatriots of similar station, much as cat-lovers, let us say, or foreigner-haters, feel they can love or hate better in company with a charter and set of bylaws.

But in this case any move is justified. Vice presidents have no hope of overwhelming their enemies save by marshaling their superior numbers; and I find myself in fullest sympathy with the Society for the Prevention of Cruelty to Vice Presidents, which, I now quote the certificate, "has been organized . . . to preserve, protect and pamper those who have been pressed, parlayed or provoked into these parlous positions."

The man who, so to speak, is president of all vice presidents, Mr. Richard Nixon, is awarded charter membership number one. Although no one will argue that Mr. Nixon was exactly pressed or provoked into taking the job. And the award to him comes at an appropriate moment, for congressmen are just now considering ways and means of giving the Vice Presidency a firmer base for its operations. One of the proposals is that a small mansion be maintained by the government in which the Vice President would live and entertain.

Heretofore the work of a Vice President has been obscure and limited save for his presiding function with the Senate. For many years political scientists have pondered ways to give more responsibility to the Vice President to relieve the President of some of his impossible burdens. A forthcoming book on the Presidency by Mr. Sidney Hyman points out that it is all but impossible to give the Vice President even some of the extra-constitutional duties of the President. He cannot act as party leader for realistic reasons; he cannot very well head an agency, as Roosevelt tried with Wallace, because then the President is not sufficiently free to criticize, change, or abolish the agency.

He can serve as the President's special advisor, as Mr.

Nixon has faithfully done, but that does not remove any of the formal burdens from the President. Mr. Hyman concludes that the one really important relief he can give the President is in taking over many of the ceremonial functions. Mr. Eisenhower is finding the endless ceremonies alarmingly time-consuming; he has already broken with protocol by ceasing to greet in person visiting heads of state at the airport, which, incidentally, almost produced a public international incident when the King and Queen of Greece arrived. Altogether, there is a strong case for expanding the Vice Presidency; perhaps the official residence is the proper place to begin.

WHO'S A HERO?

[February 9, 1954]

The Air Force has now joined both Army and Marine Corps in an attempt to investigate and hand down judgment on the extremely delicate and complex business of servicemen who in one way or another yielded to the blandishments or pressures of their Communist captors in Korean prison camps.

No one will envy the position of the five Air Force generals who must sit as a board, hear the testimony, try to imagine, as sensitive human beings, the conditions of capture under the ruthless Chinese Reds, and then, as responsible officers and as fellow humans, pass judgment upon men who experienced in their own nervous systems something the judges can only imagine themselves. The judges will find themselves caught in a serious dilemma.

They must exercise all the tolerance and mercy they can justify, but they must not whitewash what is really soiled, nor excuse the really inexcusable; for the morale of American fighting men generally is also involved here, and service morale is composed of many things. Not only of indulgence, favors, and candy bars, as many people seem to assume; but also of discipline, will, and the conviction that rules are to be obeyed, that personal stamina does have its reward of recognition and distinction from personal softness. Soldiers must try to live up to something bigger than themselves, and when they do it at personal cost, they do not look kindly upon the exculpation of those who fail to do it.

There are many special complexities in these cases from the Korean war. There are those like the notorious twenty-one, who seem to have accepted the Communist ideology wholesale and have voluntarily cast their future with it. However young, weak, or muddled these men may be, still every opportunity was given them; immense patience was exercised in the attempt to redeem them; it is hard to see how the armed services could any longer, in dignity, continue that attempt, even were it a practical possibility.

There are those accused by their fellow captives of betraying the welfare of others by accepting favorable treatment from the Communist captors. Where it can be established that this was done without torture, pressures, or threats on the part of the captors but only for personal privilege, the decisions should be clear enough; there will probably be many witnesses ready to testify, and it is likely to go hard with those found guilty.

There are those like Marine Colonel Schwable, and some thirty-three Air Force men reported to have made confessions of conducting germ warfare. Here again the main question will be whether they did what they did under duress, or out of hope of personal gain in greater comfort or privileges. And corollary to this lie the technical questions of how far normal due process should apply to military men involved in war. Normally in civil courts confessions made under duress are not even admitted as evidence. And how, legally speaking, can a man be found guilty of confessing to a crime that he never committed? In these special circumstances he may be found guilty, under military rules, of giving propaganda aid and comfort to the enemy; but by itself a confession of something that never happened is scarcely a crime. And germ warfare in Korea was entirely a myth. Individual civilians and organized soldiers are subject to differing rules of conduct. But the military judges will not be unaware that people generally may find it hard to see why a Robert Vogeler or a Bill Oatis confessed under duress to mythical crimes and came home as heroes; while soldiers who confessed to mythical crimes under duress come home as defendants.

On the side of morale and discipline, the judging generals will know better than any civilian observers. On the side of human nervous and mental endurance, they might do well to read a profound and moving little novel about the anti-Nazi underground called *The Steeper Cliff*. They will learn there that under pressures and tortures, there is no such thing as a hero. At best, there is only the half-hero, and the half-hero is very heroic indeed.

ABE LINCOLN ON TV

[February 12, 1954]

Many things about Abraham Lincoln can be argued; but no one can argue with the proposition that Lincoln never confused means with ends, technique with substance; he would never have understood a triumph of matter over mind.

With a slightly guilty bow in the direction of Mr. Goodman Ace, who employs the cold print of the *Saturday Review* to police the hot world of radio and television, I have been enjoying a gloomy private image of President Lincoln transposed upon the scene of contemporary Washington. On the occasion of the Gettysburg Address.

There's a planning conference going on in the office of the President's news secretary. The ghostwriters are going over a mass of papers—suggestions from Cabinet officers as to what the President ought to say about the farmers, working people, taxes, and the next recruiting quotas. The chief ghostwriter is beating his brains out figuring how to cover the women's angle in the speech.

A secretary comes in and says: "The boss says he's just going to make a few general remarks, two or three minutes." There's consternation in the room. The draft suggestions are thrown in the wastebasket. The news secretary puts in a pool call to the networks and says: "Sorry, boys, the thirteen-and-a-half-minute package is out." Consternation among the networks. Their teletypes chatter out emergency instructions to the radio crews to patch out with interviews of any senators who will be present;

TV camera crews are told to fade in shots of cemetery crosses and bereaved families of veterans.

At the railroad station the news secretary is half apologetic, half angry with the press party. "The boss hasn't written it yet. That's why there's no advances. Look, I know the early p.m.'s will miss it, but he's stubborn, and he's President." The *Tribune* man puts in a hot phone call to his home office suggesting they run a page-one editorial on the lousy White House public relations.

In the club car the Hollywood actor-director imported as TV counsel is talking to the national committee PR man. "I keep telling him to give them the grin, flash the old teeth. That sad look of his—the viewers will get the idea he's losing the war. He keeps saying people will just have to take him the way he is. But he makes with the jokes pretty good. If he'll get in a buffola to close with, maybe he can still send 'em home happy."

The chief ghostwriter enters, collapses into a chair, and says: "I've just seen his opening paragraph. Know how he starts? 'Fourscore and seven years ago.' Brother! After all I've told him about simplifying; if he means eighty-seven years ago, why doesn't he say so? After all, his vote strength is with the common people, not the eggheads."

At the platform on Cemetery Hill the TV pool director steps up to Mr. Lincoln, and, as conjured by Mr. Goodman Ace, the conversation goes like this:

"Mr. President, you'll open up on camera two, that's this one. When the red light comes on, you start your speech. Then we'll cut to a profile. You'll stand about here. Oh, I'll take that shawl, Mr. President."

"Well, there's a chill in the air and I—"

"But you're not going to do the show in that shawl, are you?"

"Yes, I am."

"Well, I wish we'd have known—we could have had costume send one over. I'm afraid the lights are going to pick up all that fuzz around it. By the way, I'll get the make-up girl. We ought to trim that beard a little. It's kinda straggly and it might—"

"Oh, this is quite all right."

"But, Mr. President, this is television. At least we can touch up that right cheek. That mole is going to look like—"

"No, no, young man. It will be all right."

"But, Mr. President, you know you're following Mr. Everett. He's going to look quite distinguished with that white hair— Oh, before I forget, your speech."

"My speech?"

"I'll have the boys run it off for the teleprompter."

"No, I'll manage with this."

"With that? You're not going to read it off that envelope, are you?"

"Well, I had planned—"

"Okay, Mr. President, but Mr. Everett will steal the show. They'll come away talking about him. They'll little note nor long remember anybody else."

REPORT FROM
THE INDEPENDENT PESSIMISTS

[*February 18, 1954*]

A national conference on traffic safety is going on in this capital city in the traditional American belief that if only enough people sit at enough round-shaped tables and talk enough, any problem can be solved. The problem

181

is there all right: the sad fact is that in these fifty-four years of driving cars more Americans have been killed by other Americans than by armed enemies in all of America's wars. Last year alone 38,000 were killed on the roads, which is more than our combat deaths in three years of the Korean war. And the President has pointed to the ironic fact that while we spend billions and set up elaborate world-wide organizations to prevent war, we just pick at the fringes of this far worse manslaughter of street and highway.

The conference here hasn't come up with anything exciting or concrete in the way of remedy except the general proposition that somehow public opinion has got to be mobilized to support safety education, training, and enforcement. Well, as one who belongs to no political party except the Independent Pessimists, I beg to submit a minority report, saying this just won't do the job. Neither will bigger and better highways, a program that can't possibly keep up with the increase in the number of cars and trucks, which will reach the appalling figure of eighty million by 1975. There are only two ways to approach the problem, both difficult. You can change people or you can change the cars.

The second is easier than the first. The modern car is an example of progress going so far it has circled back on itself; it is too fast, too comfortable, too quiet, and too filled with automatic devices, all of which break down at one time or another. Yesterday in a strong wind the hood on my taxi flew up, smashed the windshield, blocked off the driver's vision, and we narrowly escaped a bad smash-up. That never happened in the old days of the spring catch operated by hand. Children have been maimed and even killed in the modern fingertip-controlled car windows. That never happened in the days when the American driver was considered athletic enough to crank his windows up or down.

And how many people have been crushed against the garage wall by the automatic gear shift, which has a will of its own? How many people have been killed because the driver didn't know his brake fluid had leaked out? Under the old braking system you had fair warning. The newest idea in this so-called progress is the headlight that will automatically dip when the lights of an approaching car strike it. This is fine until it breaks down unbeknownst to the spoiled and sleepy driver, at which point more mechanical murders will ensue.

The whole point is that the instinctive self-survival apparatus of the human nervous system is dulled and blunted in the modern, quiet, comfortable automatic vehicle, which is not really driven or operated but merely sat or slept in.

Since the human brain, hands, and feet have so little to do, the only really safe drivers today are those the psychologists call "high-grade morons." That is, people who are fascinated by the gadgets themselves and, like children, can keep their thoughts upon them. The abstract thinker, the intellectual, or the man who merely has a lot of problems on his mind wanders off in his thoughts until a crash or a shriek brings him back to reality. Perhaps people can't be changed, but they can be protected. So the Independent Pessimists' Party proposes that all driving tests be given by psychologists. The high-grade morons will be allowed to drive the new cars. All others will drive only cars remade in the old image; cars that rattle, bump, and bang and require both hands, both feet, and the whole cerebral system to operate. Otherwise my party will wash its hands of the whole business, and sit by and watch in the attitude of the famous historian who said of the human race: "I wish them well."

SAVING GRACE, THE FALL FROM

[February 23, 1954]

If you've been suffering the guilty feeling that you're no better than a saboteur doing his bit to undermine the American way of life—why, I know just how you feel. I've had the same feeling for weeks now; insomnia has frazzled my nervous system, and it seemed to me if I just confessed my sin in public, I'd feel a lot better. It may even change my secret habit. I mean the habit of penny-pinching. Lately I've been pinching not only pennies but whole dollars, even though I learn from the front pages every day that I am directly contributing to the economic recession. If enough people like me are allowed to go hog-wild in this tendency to scrimp and save, the American economic structure, based on rapid turnover of goods, will simply collapse.

I wouldn't say I'm as bad yet as Calvin Coolidge. You may recall that day in 1928 when a Treasury delegation called on him, warning him that he must halt the wild inflation in the stock market. Silent Cal just gave them that icy stare, then spent the afternoon in the White House basement counting the apples in a barrel sent him by a friend in Vermont. It was Coolidge and that penny-pinching attitude of his that really brought on the '29 collapse, not anything Mr. Hoover did; about the only good thing Coolidge did for Hoover was to ensure a supply of apples when the country came to need them.

I can only plead that I inherited my subversive tendency. Jim Hill, the empire-builder, gave the commencement address at Father's graduation in Iowa and said: "If you can save your money, you'll be a success; if you can't, you won't." Until I was old enough to read, I had a vague notion that was one of the Ten Commandments. But in these recent years of the Keynesian consumer-spending economic theories I've been given to understand saving is one of the seven deadly sins. Well, I did my best—a house I couldn't afford, a car that drinks gasoline, steak-eating pets, all the rest of it. But it didn't last—the traumatic experience of early childhood proved dominant, and I began to slip, some time last fall.

It seems so innocent now that I look back—that first fatal misstep; I took a day coach to New York instead of the parlor car. Of course, I laughed it off and convinced myself I could check the tendency right there. Little did I know that the battle was already lost. Came the day I started using one filter in my holder per six cigarettes instead of five. Next thing I knew I found myself asking for regular instead of high-test gasoline. The old urge was upon me, the habit had taken hold. A topcoat off the rack, instead of one custom-made; one scoop of feed for the horses instead of two; I got old hats blocked, old socks mended; I gave taxi-drivers dime tips, counted my change in restaurants, began walking brazenly past head waiters with empty hands.

I grew wilder, bolder, as my moral sense became dulled; I outfumbled even the women over luncheon checks, hung around the canapes at cocktail parties. Old friends from New Deal days tried to take me aside for heart-to-heart talks. Republican friends began slipping anti-gloom-and-doom speeches by Sherman Adams and Senator Ferguson under my door. I was beyond redemption, it seemed. Then came yesterday and the annual Washington's Birthday sales. I sneaked out of the house at dawn, and halfway to town the car stopped. I had delayed filling the gas tank until too late. It was somewhere along the highway, as, footsore and weary, I thumbed the passing cars, that grace descended upon me. Something hard in my breast dissolved, and I knew I was saved, if only I could confess and take punishment.

So now I will sleep peacefully tonight awaiting with serenity the knock on the door. Within hours my last doubt shall be removed—I have been wondering a little if the meals really are free in jail.

MASS MERCHANDISING THE
NATIONAL DESTINY

[*March 4, 1954*]

One of the troubles with the former Democratic administration of this federal government in its later years was that it became far too rigid in defending its mistakes as well as its successes, after its policies had been put to the test. And one of the chief troubles with the present administration is that it has been far too sweeping in its claims for its policies before they were put to the test. The latest example is the painful embarrassment of administration officials now forced to tone down their extravagant claims about the discovery and discharge of the so-called security risks in government.

This general tendency set in even before the Eisenhower nomination, when a new type of strategist entered big-time politics in force; many of them were men from the national advertising agencies; they clearly saw that the old political days of the back-room boys were ended, that the new arts of mass suggestion, endlessly repeated slogans and claims could be used in behalf of a candidate or a policy as well as a commercial product. They applied to politics what they call "mass merchandising" and what their enemies call "a snow job" on the American people. Not even yet has the full story been told of the small, skillful group of psychological strategists in Chicago who saw that the delegates were inundated each day with wires and calls from their own districts in behalf of the so-called "fair play" amendment, which was anti-Taft. The general technique was applied throughout the fall campaign.

What works in the heat of an election campaign does not always, however, work so well in the practice of government; the scrutinizing responsibility of the free press and the free parliament comes into play, and sooner or later all claims are put to the test. Because the pre-inauguration tendency toward the wholesale, oversimplified claim was carried over into some areas of actual administration, this government has compounded its troubles; had the claims been less sweeping, the criticism would have been less severe when the inevitable mistakes showed up. The first mistake of this nature came in the President's first state-of-the-Union message with the announcement that the Chinese Nationalists were now "released," and mass hopes were encouraged of action from Formosa. Then the facts of life set in.

The next example of overselling was the announcement that hereafter we would pursue a "more dynamically anti-

Communist" foreign policy. The facts of life again set in. The Korean armistice and the agreement to sit down with the Chinese Reds next month scarcely represent a more dynamically anti-Red policy; and Mr. Dulles is now suffering a degree of retaliation he would not be suffering if the product had not been oversold in the beginning. Another example, last year was the happy talk about "psychological warfare" as a miraculous and bloodless trick for making the Russian specter in the world lie down and behave; it has its place, but a very limited place, and all such talk has long since died away.

Brownell badly oversold his case about Harry Truman knowingly abetting treason; the so-called "new look" in our world military strategy has been so wildly oversold that no administration official has even tried to make a public defense of the more extravagant claims originally made for this idea. The claim and slogan of administration "teamwork" was so oversold and oversimplified that the events of these last two weeks simply hand the Democrats a wicked weapon of satire. And the wholesale claims about Communists or subversives ferreted out of government—especially as blown up by McCarthy, Governor Dewey, and Postmaster General Summerfield—have now collapsed on the basis of the administration's own figures.

Mass suggestion is successful in the art of selling in a free market; it remains distinctly limited in the art of governing in a free democratic society.

TELL IT TO THE BUFFALOES

[*March 10, 1954*]

There was a time, about twenty years ago, when the name Herbert Hoover was a cuss word in this Capital; or an adjective useful for humor and derision; and nowhere was that more true than around the premises of the slightly cynical National Press Club. Today the ex-President, now nearly eighty, spoke before that club; he had a capacity audience, a warm and friendly and admiring audience. The admiration was not perhaps so much for the social philosophy he has resolutely clung to all his turbulent life, but for the man himself. He was erect and ruddy, dignified but relaxed; he spoke clearly, deliberately, in a lean, effective prose; he has acquired—or uncovered— a delightful sense of humor, benign in tone, slightly sardonic, but never bitter, about the human parade in all its glories and its foolish vanities.

There was something refreshing and reassuring about his appearance today and about his speech. First, because of the man himself; he not only has survived years of the most violent criticism, much of it unjustified, but has come through it with calmness and self-respect. He stood there today, a reassuring symbol of the truth that the political passions of the considerably violent American people do give way in time to sober second thought. His life has now spanned several eras of political orientation and he stood there as a symbol of what one might call the moral continuity of government.

189

There was something else refreshing about this appearance. For many weeks Washington has been distracted by the domination of personalities and political emotion; and it was good for all concerned to be reminded that if there is an art of politics, there is also a science of government. Hoover is no artist at politics, but he is as close to a scientist as one can be in this human and therefore extremely difficult field of governing. The great Presidents are, and must be, the political artists, but this fantastically complex machinery also requires the constant attention of engineers. And in these recent years of war and crisis, government has suffered for lack of the quiet men with the slide rule in their hands.

There is a chance now, in this present period of relative calm, for the general overhaul so much needed; and it may be an ironic eventuality that Herbert Hoover's most positive and lasting contribution may be recorded in the history books as his reorganization work first undertaken at the behest of a Democratic regime. The Hoover Commission on overhauling the federal structure is now in its second phase. Mr. Hoover is convinced that if Congress would grant all his recommendations, his commission could save five to seven billions a year without injury to essential functions. But he is wise in the ways of Congress, well aware that every Congressman's general desire for economy is cut across, again and again, by his specific desire to get more and more for this constituent or that project back home.

He is also aware of the two hundred thousand or so pressure groups, each of which is all in favor of every single item of reorganization—except that one which affects itself. "If they would all just take a holiday for two years," said Mr. Hoover, "they would get a possible reward in heaven and a positive reward on this earth in the form of reduced taxation. And, finally, Mr. Hoover casts a wary eye on the self-styled efficiency experts who would condescend to give government a few quick weeks of their specific wisdom. They remind him, he said, of the efficiency expert who arrived in a snowstorm at a Western town. In the sleigh he objected when the old Irish driver tucked the buffalo robe about him with the hair side of the robe on the outside. "It would more efficiently keep the cold air out," said the expert, "if the leather side were on the outside." After a while the driver chuckled and said: "Mister, I was just wondering why somebody didn't tell that to the buffaloes."

A LITTLE BOY SHALL LEAD US

[March 12, 1954]

I should like to tell a little story tonight, about three small boys, a dog, and a bird. I am indebted to the *Washington Daily News* for this story, but not so much professionally as personally. This has been a week of sickness in Washington affairs, a moral sickness; its symptoms have been slurs and slanders, man to man, sneers and innuendoes, assaults on honor and truth, all of it presided over by a kind of neurotic tension, by brooding fears and hatreds; and in the process the majesty of the greatest free government on earth has been, for the moment, despoiled and reduced to shabbiness. I will not try to draw any moral from the little story; I tell it only because it made me feel better and perhaps it can make you feel the same. It is a story of love, not hate; of courage, not fear, and of the pure in heart, whose strength is as the strength of ten.

The Hazenner family lives at a little crossroads cluster called Tyson's Corner, Virginia, just outside this Capital City. Irving Hazenner is twelve, Frankie is ten, and Wayne is six. They were in the woods the other day, hunting for flying squirrels. They had with them their three-month-old puppy, named Whiskers. Whiskers strayed off and the three children heard him scream in terror. And then they saw Whiskers, sailing up in the air, in the claws of an eagle. The eagle took Whiskers to his nest in the top of a tree. Whiskers was about to die, and it was three little boys against a great eagle and high in the eagle's element.

The little boys did not run away for help, nor did they cry. They ran to the eagle's tree; it had no branches near the ground. "But there was a smaller tree next to it," Irving later explained. "Frankie climbed up. Then we pushed the little tree over toward the big one and he got onto the big tree." Frankie climbed up, and up. Frankie described it this way: "That eagle was flying around me," he said. "He was grabbing at my pants and he tore them. So I hit him. I just hit him a good one with my fist. He flew off to a branch and sat there. There was a baby eagle and two big rabbits there in the nest, too. I got the puppy and climbed down." Frankie added: "I sure was scared."

But Frankie couldn't have been quite so scared as one would think. For what did Frankie do, but climb right back up the tall tree and bring down the baby eagle, too? The three little boys walked calmly home through the woods, with the puppy and the baby eagle in their arms, and all the while the big eagle followed them, circling and swooping near. But not even the six-year-old was frightened of the eagle by then, and when it took up a station in a tree near the house, they all three shouted at the eagle as hard as they could and the eagle, which had clearly lost *his* nerve, took fright at the shouts and flew away.

But, as sometimes happens even among grown-ups, what courage has done, carelessness can undo. When all the excitement was over, Irving went down to the deepfreeze, to get some candy for a victory feast for all hands. He took Whiskers with him. Then the boys sat down to look at television, though how the flickering adventures of cops and cowboys could ever excite them again, I cannot imagine. In a half-hour Mr. Hazenner came home and heard the tale of the day's mighty doings. He wanted to see how Whiskers was getting on. So, after a search, they found Whiskers—locked in the deepfreeze. This time not even his screams were doing him any good.

Frankie said later: "Whiskers was pretty weak that night, but he's doing all right now."

The baby eagle they keep in a box; they feed him hamburger, and call him Squeaky because he makes a squeaking noise. Squeaky does not seem particularly out of place in the house. The three boys have eleven dogs, besides Whiskers, a cat, and a rabbit. "We did have a pet skunk," said Irving, "but he got away."

FOOTNOTES

[*March 22, 1954*]

This is probably the most superfluous discourse since the day the big war broke out and H. V. Kaltenborn analyzed the Archbishop of Canterbury's prayer. But the great affairs of state will have to get along without my advice for one evening while I consider the burning question of the human foot. Several pairs of distinguished feet are burning in this region right now, though the latest word from the world of science is that feet really don't *have* to burn.

The burning feet in question belong to some misguided Washington editors who foolishly took up a challenge flung down by Supreme Court Justice Douglas, a fellow with happy feet, who climbs mountain peaks before breakfast because they are there. The editors took their feet off their desks long enough one day to write an editorial saying there ought to be a parkway between Washington and Cumberland, along the Potomac and the old C and O Canal. Douglas retorted that the area ought to be left in its natural state and challenged them to hike the hundred and eighty miles to test the two theories. The editors accepted, violating a fundamental precept of journalism, which is that any editor or commentator who consents to test out his own advice to others is jeopardizing everybody in the trade and ought to have his union card taken away from him.

Thirty-seven normally immobile characters started out with Douglas on the hike three days ago; they are now down to about twenty. Some have been sneaking rides on trucks; some have just been sitting, under the pretext of bird-watching. One paper, last night, got a dispatch from its reporter with the party beginning with the words of Robert Louis Stevenson: "Glad did I live and gladly die; and I laid me down with a will." As things are going, the Justice is likely to reach Washington as a minority of one—a natural position for him, anyway.

I relate this sad affair as an example of what need *not* happen to the human foot, according to some orthopedic surgeons now meeting in Cleveland. The doctors' general conclusion is that the trouble is not so much with our feet as with our shoes. Our shoes boss our feet, instead of the other way round. And in the good old American tradition of action, these doctors not only think something should be done about it; they are doing it. They are designing shoes equipped with a kind of automatic gearshift. The thing is, when we walk, our bones and muscles shift in a pattern, but our shoes don't shift with them; result—bunions.

The doctors want to see shoes with heels built on the offset, so the weight is directed toward the big toe, where it's supposed to go. They also suggest a movable center in the rubber heel, to give the foot a rolling, rocker motion.

As a fellow who once had to walk a hundred and fifty miles on blisters the size of a silver dollar, I am tempted a bit by this prospect; but as a reactionary who disbelieves in most mechanical progress, as a nay- rather than a yea-sayer, on sober second thought I immediately conjured up the negative. The gearshift shoe would immediately proliferate complications, and accessories. Salesmen would urge you to buy their special oil for the gears; we'd all be carrying guaranteed lifetime oilcans in our vest pockets like cigarette-lighters. We'd be out of the spare parts just when we needed them. Rotary Club board meetings would break up into arguments about the pros and cons of the newest model shoes with overdrive. Guests would be taking off their shoes to demonstrate during the brandy period. Kids would be begging to borrow the old man's foot-o-matics for the senior prom.

This thing could even resurrect the bunion derbies and the walkathons of the thirties, and everybody knows what followed that—world war.

In the words of Patrick Henry, I know not what course others may take, but as for my feet, they will remain in their normal condition; that is to say, on top of my desk.

TWENTY-THREE SKIDDOO,
SENATOR

[*March 25, 1954*]

The Senate has been winding up debate on the excise taxes—Democrats like Douglas wishing to reduce them not only on furs and jewelry but on household appliances in order to stimulate buying among the lower-income groups; Republicans like Millikin wishing to go slowly on such cuts in order to keep a balanced budget at least on the visible horizon. It was quite a debate; it had everything, including sex, psychoanalysis, crap games, home and mother, the Stork Club, and the Icarian syllogism.

It started off in fine style with Millikin accusing Douglas, who is worried about the recession, of wallowing in gloom and doom. Douglas promptly suggested Millkin was an apostle of zoom and boom.

But things began to jump track a bit when Millikin, dyed-in-the-wool conservative Republican, quoted Franklin D. Roosevelt on fearing nothing but fear itself. From then on the quotations came thick and fast until the two statesmen were furiously belaboring each other with couplets, quatrains, Alexandrines, and finally rabbit-punching by misquoting each other. Douglas scorned the needs of bejeweled, befurred women and said the Republicans were gilding the lily that toils not, nor spins, thereby not only mixing up Matthew VI with Shakespeare's *King John,* but misquoting Shakespeare in the process. You gild refined gold; lilies, you *paint.*

At one point Millikin mentioned "expensive democratic minks." Douglas finessed this and came out with "simple democratic cloth coats," which concealed a counter punch at Vice President Nixon, and then aimed a right cross at Millkin with the statement that sales of minks and sables have greatly increased in Washington over the last fifteen months. Later, with scorn, Millikin referred to Douglas's description of the poor ladies suffering on their knees while the rich cover themselves with diamond tiaras and blue mink or fox furs. Douglas: "I said sables." Millikin: "The only sable . . . is to be found on the black, funereal clothes of the Senator from Illinois."

They got on to the cabaret tax. Douglas said righteously that he had never been in a night club in his life, and proved it by insisting that the Twenty-one Club is the Twenty-three Club. Millikin was slightly doubtful, but gave up when Douglas cited Walter Winchell as his authority for this. Millikin then proved his own happy innocence of night-club knowledge by suggesting that Douglas must be thinking about the "toothsome chorus line" at the Twenty-three Club. This completed the day's rout of all accuracy, inasmuch as the Twenty-one Club is the place people go because it does *not* have a chorus line. They got into more argument about the Republican "trickle down" economic theory versus the Democratic "percolate up" theory, but they were soon back to sin. Millikin accused Douglas of pulling figures out of the air as if he were shooting craps, and Douglas solemnly announced that he does not shoot craps. Millikin: "The

Senator will soon stand in an exalted position and we will all have to act like disciples of Father Divine in his presence. Good Father, please spare us from that."

A happy accident happened to Millikin. He spilled the glass on his desk; it contained—*milk*. He pointed to this with a glad cry as proof of his virtue and armor against temptations of the flesh. Later Douglas asked if Millikin believed in the sale of home appliances; Millikin said he not only believed in the sale of home appliances, but in the Bible, God, home, mother, and the flag. This projected Senator Humphrey into the debate. He reminded Millikin of the man who believed in Cleveland and Akron and in Santa Claus, but had his doubts about Toledo; Millikin rose to the new challenge.

He believed in Akron, Cleveland—*and* Toledo.

TOLERANCE, VARIETY, AND CALM

[March 26, 1954]

This happens to be the eightieth birthday of that irreplaceable American, that statesman of the soul, the Vermont farmer and poet, Mr. Robert Frost; and, as the woman said in the play about the salesman, attention must be paid.

Thinking of Mr. Frost, a vague and vagrant theory of wartime has recurred to me, which, I almost believe, has something in it. When England came to its mortal peril, its people turned to an old man named Churchill; when

Small Sounds in the Night

Mussolini's regime collapsed, the men to whom the people turned were not its men of middle age, but elderly men, like Sforza and Croce and Orlando. When the new France emerged, only partial faith was extended to the middle-aged men like De Gaulle, and it was to the old men like Herriot that the people gave their trust. Here in our own Capital there is today a sense of unease with the men of the prime, middle years, and a vague yearning for the calm solidity symbolized once by elder statesmen like Stimson and Root or Cordell Hull. My vagrant theory was that perhaps something has broken in the succeeding generation of leadership, those now of the middle and active years. They reached maturity amid crisis and uncertain change; they tend to think in the short term; they do not seem to have the sense of continuity possessed by that older generation who matured in social stability, before the first great war; current winds and modern quakes did not slip the footing of such men, for their footing was lodged in rock, the great rock column of our institutions, reaching down deep to our founding strata.

Perhaps this is fantasy. But if we ever have to trade off our democratic form of government, my own vote would be for a patriarchy. The thoughts of the very old, like those of the very young, are long, long thoughts. A vast amount of the thinking we have had the last few years has been compressible into the width of a headline, and not even the eight-column streamer is long enough for the long, long thought.

So the headline-writers had a little trouble with Robert Frost and his birthday remarks. The needs of the next edition or broadcast are not likely to impress a man from that vanishing breed, a man who builds fences, stone by stone, and lets a poem ripen six or eight years before he permits its publication. "When you can't pin me down," said Frost to the inquiring reporters, "it's due to my quality of uncatchability"; the only proper answer from a man who has spent eighty years trying to pin down truth with his pen and therefore knows its elusive nature.

But was he hopeful about life any more? "It goes on," he said. "It goes on. I don't hold with people who say, 'Where do we go from here?' I wouldn't get up in the morning if I thought we didn't have a direction to go in. But if you ask me what the direction is, I don't answer." Still, he did say it was not in the direction of the dogs. Juvenile delinquency, atom bombs, McCarthyism—he refused to be excited about any of it. Politicians, he said, were slinging the word *fear* around so much, he hardly knew what it meant any more, but thought he knew what freedom means; "Freedom," he said, "means feeling easy in your harness."

If he had one piece of advice to give, it was this: we are all too crowded and too hurried, and a man must, by craft or by courage, temper himself to this condition, and go on.

This, I might point out, is what all the old men, the great men with their feet in the rock, are telling us. This is what my old friend Carl Sandburg means when he instructs his household not to bother him if the house catches fire—he has to get on with his work. This is what Winston Churchill meant in his Nobel Prize advice, to confront the clatter and confusions of the world with "tolerance, variety and calm."

THE ALL-AMERICAN DREAM

[*March 26, 1954*]

Around six p.m. today, when it was all over, I had that funny feeling you get sometimes that the whole thing had happened years before; and, of course, it had. It happened lots of times, just the way it happened this afternoon. There I was, facing the Yankee pitcher in the last half of the tenth inning. The roar of the crowd was drumming in my ears; out of the corner of my eye I could see the President of the United States, staring at me with an imploring expression. His name was Coolidge. (It was years before I found out that any expression at all in his face was an optical illusion.) Sometimes, in those tenth innings, the President's face faded out, replaced by the heavenly image of Helen Bloomquist, who had yellow hair and sat right in front of me in the sixth grade. Anyway, I always hit the ball over the fence for the winning run. My shouting teammates would carry me out on their shoulders and the President would lean over to shake my hand, saying: "Young man, your country is proud of you this day."

Well, that's the way it happened this afternoon, except that it was Mickey Vernon, the Senators' first baseman, and Eisenhower, instead of me and Cal Coolidge. For a moment I felt a little resentful at Mickey Vernon for stealing my dream, but, after all, I had got my use out of that dream, long ago, and Vernon sort of needed it, after

201

nine innings of very medium batting indeed, to say nothing of his blooper at first base on that silly Yankee bunt play that put a man on first when he had no business there. Altogether, the 1954 version of the universal, eternal, all-American dream of the male species couldn't have gone to a more deserving fellow. Vernon led the league in batting last year, but still had a hard time getting a raise from Clark Griffith, a very languorous man with a dollar; so, as I say, the '54 gold-framed, cloud-tinted, all-American dream—this country's equivalent of the Nobel Prize and the Croix de Guerre—the award couldn't have gone to a more deserving fellow.

It was the right-field fence: distance from ground, forty-one feet.

President Eisenhower did lean over and shake Vernon's hand, all right; but he didn't really say: "Your country is proud of you this day." As far as I can find out, what he said was: "What a wallop!" But people are more informal these days. It was a pretty informal ball game all around; downright unorthodox. For example, when a President throws out a second ball, for the photographers, the player who catches it doesn't, according to protocol, pitch it back to the President; and the President certainly doesn't catch it and throw it back again to the player. But today he did. Bucky Harris doesn't normally force Casey Stengel to use five pitchers, but today he did. No team normally makes two costly errors in a row against the Yankees and still beats them, but today the Senators did. Presidential Assistant Sherman Adams normally doesn't permit a smile to disfigure his firm New England countenance, but the lady next to me, with the binoculars, claimed she saw one, today. And Mamie Eisenhower doesn't normally chew gum, but I noticed she was chomping rapidly in that terrible ninth inning, which, I suppose, is one way to keep from biting your nails off.

The President doesn't normally miss a round of golf for baseball, but today he was there to the glorious finish, and by the time he reached Augusta tonight he couldn't have had time for anything more than putting practice on the living-room rug.

And normally, my fourteen-year-old Mike would be rigid with awe in the presence of a President; but the way he pummeled through the whole covey of dignitaries to get to Vernon with a ball for autographing, you'd think he'd never learned any manners at all.

But about the dream—I'm just waiting. The first time the fourteen-year-old hints that he'd sort of rather be called Mickey, I'll know the dream is still around the house.

THE LADY'S NOT FOR BRANDING

[*April 26, 1954*]

It's not very often we get a new Senator in mid-term around here, and it always causes a certain stir, not only inside the club, but among those who chronicle the doings of the members; it's like a new boy joining the class in mid-semester, or a new girl showing up, a little defensive, at the sorority house after her folks move to town. So there was a fair amount of neck-craning and first-impression-exchanging today when the new lady Senator from Nebraska was sworn in, the attractive Mrs.

Eve Bowring. She's a grandmother and runs a cattle ranch that consumes a considerable proportion of Nebraska. This gives us two women in the Senate now, and therefore twice as much opportunity for the male Senators to demonstrate their gallantry. Sometimes Senatorial gallantry is a little on the heavy-handed side; sometimes it gets a little obscure. Today it was obscure.

As she came down the aisle to take the oath she was escorted by Senator Butler of Nebraska, and Vice President Nixon remarked: "Senator Butler has asked me to inform the Senate that no implication should be drawn from the fact that the Senior Senator from Nebraska is a widower and the Junior Senator is a widow." Nixon must have meant *inference*, not *implication*, but I'm still not sure just what he had in mind. My guess is that Butler was disclaiming any romantic notions toward the lady. Was he, then, informing the other Senate bachelors that the field was wide open? Or was he, by this negative approach, slyly putting the notion of possible romance in the lady's mind? Recently I've been compiling an innuendo and implication dictionary to help me report the Senate in this new era, but I don't find anything in my files covering this particular situation.

The situation got considerably more obscure today when the new Senator Bowring held her first news conference. She showed that she has already learned Senatorial lesson number one—how to confuse by saying too little. Later, I suspect, she will learn the final lesson—how to confuse by saying too much. She showed herself already competent at the Washington art of question-parrying, and she made it even tougher for the reporters by doing it in cow-country language; it was a little like the new boy in the class answering the other kids in pig Latin to show he knew a thing or two but wasn't going to commit himself until he found out the general attitude of the bigger kids.

One question was: did she intend to run for the full Senate term in November? This, she replied, was an "amusing" question. It struck the reporters that the reply was more amusing than the question, but they held their ground and went on. How does she stand on foreign affairs? Reply: "May I tighten my cinch before I tell you my views?" Well, the reporters were perfectly willing if she wanted to excuse herself a minute and tighten her cinch, but she didn't seem to mean that. She seemed to mean that she wanted to tidy up her ideas a bit before speaking out. Thinking back to my own Western days, I just assumed myself she meant she wanted to be sure the saddle was secure before she rides off in all directions.

Question: how does she stand on the farm price support argument? Answer: "Sir, I didn't notice you came in with your spurs on." This completely baffled us effete Easterners; there's nothing to do but wait for a translation at the President's next news conference; he keeps up on Wild West dialogue better than anyone else around here. Question: how would she describe her political position? Answer: "I am a forward-looking Republican, but," she quickly added, "we must also remember to look back." Obviously, this is a lady who wasn't born yesterday, can put the water on both shoulders to the wheel, and put both ears to the ground without burying her head in the sand. But I'm still worried about her last phrase. I'm a little weak on Westerns, but I know my Bible pretty well, and I'd like to remind the new Senator that around here ladies who look back are apt to turn into a pillar of society.

RISE AND SCHINE

[April 29, 1954]

If there is any sense of political humor left in the country, which I frequently doubt, we will probably have
a new musical comedy one of these days entitled *Rise and
Schine*, in which a basso profundo in the wings will repeatedly sing the theme song called "Point of Order"
(not to be confused with the novel entitled *Point of No
Return*). With or without music, a re-run of the current
Washington soap opera can be a distinct service to the
public, provided the program prints a clear outline of the
plot and identifies the part each of the characters is playing.
By five o'clock this afternoon the folks in my neighborhood, whether they were pro- or anti-McCarthy, couldn't
tell, any more, who were the good guys and who the bad
guys.

There was a newcomer in our group and he gave us
expert spectators quite a rough time with his questions.
The conversation in front of the television set went, in
parts, about like this:

"McCarthy and Stevens, they're both Republicans,
aren't they?"

"Yes."

"Well, how come they are fighting each other, then?"

We said they were probably also human beings.

"Well, now, that Jackson and McClellan and that
Symington, they're Democrats—how come they seem to
be defending the Republican Secretary of the Army while

the Republican members on the committee don't seem interested in defending him?"

All we could answer was that Washington is full of wheels within wheels, sometimes big wheels within small wheels.

"What's so funny about Private Schine being out in front of a bunch of generals? Isn't that the way it usually is, in a war?"

We said it was, but in this war the men in the rear weren't exactly supporting the private at the front.

He said: "Who's Schine scared of? That lawyer in front of him or his generals in back of him?" We thought this was probably the first time in history a private has been more scared of a civilian than of a general.

The newcomer said: "Isn't that Mundt in the middle?" We said Mundt was in the middle all right. "Why doesn't he use that hammer?" We said he probably saves the hammer till after the sessions to hit himself over the head with because it feels so good when he stops.

He said: "McCarthy must be reading somebody else's lines. There he is objecting to a witness being browbeaten." We replied that McCarthy does not like to see privates browbeaten, only generals, especially generals who undignify themselves by sitting next to assistant secretaries of defense.

"Look," he said later. "There's Senator Dworshak squabbling with McCarthy about that letterhead. I thought McCarthy handpicked Dworshak to represent him on the committee." "Well," we said, "in politics when you grab for a rose you often get a thorn; besides, Dworshak also represents a lot of people in Idaho, where television is believed to have penetrated by now."

The newcomer said: "Is Private Schine a Communist?"

We said: "Of course not; what gave you that idea?"
"Well," he said, "they keep talking about the Army
'coddling' him, and according to McCarthy it is Communists the Army coddles." "Well," we said, "the Army
is a big melting-pot, where anybody who falls into it is
likely to be coddled, steamed, or parboiled. In any case,"
we said, "Schine is not being coddled at the moment;
Schine is being roasted."

The newcomer observed that this was not very funny
and went on to say: "With all those generals and secretaries tied up there, who is minding the store?" All we
could say to that was that it's pretty hard for anybody to
wait on the customers when a couple of small boys keep
throwing bricks through the plate-glass window.

The newcomer said we were confusing him more than
the hearing. We said if that was true we would immediately put a bullet through our head or run for the Senate.
And on this inconclusive note the conversation ended;
which, come to think of it, is how the hearing ended, too.

THE DECISION ON
DESEGREGATION

[May 19, 1954]

It is a fair statement, I think, to say that the over-all reaction by the press and community leaders in Southern
states to Monday's Supreme Court decision has been a
matter of profound relief and encouragement to responsible men in the federal government. The decision struck a
deep blow at what millions of Southerners look upon as a

way of life, and yet with some notable exceptions, the Southern reaction as far as it can be judged here in the Capital, has been steady, clear-headed, and high-minded. Coming in the midst of a distracting period generally, when there appears to be deep intellectual and emotional disunity in the country, this reaction to a most intensely personal development is the most magnificent kind of reassurance that Americans are one people, that this house is not divided in any of its foundations, and will not be divided. As the decision itself sweeps away a peculiar and non-typical American institution, so the Southern reaction should sweep away any lingering notions in the North that Southerners are somehow peculiar or non-typical as Americans. There have been a few explosions of wrath among some Southern political leaders, but not very many. The South is represented, these days, by extremely few professional anti-Negro politicians of the type of a Rankin, who used to be described as the man who believed what Bilbo said.

In terms of history, there is a kind of fortuitous timing about this drastic Court decision. It is doubtful if it could have been done, and made to stick, without violent dislocations, even a few years ago. But no section of the country has changed so much as the South has changed in the last twenty years; the old image of an agrarian, torpid South, brooding in the weeds of its memories, letting the world of events and ideas pass it by—that image bears no resemblance to the reality of today; today the true image is one of an industrializing South, prosperous, electric with energy, new people, new ideas, developing a creative intellectual life perhaps more effectively than any other part of the country. All this, particularly the economic prosperity and its accompanying sense of confidence, has greatly reduced the racial tensions; for when fear diminishes, the irrational prejudices growing out of fear must also diminish. And the Court's decision comes at a time that finds most Southern states by no means unprepared in practical terms. Advances in schooling practices, facilities, and standards have been greater in the South in recent years than anywhere else. The whole picture has changed in this respect. The over-all average for the seventeen states with segregation shows somewhat less money spent per Negro than per white child, but in many places Negro children have the best schools and, indeed, the best teachers, because the cream of Negro intellects of necessity goes into teaching, more often than does the best of white intellects. Consider the educational revolution in the state of Florida; twelve short years ago, the state spent a little over six dollars a year per white pupil and eighty cents per Negro pupil. Today it is around seventy-five dollars per white child and eighty dollars per Negro child.

Altogether, the seventeen Southern states spend a greater proportion of their income on education than do Northern states; if the average amount per child is smaller, that is only because the income is smaller.

So the South is not unprepared. But no one would pretend that the practical difficulties, financial, material, psychological, will not be extreme and lasting over several years ahead. It would be hard to think of any American parallel, where so many communities have been ordered by simple decree to make so difficult a readjustment in their normal way of living; how they do it in the period ahead should be a matter of the most intense and sympathetic interest for all Americans.

Somehow and one day, it must all shake down, and work. It is hard to believe to the contrary.

THE RUSTY HACKSAW HAIRDO

[*May 21, 1954*]

With the cowardly courage of a fellow who's about to flee to Europe and thus can't be got at, I propose to analyze the new female haircut, known variously as the "Italian," "Ondine," or "Mermaid," but hereinafter referred to as the rusty hacksaw hairdo. You know what I mean—the new arrangement of woman's former crowning glory which looks like a boy's fallen flattop hairdo after a swim at a beach where no fresh-water shower was available. I have investigated this new bit of evidence, raising again the question whether the female sex is here to stay— or even *wants* to stay—and I find its sociological history somewhat confusing.

Hairdressing experts I have consulted indignantly reject my own original hypothesis, which was that the whole idea came from that page in *Tom Sawyer* wherein Aunt Polly clamped the soup bowl over Tom's head and went to work with the kitchen shears. They have also spurned my secondary theory, which was that the idea originated in rural sections of the Midwest through careful observation of what a strawstack looks like in August after sufficient forming and shaping by sufficient cattle seeking shade. No, the thing just growed, like Topsy, who, as far as I recollect, never did grow very much. The thing just ungrowed.

It ungrew from rather obscure beginnings. One school of fashion experts holds that it was started by the actress Audrey Hepburn, who appears in *Ondine*, the play, with a quick assist from the French dancer Jeanmaire, who appears in everything, mostly magazine covers. Other fashion historians dispute this and claim that it was originally the property of Miss Anita Loos, the writer, who presumably tore her hair out in patches while trying to perfect the book *Gentlemen Prefer Blondes*. Either that, they say, or it came from Miss Carol Channing, who played the leading role in the stage version of that book. If either of these latter two identifications is authentic, there is a certain splendid irony in the whole development. For Miss Loos wrote about blondes, Miss Channing was a blonde on the stage, and yet, so the experts have informed me, the new hairdo has reduced blondes to wretchedness; it simply does not *do* for blondes. Why, I still don't know—something to do with contrast or skin textures or something; anyway, the rusty hacksaw hairdo is just fine for brunettes. This has resulted in the further irony of brunettes who dyed themselves into blondes now having to dye themselves back into their natural shade. What this is going to do to the peroxide business hardly bears contemplation; the whole thing is already raising havoc with the hairdressing business; the new operation takes only about seven minutes and a pair of scissors; most hairdressers can't charge more than a couple of dollars. The chain of historic irony goes even farther; for centuries, women with naturally curly hair have been the despairing envy of straight-haired women, who spend vast annual sums achieving curly hair, and this thing, I'm told, is no good with curls. After centuries of pre-eminence, the curly-haired blonde has had it. Well, this is an era of revolution everywhere; any day now, some desperate ad-writer may even go so far as to revise those immortal lines to read: "Which twin is named Toni?"

This concludes my offerings on the latest organized madness of the sawed-off half of the human race. There is no use trying to enlighten me. For the next two weeks I will be in Italy, incommunicado, and incognito in a duck-tail haircut, reat pleats, and stuff cuffs. Address all tele-grams, and letters of protest to the gentleman who will be struggling with these shattered five minutes—Mr. Dallas Townsend. What I don't know about women I will learn from him when I get back. Remember the name—Town-send.

This is John Doe in Washington.

THE STRANGE PROPORTIONS
OF FEAR

[*June 7, 1954*]

This reporter has spent the last two weeks in Italy, chiefly in Rome, where the sun is bright, the people busy, and where the general tranquillity is marred by the incessant popping of motorbikes on the street, not Sena-tors on television. It is perfectly astonishing how well the people there get along with a minimum of television and a dearth of Senatorial hearings; in fact, the Italians seem to insist on doing things in *reverse* from us. We have very few Communists and a vast excitement about them, whereas they have a vast number of Communists and very little excitement about them. I wouldn't care to trade positions with them, for the long run; but in so short a run as two weeks the effect is rather soothing on raw

213

political nerves. This is like trying to cure vertigo by standing on one's head; the cure will certainly turn out to be worse than the illness, but for a moment, at least, the changes does produce a pleasant illusion of relief.

It could be that I *have* been standing on my head for the last two weeks and thus seeing everything in the focus of upside-down. Anyway, quite a lot of things did look different from the way they look in Washington.

In Italy, Communism is a matter for debate; here it is a matter for battle; here Communism is a conspiracy against the state; in Italy it is not only that but a vested interest *within* the state. There, it is not only a revolutionary movement, but a vast, settled bureaucracy; here it thrives, when it thrives at all, on poverty; there it exploits prosperity as well as poverty; like an efficient, established labor union, it gets its members the jobs where jobs are scarce; and it gets its members the raises, promotions, and perquisites where there are plenty of jobs. Here Communism involves a few intellectuals and a few workers; there it involves every class; many rich men pay money tribute to it, and you will find even members of the so-called aristocracy, the most decayed aristocracy in Europe, professing adherence to it. Here vigorous anti-Communists say we must prosecute the Communists; there they say: "We must *liberate* the Communists." Here we hate the person of the Communist as well as his ideas; there, they will tell you, "We can love the sinner while hating his sin."

Here one Communist in a family jeopardizes all relatives, including the in-laws; there Communist and right-wing conservative regularly dine at the same family table.

There is no doubt that Italian Communism is widespread and powerful; and yet, even if Italy's poverty grew suddently worse than it is, I would hesitate before betting hard cash that the country would go under Red control. There are strong political, moral, religious, and traditional forces balanced against it; and, after all, Italians are used to poverty; they do not fear it; what they fear is war.

And therein lies our current trouble. The painful truth is that years of patient Communist propaganda, coupled with much too much impatient talk from Washington, has persuaded millions of Italians that Soviet Russia is a greater force for peace than the United States. It is still a minority so persuaded, I would think, but a disturbingly large minority. All men, wherever they live, think, not only in accord with objective evidence, but also in accord with their historical experience; and so Americans in Rome are told by their Italian friends: "We have been invaded by the Germans, the British, the French, the Americans— by every great power at one time or another, *except* the Russians; and you are asking us to get alarmed about the one country that has never bothered us."

When you hear this argument, you know in your heart it represents a kind of visceral rationalization; but try answering it in any circle of Italians so sick of armies and destruction that it's almost bad form even to mention the chances of war. The answers do not come easy.

THE SOLID SOUND OF WRATH

[*June 10, 1954*]

The McCarthy-Army hearings—so saturatingly familiar now that the preposterous has come to seem sensible, the incredible commonplace—the hearings have entered the last days; and the Mundt Subcommittee is rediscovering what the Tydings Committee discovered four long years ago, the last time McCarthy took the stand. They are discovering that where McCarthy sits is the head of the table, even though he be in the witness chair; that to extract a yes or no answer from the Senator is a physical impossibility, save when the situation suits him.

And, as the weary end approaches, many observers are saying again what some of us said before the hearings ever started—that despite the flattest contradictions of testimony, no perjury indictments are likely to emerge from all this; that so far as any majority committee report is concerned, both McCarthy and Stevens will emerge relatively unscathed, that if anybody does suffer in such a report it can only be Adams on the Army side and Cohn on the McCarthy side. The basic weakness of the whole business, in terms of any real showdown, is what some observers perceived before it all began—that each side had negotiated with the other, during fall and winter, *not* at arm's length, in a formal manner, as representatives of the Senate's dignity or of an august military department; they had negotiated in a footsie and foot-loose manner, in the phony friendliness of "pass the cheese and the beer, we're all good guys together." That is basically why the respective charges have a certain hollowness and why expressions of neither moral indignation nor outraged innocence from any of the principals is ever quite convincing.

It is, no doubt, a sign of the fading integrity of American politics that almost no one in political life can drop the coin of moral indignation and make it give forth a pure and solid sound; it took a stranger to the shabby spiritual corridors of federal politics to drop that coin and make it ring; Joseph Welch of Boston, who yesterday cried out from the depths of a believable heart against McCarthy's sudden poisoned arrow directed at the personal honor of a young man who has no conceivable connection with the matters at issue.

Its *immediate* target was not the young man but Mr. Welch himself; the tactic was the familiar McCarthy tactic —to step out of a tight corner, not by destroying his opponent's arguments, but by trying to destroy his opponent's credibility by impugning his honor and loyalty. In that moment, as he intimated, a blinding revelation was bestowed upon Mr. Welch's normal mind and he understood for the first time the gargantuan abnormality he had been dealing with. Millions of Americans apparently do not grasp it even yet, but Mr. Welch surely should have known before. In the first day of the hearing, he had heard McCarthy try this with General Reber; the day before yesterday he had heard McCarthy try this with Senator Symington.

No less revealing was the reaction of McCarthy himself when the flame of anguish and indignation from Mr. Welch ignited an explosion from the ranks of the audience. He appeared, for a moment, astonished that one more thrust at one more helpless, absent victim should arouse any feelings, anywhere; and no less revealing was his immediately succeeding attitude. Clearly, he did not sense that the audience was crying shame upon him; he had no feeling that he had done anything morally wrong; clearly, his only feeling was that he had done something tactically wrong, that he had merely lost a point in that particular round; and what has long been clear to many observers here and what one may surmise became clear to thousands of others in that moment, is this: that those *were* his only feelings, because the capacity for other feelings is simply

not there. He cannot help it. The personal tragedy of Mc-
Carthy is that the nerve or chord or cluster of cells that
produce what men call conscience was not granted to him.

McCARTHY VERSUS THE
CONSTITUTION

[*June 18, 1954*]

The sun was shining in Washington today and a cool,
cleansing breeze blowing away the vaporous fogs.
This change in the weather seemed a timely act of symbolism to mark the end of the McCarthy-Army hearing; and,
one may hope, the start of a new moral climate in this
Capital. The hope may be a vain one. Much current evidence suggests that it is.

The Committee Majority Report is hardly expected to
be a model of statesmanship, reaffirming the dignity of the
world's greatest government against the swarm of little
men who fail to understand that dignity is an integral part
of authority; that in a free society when dignity is lost,
authority must wither. There are no grounds for the hope
to be found in the astounding invitation from Senator
Mundt, who wants all the participants who have challenged each other's honor, competence, and sanity, now
to gather round the cup of cheer at a party and slap each
other's backs in the phony good-fellowship of poolroom
politics; no grounds for the hope in the astounding statement from the Secretary of Defense, the Department on
which our safety rests, and which was vilified and as-
saulted in its very integrity—his statement that everybody

in the hearings should have let their hair and whiskers grow, et cetera.

And yet there *are* some reasons for the hope that the ground fog that has obscured the imperatives of constitutional government may be slowly drifting away, and that these hearings have helped in this respect. The issue has never been Private Schine; the issue in these hearings at least has never been Communism; the issue has been that other radicalism known as McCarthyism; it is possible that millions more Americans now understand why this ism *is* radical, has nothing to do with conservatism, very little to do with patriotism, and, like Communism, operates not only outside the constitutional forms of government, but directly against them.

There are grounds, not only for hope, but for belief, that the administration has now cleared its decks in its confused, and long compromised struggle with McCarthyism. Despite the attitude of a few officials like Secretary Wilson, it is possible to believe that White House, Justice Department, State Department, and the operating levels of the Defense Department have finally accepted the impossibility of appeasing the Wisconsin Senator, have understood that all who try it reap none but bitter fruit. Secretary Stevens was naïve and bumbling, and his specific factual case was not a strong one; and yet he goes down as the rather unwitting champion who, by carelessly making himself a hostage to fortune, forced the whole administration to defend its authority against the wrecking crew. And the course of the hearings themselves, whatever their evils, forced the Wisconsin Senator to declare himself frankly; his own words tore away his veil. He declares that he and he alone shall be the investigator-in-chief, prosecutor, judge, and executioner-in-chief, in all that pertains to loyalty, the very spiritual distillation that holds this society together; he shall preside over it all, regardless of President, Attorney General, loyalty boards, procedures, rules, or law. He has said, in effect: "*I* am the law." And he has said it so loudly and boldly that no one save fools or knaves can possibly have failed to hear.

As the *New York Times* puts it today, this has been, in the larger sense, the case of McCarthy not versus Stevens, not versus the Army, not versus the President, not versus the Senate, but Senator McCarthy versus the Constitution of the United States.

The Constitution is defended, in this time, by a government that seeks to follow the middle of the road. It can be believed that this government has been forced to conclude that there is no middle of the road on McCarthyism; that, as with Communism, you have to be totally for it or totally against it; and the reason for this is that the one ism, like the other, is in itself totalitarian.

THE FANCY FOOTWORK OF
FARMER JOE

[*June 22, 1954*]

Washington politicians have been rewriting our history like mad for the last several years, and that's bad enough; but when they show signs of re-jiggering our *folklore*, it's time for all believers in the good, the partly true, and the beautiful to take alarm, to say nothing of

220

umbrage. Take away a man's facts, and he'll manage to survive; but you take away his *illusions*, and he's finished.

Twice now politicians have interfered with popular illusions about the American cowboy and Injuns saga; and this has caused me, as one who was raised on those illusions through the medium of the dime novel, considerable personal distress; I am beginning to fear for my children, who were raised on cops 'n robbers illusions; they're apt to get to a comfortable middle age, at peace with the world, and then some politician is going to prove that Dick Tracy couldn't hit the side of a barn or that the T-men were all a bunch of round-shouldered clerks, and their life is simply going to sour on them.

It was just this winter that President Eisenhower was retelling the grand story of how Wild Bill Hickok, and other Abilene folk, lived by the code of meeting your accuser face to face; immediately some politician, probably a treasonous Democrat, proved that Wild Bill, far from fightin' "far and squar," was a real dirty fighter who used to shoot people in the back. Now along comes Senator McCarthy with his story about the Indian named Charlie, which almost brought me to the point of burning my whole Fenimore Cooper collection. You know what McCarthy said to Mr. Hensel. He said he had once learned on the farm from an Indian named Charlie, that when a foe advances upon you, the best defense is to kick him as fast as possible below the belt until he is helpless. This is character assassination of a whole race; it's genocide; McCarthy has finally gone too far.

He has planted the big doubt about the erstwhile noble red man and half of America's literature. This is postdated guilt by association. It won't be long before any reservation Indian, to collect his government stipend, will have to prove that his name is not Charlie, that he is not related to any Indian named Charlie. Anybody at all named Charlie will have to prove that he has no Indian blood in him, has never met McCarthy, and never been near Wisconsin.

This revelation by McCarthy shook me pretty deeply, for a time. In the wild surge of thoughts it produced, many mysteries seemed to be resolved, unrelated facts seemed to fall into place. Obviously Indians rarely wore belts because that would help an enemy's aim; no wonder, the tragedy of Custer's last stand; if he'd been seated, like Sitting Bull, instead of standing, he might have escaped destruction. No wonder the Indians have been rapidly declining in population.

For hours these wild thoughts of disillusionment took possession of me; I was at the desperate point of washing my brain of everything I had read between the ages of six and sixteen and filling the void by memorizing the public speeches of Herbert Hoover; but finally I got a grip on myself by running three times around the Senate Office Building, and reason began to prevail.

Maybe McCarthy never said it. No, that would make an Assistant Secretary of Defense a barefaced liar, and *that* thought was too painful. Maybe Mr. Hensel had misunderstood McCarthy. That was it. What McCarthy had really said was this: "I once learned from an old Indian named Gandhi that when a foe advances upon you, the best passive defense is to smile and put your best foot forward."

It *must* have been something like that. The corroborative facts at hand simply do not support the Hensel version. Such facts as these—that McCarthy's whole record proves his devotion to the *jawbone* as the weapon for defeating armies, not to the feet; that Indians either went barefoot or wore soft moccasins—very poor equipment for kicking—

and that it would be equally futile to go around kicking with feet of clay.

So I restored all my illusions and felt ever so much better.

UNRULY GENIUS AND THE RULES

[*June 30, 1954*]

Yesterday's decision of the Atomic Energy Commission majority means that the public career of J. Robert Oppenheimer is finished. The man whose genius and energy, more than that of any other single person, gave us the atomic weapon is now cast aside. He will no longer have access to secrets in government files, and government, presumably, will no longer have access to secrets that may be born in the Oppenheimer brain.

Only the emotionally pre-committed can instantly approve or instantly disapprove the conclusions of the Commission majority; and as for those few writers and politicians who reveal personal *pleasure* in the outcome—for them there is no easy description; for whether yesterday's verdict is basically right or basically wrong, there is tragedy here, on the heroic scale. If there must be tragedy, the audience can at least accord it the dignity inherent in all Greek drama. Those in the gallery seats who are whistling their approval *or* throwing dead fruit at the cast might be escorted down the street to some cops-and-robbers thriller to which they are better conditioned.

When the Commission finding was announced yesterday

223

in the House of Representatives and some members actually *applauded* the announcement, this observer, at least, could not help remembering another occasion, long ago, in another parliament. In the anxious summer of 1940 Winston Churchill rose to announce, in grief, that British gunboats had destroyed at Oran the fleet of Britain's ancient ally, France, not daring to take a chance on its future course of action. In the tension of those frightening days, when none knew whether Britain would live or not, members of Parliament forgot themselves and cheered the announcement. Most of them felt instantly ashamed; loyal Frenchmen in the gallery walked to the doors, tears streaming down their faces. They did not know whether the destruction of the fleet was required or not; the cheers, they knew, were not.

This reporter does not know, in terms of either present fears or history's probable conclusions, whether the destruction of Oppenheimer was required or not. Because this is not so much an issue of the facts, not so much an issue of regulations; this is a matter of human wisdom, in all its baffling labyrinths. Part of the core of the issue Oppenheimer's judges had to meet, it seems to me, is this:

In an extraordinary case, shall the ordinary rules and procedures apply? Shall a man like Oppenheimer, because of his exceptional qualities, his exceptional contributions in the past and possibly in the future, be given *more* leeway in his personal behavior; or, because of his exceptional qualities and exceptional opportunity for doing injury, shall such a man be held to *stricter* accountability in his personal behavior? No rule book can possibly provide a final and completely satisfying solution to such a question as this; men simply decide in their own hearts, subject to their own knowledge or ignorance, independence or sense of conformity; they have so decided, four to one, and their decision will be debated for years to come.

It is not convincing enough to say that a great man was judged by lesser men; nor is it convincing enough to say that Oppenheimer showed contempt for security rules. It is clear, on the one side of the case, that he was obstructionist at some points, evasive, contradictory, and untruthful at others; that he persisted in seeing personal friends who were deeply suspect; it is equally clear, on the other side, that his personal contributions to our strength and security are prodigious, that there is no shred of evidence that he has ever betrayed his secret trust to our enemies.

It is clear that he *could*, if he chooses, injure the country badly; equally clear that he could, if kept on, help the country greatly.

Caution, and the rule book, have won the case; the case of a man, ironically, of that rare stripe of men who achieve such feats as atomic fission, simply because, in their own field, their minds reject rule books and caution.

TAXI-DRIVERS VERSUS
THE WORLD

[June 15, 1954]

One of the subtle skeins that hold the Republic together is the fact that all citizens consider themselves authorities on, and therefore have a common interest in, the weather, politics, and taxicabs. This citizen has an *un-*

common interest in taxis, having spent therein half his own life and the company's liquid assets, and is always prepared to dissertate thereon at the drop of a flag.

Today New York City licensed its first small-size taxicab —that is, a normal, five-passenger sedan, instead of the locomotive-length limousines that now so clog the cross-town streets that it is faster to get from East River to Hudson on foot, leaping from cabtop to cabtop in the manner of Eliza crossing the ice. New York is now so jammed that inches count; and if they can remove the extra inches on their taxis, a hackie will be able to make a U-turn in the middle of the block in *one* graceful movement. At present it requires three graceful movements, snapping the passenger's head backward, then forward, then backward again, and stalling traffic for five blocks in both directions. Further evidence of what I have always maintained—that New York is a nice place to live, but a terrible place to visit.

Londoners never did make the mistake of confusing big-ness with quality, and the high-backed, snub-nosed London cab can turn on a sixpence, to phrase a coin.

In some cities, of course, the *driver* is the dominating element in the transaction, not the vehicle. All cab-drivers in all cities are united in their hatred of the pedestrian race, but their modes of self-expression seem to differ. The drivers in Lisbon express themselves by leaning on the horn, except the one I once engaged who had a brother in Manchester and loved to shout English phrases over his shoulder. He had an engraved card that he handed to all foreign clients. It read: "Louis Garcia, Inglis Aespinking Driver."

Paris taxi-drivers hate other Paris taxi-drivers almost as much as pedestrians and express themselves by spinking

French to each other at the stop lights with an eloquence that is music to the ears of those who are partial to the brasses and percussion instruments. Except that fellow who was always stationed on my corner in Montmartre before the war. In those days radios in cabs were a novelty, but he was a hold-out. He had a little sign on his windshield which read: "No wireless here. The chauffeur sings."

I don't remember any taxis in the Far East, except a rickshaw in Chungking, from which I descended in mid-journey and paid off the sweating coolie. The whole thing made me feel ashamed of myself; the coolie, however, did not take my behavior as a humanitarian gesture. In fact, he got sore.

Then there was the horse-and-cab taxi ride at midnight in the more mysterious reaches of Calcutta. All went plod-dingly well until my co-passenger, Henry Cabot Lodge, lifted his voice in a very Senatorial-bass rendition of *Harvest Moon*. In the dark recesses of the street, shutters began to clatter, dogs began whining in the alleys, and our horse and driver began acting strangely. It was nearly dawn when we reached the Great Eastern Hotel, and with the doorman as translator, our driver, in tears, explained that this was the first time in his life he had ever got lost in his own city. I notice that at the UN, Lodge takes a pretty anti-India line and I've always sort of wondered. . . .

Taxi-drivers both contribute to and reflect the personality of their city. Detroit, for example, is an angry city, and I have never forgotten the story of the hackie there who blew up when he got his ten-thousandth command to drive to the Book-Cadillac, a thirty-cent run from the station. He drove hack, passenger, self, and all—right into the river. But that is another story and, come to think of it, I've told it before.

THEY WANT TO BE ALONE—
ON PAGE ONE

[*September 3, 1954*]

A fellow who lives by making amplified noises in people's parlors probably has no business getting into the subject of privacy; still, there's been so much public concern about privacy in press and radio recently—those natural enemies of privacy—that raising the general decibel range another notch won't do much harm. One school of diplomats has been arguing that diplomacy by public conference, speeches, and mimeographed statement is paralyzing all possible progress toward peace in this world. They think that if we could somehow get back to the old-fashioned practice of private negotiations without reporters and congressmen peering over the negotiators' shoulders, ready megaphone in hand, there might be some real give-and-take and the world would get somewhere.

In the last few days distinguished citizens have been publicly arguing the pros and cons of keeping congressional hearings private—*semi*-private, that is, since the question is whether microphone and camera add something fundamentally different to the scratching of a press reporter's pencil, so far as decorum is concerned.

And a couple of days ago Mr. Herbert Hoover had something to say about *Presidential* privacy. He watched Eisenhower being watched by reporters while Eisenhower fished trout, and he lectured the reporters—to wit, that the press used to respect a President's privacy in fishing as well as in prayer; that fishing privacy is now destroyed and, he said, this is one of the degenerations of the last thirty years.

This, I find, produces a certain confusion of thought, at least in me. *Hoover* allowed the fish pictures when *he* was President. We older and more jaundiced President-watchers recall no more famous photograph than the one of President Hoover, in stiff collar and business suit, sourly regarding a six-inch trout. Some people figured he lost a million votes with that picture, so it could be, perhaps, that his whole philosophy about Presidential fishing privacy is founded, not on objective reason, but on that traumatic experience of his earlier life.

It's the fad nowadays to go around suspecting others of *something*, and I go around suspecting public figures of a sort of unconscious hypocrisy on this matter of privacy. What I mean is, it isn't the publicity they object to, it's the *kind* of publicity. Mr. James Hagerty, the President's Press Secretary, is an expert at laying the wires, pushing the button, and releasing a flood of Eisenhower publicity—or non-privacy—when it's the kind of non-privacy he wants. But Mr. Hagerty was *furious* with one of the fish stories this week, not because it was an invasion of privacy but because it stated that the President had exceeded the legal limit on trout. (I don't know who cares, since they were private-enterprise trout just dumped into the stream by their owner.)

You take your average combat general in the war. I found that if I wrote about his occasional brilliance and victories, he didn't mind my invasion of his privacy a bit and I was a valued force for army morale. But when I wrote about his occasional mistakes and defeats, he minded a great deal and I was practically a foe of the Republic, as well as of his privacy.

Some public figures seem to want it both ways, and get it. Greta Garbo was never more publicized than after she announced that she wanted to be alone. Lindbergh had a genius for the darkest privacy when he wished, and then suddenly the brightest publicity—when he wished.

But, normally, privacy for public figures is a contradiction in terms. It might save nerve strain all around if they would just accept the fact. Nobody in public life for a long time has said: "Paint me as I am, warts and all." I haven't met a politician in years who followed the philosophy of the one who said: "I don't care what you say about me, boys, just so you mention me."

It would be nice to have a few like that around. Just for variety, if nothing more.

ULCERS GROW ON GLASS

[September 9, 1954]

It may not be possible for an empire to rise and decline at the same time, but one quick look around here in New York is enough to persuade even a visitor that it's quite possible for a city. The greatest city of our land is falling into the pit while reaching for the skies, a matter that ought to be of some concern to the general citizenry, or that portion thereof that can get its mind off the Giants and the Braves.

Remember Park Avenue, the one Manhattan street that

retained some charm? Forget it. It is almost gone, and the enemies of calm, space, tradition, and continuity have blue-prints ready for its finish. The solid stone buildings of somber hue that accommodated twilight and the colors of the dawn—they are going. They were built to last for a hundred years of family-raising, dog-walking, and Sunday calling after church. They are tearing them down, stone by stone, and throwing up meaningless metal and anony-mous glass, sheet by glaring sheet. The adjoining streets were noisy enough and this is more noise, a clamor in the eye and a screeching in the inner ear.

The trees will go one day, as a bother to the conspirators' lingering conscience, and then the dogs and the Sunday strollers; the twinkling colored lights of Christmas time will be stored away, and the ulcer, the only living thing that grows on glass and metal, will move over from Madi-son and Lex.

Grand Central, which anchors the Avenue and shelters it from the world of the quick lunch and the neon sign, is to lose its character, if the imperious will of the little Na-poleon, Robert R. Young, is to have its way. Grand Cen-tral was good enough for a generation of artists and writers and wide-eyed maidens come from the country; but it's not good enough for Mr. Young. He will build upon its site and memory, so he says, the tallest building in the world. It will be shaped like the bell tower of San Marco in Ven-ice, Italy; Mr. Young, no doubt, will provide the peanuts and the pigeons. Vitamin-treated peanuts, I presume, and two-toned pigeons with lacquered wings.

It will be an office building. You see the plan. Com-muters can step from air-conditioned station wagon to air-conditioned train, be rushed underground right to their office building, and whisked up to their offices in air-conditioned elevators. They can repeat this in reverse at night and fall to sleep, safe in the knowledge of their sanitary day, unblemished by a single touch of unpasteurized rain or the unconditional sun. I see by a gossip columnist that every elevator in Mr. Young's building will contain a bar, but this I disbelieve, even of Mr. Young.

If I sound unduly bitter, hear me out. My grief has personal cause. My own hotel on the Avenue, where I have lodged these many years, has fallen to the blight. The spacious lobby, with its carpets and its calm, is gone, a narrow maze now of glass and glitter. The great chandelier in the gracious dining-room is torn away; the oasis of the barbershop, where a man could doze in the sweet mingled scents of cigars and oils—all gone. A night club, God help the weary traveler, is coming in.

I asked a friend today what makes men do such things; he could only say that it must be nerves. *I* can only say that if this be the future, I'm going home to the past. If this be progress, I want my decadence back.

THE FTC AND THE T-ZONE

[*September 15, 1954*]

Secretary Dulles is flying off on another trip, speculation on the Maine elections still fills the air around here, and Ike has gone fishing again; but it's pretty hard to put one's mind to such matters, in view of today's quiet little announcement from the Federal Trade Commission. Nobody expected such a body blow to free enterprise—or, at least, advertising enterprise—from a conservative administration; but the startling fact is that the FTC is asking the cigarette industry to stick to the truth in its advertising. Or, as they put it, I quote, to eliminate "all claims and implications which are questionable in light of present day scientific knowledge."

Well, science is always taking the joy out of life, and this ominous move threatens to destroy half the fun of leafing through the three-color magazines and flipping the television dial. The FTC—no doubt composed of pipe-smoking bureaucrats who spend *their* evenings reading statistics to their kids—wants the advertising boys to leave out any mention of throat, larynx, lungs, nose, digestion, energy, nerves, or doctors. I just wonder if the FTC people have had the proper liaison with the mental-health people over in PHS. What is going to happen to the self-confidence of all those Americans who have protected their T-zone with brand X, their H-zone with brand Y, got their morning pep from brand A, their five-o'clock pickup from brand B, and went unafraid to sleep, relaxed by brand C?

The FTC is suggesting that the cigarette copy drop the word *non-irritating*. A whole generation of copywriters have made a living out of that word. It even suggests that the word *smooth* be dropped. The FTC will have only itself to blame if it learns tomorrow that a couple dozen TV announcers have written farewell notes and cut their T-zones. They trained hard, learning to pronounce it "smooooth," and it's pretty tough for a man in the full flood of his career and talents to turn to something new, even to real estate.

Nor does this complete the story of the FTC's sudden attack on the American way of life. It goes so far as to suggest that cigarette testimonials by celebrities be only what it calls "genuine testimonials," representing, I quote, "the current opinion of the author of the testimonial, who currently smokes the brand named" in the ad. If the financial panic in Hollywood was bad up to now, wait till *this* news reaches the coast. To say nothing of major-league ball-players, who've got to make their summer earnings stretch through the winter somehow. They can't *all* endorse razor blades, in spite of indications to the contrary.

Still, the FTC did put in that word *currently*, which could save the situation; obviously, the patronage drive here hasn't entirely cleaned out the old Civil Service. What I mean is, no law or government proclamation is considered complete without its loophole, and the FTC's loophole expert is still on the job. The native ingenuity that built this country isn't destroyed yet; therefore we may be confident that our favorite stars and players will exhibit considerable versatility in their opinions and purchases of cigarette brands. Of course, if FTC works up liaison with FBI and they bring in lie-detectors—then I'd hate to predict.

As a hint to the worried testimonial-signer of the future, I might cite the example of a British M.P. with whom I spent a week-end once. The lady next door wrote popular, and horrible, boy-meets-girl novels. She'd presented the M.P. with her latest novel the previous week. Now the doorbell rang; she sailed into the drawing-room with an expectant look on her face. The statesman grabbed up the book, banged it with his fist, and exclaimed: "That's what I call a *book!*"

LET ME TELL YOU ABOUT
MY ULCERS

[*September 23, 1954*]

The law says broadcasters must serve the public interest, convenience, and necessity, and what I wanted to talk about hasn't a blessed thing to do with any of those commodities, though I suppose you could argue that helping insomniacs get off to sleep is a public service of a sort. But I notice a lady producer in New York says that television is turning out better child actors than radio did, because they aren't nailed down by the microphone; they feel *freer,* more natural and at ease.

As a fellow who has been nailed by microphones, and spiked by cameras, and frequently felt pretty childish in both processes, it occurred to me that the public deserves to hear the truth from somebody on the performing, or gastric-ulcer, end of the mike and the camera.

In a nutshell, the difference is that in radio you are paralyzed by one clean bullet so to speak, the mike; whereas in television you bleed to death from a dozen buckshot called camera, teleprompter, cues, cards, monitors, lights, clock, film—*and* a mike. The post-shock treatment is different, too. Everybody understands what has happened to you in simple radio paralysis called mike-fright, so you are allowed to slink away alone while the normal healing processes of the body take over. The multiple-injury phenomenon of television, however, has, as yet, no definitive cure;

one diagnosis is as good as another, and everybody wants to help with his favorite home remedy. So you do not slink away unnoticed. You are assisted to the telephone immediately and propped up for an hour so you can hear friends, enemies, relatives, and associates tell you everything you did wrong. You gratefully receive these opinions, too numbed then to realize that most of them are contradictory and cancel each other out; you then drag yourself to bed, awake in the morning, and read the newspaper critics' opinions, by which time you are alert enough to notice they cancel each other out too.

The process of conducting a television program from the wrong, or bull's-eye, end of the camera can best be compared with the task of accurately charting the movements of each one of thirty-seven bats suddenly let loose in a closed room. There is no requirement for eyes in the *back* of your head, but one in the top of your head helps to avoid cracking your skull on the overhanging microphone; and eyes in each side of your head help you to watch the monitor at the right while watching the floor director at the left. You may have noticed a television performer's head, at times, suddenly go freakish and lopsided; that does not necessarily mean your set is out of sync; it probably means the performer has been staring with all five eyes a little too long.

Perhaps I can make myself clearer by explaining what goes on back-stage, or back-camera, in terms of what *you* see on the little screen simultaneously. You see the performer change from a straightforward, trusting gaze to a sneaky look out of the corner of his eye. This means the red camera light didn't go on and he has to look at the monitor to see if *he's* on the air or Miss America, on the film, is still dabbing at her tears.

You hear the performer hesitate, as though groping for a profound thought. This means the teleprompter is slow and he's waiting for it to catch up.

You see a smug, sort of secret smile. This means the floor director threw him the wrong cue but he didn't fall for it.

You suddenly see the performer in a strange posture, resembling that of the praying mantis. This means the film has broken and the camera switched to him without warning.

When you see his mouth open and close several times without producing sound, this does not mean the mike is dead. It means his sponsor has just walked in the studio door and he will be dead tomorrow.

I might add that the social term for television performing is "technological overemployment." There is probably no area of American life today in which a share-the-work plan would be of more benefit; and I personally intend to vote this fall for whichever party adopts this plan in its program.

THE PILGRIMAGE PERSISTS

[*October 7, 1954*]

This week it was Washington, D.C.; last week it was Baltimore; but in both these great border cities—laboratories, in a sense, for testing the integration of white and Negro schoolchildren—the sporadic, half-hearted street demonstrations seem to be over; it is possible the country will be spared from having to look at more photographs of the most humiliating spectacle in some time—the spectacle of the bobby-soxed beneficiaries of a free education in the freest land in the world parading with placards demanding their "rights."

Ninety years ago a half-million of the finest men of the country, North and South, died terrible deaths trying to decide what rights were whose in this complex and tragic question of racial democracy; since then, generations of statesmen and lawyers and philosophers have struggled with the question, trying, with the sweat of their minds and hearts, to hammer out the workable answers. But in the sweet simplicity of adolescence, apparently, all is simple. "We demand our rights," the placards said, leaving the onlooker a little mystified as to what they meant, unless it be the right to feel exclusive from and superior to—somebody. A natural, immutable human craving even in the lowliest, and one susceptible of gratification in many private ways; but hardly at the expense of general laws and public institutions designed to serve all and serve them equally.

In spite of these scenes of the last two weeks, the general pattern of school integration in the areas where it is really being tried for the first time shows more success than failure. In states like Kansas and Arizona and New Mexico, on a local permissive basis before, obligatory integration is working smoothly enough; it is working so far in Missouri, in some areas of West Virginia, despite one setback there; definite plans for it are ready in Oklahoma; and it is proceeding in various parts of Deleware despite the failure at Milford. There seems, right now, every prospect of success in Baltimore and Washington.

These results are about as many had predicted, who realized long ago that integration would come first in the areas where Negroes are more sparsely settled and last in the areas of heavy population, where racial feelings are deeply embedded. And so all the states of what some call the "old South" are standing by, discussing ways and means or alternatives, and waiting for the next Supreme Court ruling, on the mechanics of carrying out the unanimous decision of last June. It is not possible that integration will come in those states save very, very slowly, and in some states which may carry through their threats to abolish all tax-supported schools rather than integrate them racially, it may not come at all. It is conceivable that the law could be technically complied with in some big Southern cities, simply because Negroes are already segregated in their housing districts and could go to the schools nearest their homes; in the back country, farming areas, where the boundary lines are not fixed but where emotions and attitudes are even *more* fixed, in these rural districts which can support but one school, the problem of integration will tax the wisest and the most patient, to the limit. One familiar with such areas finds it hard to believe it really can be done.

But someday, somehow, it can and will. For wisdom and tolerance and generosity in these matters have grown; they have not diminished; ever since Jefferson's day, the main current of this long, slow, and troubled American pilgrimage toward racial democracy has shown a forward motion. It does not move backward and it never really stops, in spite of what the propaganda of our foreign enemies may tell the world; in spite of the unhappy little street scenes around a few schools in a few of our cities, these last two weeks.

BIRD AND KENNEL DOGS

[*October 12, 1954*]

It is a matter of pride among the new team around the halls of the Pentagon that politicians and political instincts play practically no role any more in the running of the defense establishment. Most weeks of the year this is probably a good thing for Eisenhower's administration and his political party. But this is not one of those weeks. Only a man with Secretary Wilson's total lack of political instinct could have said, three weeks before a critical election, what he said last night about bird dogs and kennel dogs in reference to the industrial unemployed. Of course, he does not think of workers as dogs, but the unfortunate analogy, with its tone of aloofness to the plight of the jobless, cannot be recalled; the fat is in the fire. No better evidence can be found that this offhand remark may seriously affect the election and control of Congress than the fact that the President's advisers quickly persuaded him to issue a statement reaffirming belief in Wilson's humanitarian nature.

Republican Senators Ferguson and Saltonstall did not immediately repudiate the Wilson remark just to hear themselves talk. Ferguson—right there in Michigan—has something of a fight on his hands for re-election, and it is not impossible that the Wilson remark could lose that seat to the Democrats; Saltonstall is chairman of the Armed Services Committee, must work closely with Wilson and

240

defend his policies; but Saltonstall is in a hard Massachusetts race for re-election, and it just happens that there are
many unemployed in that state, too.

There can be no doubt that, in the view of experienced
Republican strategists, the Wilson remark hurts their cause,
right where they are weakest already—in the areas of unemployment; and there are probably enough of these areas
this fall to decide the balance of congressional control.

Well, American political history is strewn with unfortunate remarks, some of which probably did decide elections. When the elder Vanderbilt said: "The public be
damned," he wasn't a member of the federal Cabinet, and
the whole context was different. But in '32 Vice President
Curtis, running for re-election with Hoover, lost his temper
and told a heckler at an Iowa county fair: "You're too
damn dumb to understand," and it could be this was one
reason the stanch Republican state of Iowa went Democratic that year.

The phrase "Korea, Communism, and corruption" may
have brought the Republicans quite a few votes two years
ago, but the phrase "party of treason," ascribed to
McCarthy this year, seems to have had some boomerang
effect. "The forgotten man," helped Roosevelt in thirty-
two, but "We will tax and tax, spend and spend, elect and
elect"—ascribed to Harry Hopkins—grew to haunt the
New Dealers as time went on. Bryan's one paragraph
about crucifying mankind on a cross of gold probably won
him his first Democratic Party nomination.

But the two episodes of *carelessness* that did decide
Presidential elections, in the view of many historians, were
both at the expense of the Republican Party. One was a
careless act; the other a careless remark. The act was

241

Hughes's failure to greet Senator Hiram Johnson, one campaign day in San Francisco in 1916, which appeared to cost Hughes California's electoral vote and the White House. The careless remark, or rather the failure to instantly repudiate it, was of course the remark of the Reverend Samuel Burchard in 1884. This pastor of the Murray Hill Presbyterian Church in New York was substitute spokesman for six hundred clergymen who called on Republican candidate Blaine; Burchard made his remark about the Democrats as the party whose antecedents, he said, were "rum, Romanism and rebellion." Blaine failed to see the dynamite in this, at first; there was an uproar, worse than today's uproar over Wilson's remark, and Blaine lost New York State by a thousand votes and thereby lost the White House to Cleveland.

Blaine never forgot this. He said, later: "I have been beaten by an ass in the shape of a preacher."

B. AND K. DOGS, CONTINUED

[October 13, 1954]

The political effects of Mr. Charles Wilson's moralizing are still a matter for speculation, but nothing is more certain than that the standards of wit and humor around this Capital have collapsed. Every guy standing at the water-cooler fancies himself a wag—you see, it's contagious—and I have been informed all day that the Democrats have changed their song to read "Happy dog days are here again," that Wilson is in the Republican doghouse, that when a man bites a kennel dog, *that's* news, and that Republican candidates are trying to forget their troubles with the hair of the dog that bit them. The amount of— I almost said "doggerel"—passing as verse and limericks is positively exhausting, and I have even heard serious discussion whether the canned pet food put out by the Wilson Packing Company is headed for a boom or a collapse.

And all poor Charlie Wilson was trying to say is that he admires people who go out and find a job more than those who bewail their fate and expect the job to come to them. Back in Coolidge's day, men used to get elected President by uttering such maxims. The *Reader's Digest* waxed great on that central idea, before it decided the answer to national problems was a warm chuckle and air power; the idea still sounds reasonably logical to anybody who retains even a faint memory of Horatio Alger.

But there is a paragraph in a little book called *How to Win Friends and Influence People*—a book Mr. Wilson doubtless has never read. It says: "When dealing with people, let us remember we are not dealing with creatures of logic. We are dealing with creatures of emotion, creatures bustling with prejudices and motivated by pride and vanity."

Greater men have said worse things than Wilson said. One fellow around here was going to send Wilson a wire reminding him that Alexander Hamilton once said to Jefferson: "Your people, sir, is nothing but a great beast." But then he remembered that Hamilton got shot.

The Wilson remark may or may not be revealing of his state of mind about people, but the general reaction reveals the people's state of mind about dogs. It's schizophrenic. People love dogs, but they will not stand for being compared with dogs. Other creatures, yes. Teddy Roosevelt

243

was proud to call himself a Bull Moose. Huey Long was proud to call himself a Kingfish. Churchill called Cordell Hull a grey eagle and Hull was pleased. Call any man a workhorse, a racehorse, or a bantam rooster; tell any woman she's a gazelle, a bird of paradise, or even a little pigeon—and they love it. But you cannot compare anybody with a dog, of any kind, shape, color, or disposition. And yet the dog remains the world's favorite, most intimate pet. Obviously people have *got* to have something they can feel completely superior to.

The Wilson business has sent me to the books on American political history, and it's amazing how rarely dogs figure in the long story. You can find ducks, wild and lame; you can find horses, both dark and stalking; you can find copperheads and mugwumps; you find the familiar elephant and donkey, of course going back a hundred years. You will find Cactus Jack Garner's lines to an enemy in the Congress: "Hampy Moore is a Hell of a poet; he don't know a sheep from a goat."

But you find nothing about dogs—until you come up to Roosevelt's little dog Fala, who didn't either have a destroyer fetch him back from Alaska; and Nixon's little dog Checkers, which his children were *not* going to give back, no matter what the bad Democrats said.

Both were kennel dogs. Which reminds me. Whether Wilson was *morally* wrong or not, he *was* literally wrong. No good bird dog is allowed to hunt his own food. Ruins him for shooting over. He's fed in his kennel. Another thing—if Wilson will observe the kennel dogs more closely, he'll probably find they're not yelping for food, so much, as for *freedom* to run—and hunt.

GIVE THEM TRUST

[*October 28, 1954*]

As of right now, the permanent career corps of federal employees aren't quite sure whether they are coming or going. When the Republicans took over the apparatus here two years ago, they held several fixed notions about the bureaucracy. One was that it was too big, so they have cut it about ten per cent; another was that it was lazy, so various orders about coffee-hours and such were issued. Another was that it was loaded with subversives, so firings under the undefinable phrase "security risk" became a major industry here, without, so far as I know, one certified Communist having been uncovered.

Another article of faith was that government ranks were filled with card-carrying Democrats. Republicans argued that Truman had blanketed into the permanent protected Civil Service ranks great numbers of ordinary employees who shouldn't be there. In order to force open these jobs, they blanketed out a number of these people and then fired them. On a test case, last Monday, the Supreme Court decided this was illegal, and shouts of joy were heard from spokesmen of the organized federal workers, who had been saying publicly that general morale among government employees is lower than it has been for forty years.

By today confusion returned. At his news conference yesterday the President declared that political motives shall not operate in filling Civil Service jobs, which are competitive, and filled on a merit basis. At the same conference, however, he candidly endorsed a new system set up recently by his assistant, Sherman Adams. Under it, not only will the Republican National Committee receive, scrutinize, and forward job applications, but all federal agencies must give the committee monthly and weekly reports on job vacancies and jobs filled. This covers everything, apparently; the Civil Service merit jobs are not exempted and printed cards sent out from Adams's White House office some time ago to all agency heads state frankly that a main objective of the patronage program is to win elections for the party.

There is nothing new about the spoils system; the Democrats were artists at it; but this order is new at least in *degree*, in its systematic, wholesale technique and scope. In fact, in the view of some authorities here, it is also illegal, more clearly illegal than the maneuver the Supreme Court ruled against this week.

The very premise the Republicans operate upon—that federal employee ranks are overwhelmingly Democratic —is itself debatable. This is hard to put to a real test. But there have been some partial tests; while employees living in the District of Columbia cannot vote, those tens of thousands living in adjacent Virginia and Maryland counties can. And in both '48 and '52 those counties gave their majorities to the Republican candidate for President. It is at least permissible to suspect that those men and women making a career of the federal service regard themselves, like other Americans, as free citizens, voting their personal convictions as to who and what is best for their country.

It is dangerous to generalize about the spirits of a large body of persons; there is no way to prove that government employee morale *is* at its lowest in forty years. But where it is low, that is probably due, not so much to new variations on the spoils system, but mostly to the indignities—the statements about laziness; the wholesale security-risk accusations; the secret order this summer for surveillance of employees' private behavior, such as the kind of parties they attend. In short, to the attitude of some administrators that government employees are suspect, second-class citizens, to be watched and proctored by those who assert for themselves a greater virtue.

A maxim often expressed by a very great Republican, Henry Stimson, has been ignored. "The way to make people trustworthy," he used to say, "is to give them trust."

THE MEASURE OF A MAN

[November 8, 1954]

Sometimes, to add to the meaning of the headlines, a reporter must be personal. Eleven years ago I was a war correspondent, flying toward China over the infamous "Hump." There came a terrifying moment when the passengers, mostly GI's, stood near the door, trying to summon the courage to bail out of the crippled plane. Precious moments passed. Then one of the three civilians aboard, the diplomat who clutched a dispatch case to his chest, gave us a wry smile and leaped out. His action broke the paralysis; we all followed; and all of us, but one, survived.

In the weeks that followed, we were never entirely sure we would get out of those jungle mountains. In such circumstances men learn truly to know one another; who is weak; who is afraid; who is impetuous, and who is strong, and calm and prudent. As the time passed, the GI's and I began to recognize the civilian with the carefully guarded dispatch case as one among us with a calm and natural courage, as one who would never panic, who never complained. He was the one we chose, for common sense and discretion, to deal with the touchy and dangerous Naga head-hunters, our undecided hosts. Mostly we feared Japanese patrols, and a day came when we heard there was a Jap patrol not far away. The colonel in charge gave orders that we three civilians, in case of attack, were to take our guns and try to escape, while the soldiers remained to fight. It was the diplomat who said: "In the first place, this would be dishonorable. In the second place, we'd never get out." Fortunately, there was no attack.

There was, however, a long and painful hike in rain and heat for all of us. There were moments when another step seemed quite impossible. In such moments it was generally the diplomat who would sing out with something like "Onward and upward with the arts," and we would laugh and gasp and keep on climbing. I began to faint with heat and thirst on one suffocating slope; the man who left his half pint of water with me—all he had—was, of course, the diplomat.

After we emerged into India and the military reports were in, there was a move in the Air Force to decorate our diplomat for his outstanding personal conduct. I do not know if he ever received the decoration, but none of us in that strange party, I think, would have disputed the choice. For I thought then, as I think now, that if ever again I were in deep trouble, one man I would want to be with would be this particular man. I have known a great number of men around the world, under all manner of circumstances. I have known none who seemed more the whole man; none more finished a civilized product, in all that a man should be—in modesty and thoughtfulness, in resourcefulness and steady strength of character.

The name of this man is John Paton Davies. He is the man Secretary of State Dulles, on the recommendation of a five-man board, has just broken on the wheel of official disgrace. The Foreign Service officer dismissed, three years short of retirement and pension, after giving twenty-three years of his life—and almost life itself—in the arduous service of his government. Eight times he was investigated; eight times he was cleared. One by one the politically inspired charges of Communism or disloyalty or perjury were dropped; the ninth board came up with something new, called defects of character. Mr. Davies is not, concluded the board and Mr. Dulles, of sufficient judgment, discretion, and reliability.

Sufficient, one may ask, unto *what?* Their test can only have been of supernatural design. I saw their victim measured against the most severe tests that mortal man can design. Those he passed. At the head of the class.

THE GADGETS 'LL GETCHA EF YOU DON'T WATCH OUT

[*November 12, 1954*]

Like everybody else, I have been looking at the new car models, the *next* year's models, which always come out around this time of *this* year, along with the pre-pre-Christmas decorations and the new Miss Rheingold.

The fall of the year is a lovely lingering time, celebrated by poet and painter, but I suppose it is the tinge of melancholy, nature temporarily dying, that causes Americans to seem to hate the autumn, look right past it, and make like the new year of fresh beginnings is already with us. It has something to do with the youth cult in America—but perhaps that's another story.

Anyway, as a fellow who prefers old things to new things and does everything possible to stop progress before it kills us off, I have been looking at the new cars to see if my anti-progress movement has been having any effect in the vehicular world. Not a great deal, I must confess. I seem to have completely lost my campaign against the automatic gearshift and the finger-controlled window, two serious contributors to the ominous decline of human muscle and two gadgets with a will of their own, which think nothing of throwing people against garage walls or throttling curious children. I'm not doing so well on the braking systems, either. The Lord clearly intended the *right* foot to be used on a car brake, and after a generation of training in this respect, the new brakes are so broad they can be pressed with either foot—or both. This is going to mix up established reflexes still further and I darkly predict a rise in the incidence of highway accidents.

The new cars, of course, have the standard, basic equipment, as does the new Miss Rheingold, and I make no objection to this at all; but if I must accept the automatic transmission in the face of overwhelming forces, I see no particular reason for moving it to the dashboard; at least, we were getting accustomed to it. Now we face the hazard of reaching for the cigar-lighter and finding ourselves in neutral on a steep decline.

Small Sounds in the Night

I'm pleased to see bits of evidence the new cars are moving backward in time, even though it's in a sort of synthetic, half-hearted way. Some years ago, they built a solid car to *look* like a convertible, in recognition that people prefer illusions to reality, anyway; and now they put a phony ridge across the top to make it look like the old-fashioned phaeton with the disposable back top. If these small tendencies could only be encouraged, there might be some chance of getting back to days of the old family Overland, which could be open-aired on all sides, the time before Hitler and Malenkov, atom bombs and security risks; but I am afraid that is too much to expect. Some things about the new cars I just don't understand at all; the two-color paint jobs, for example; unless this is the only way they could think of to make cars twice as gaudy for the price of one. I don't quite understand the obsessive impulse to make the Ford look like a big car, when the whole love of the Ford was always based on the very fact that it was *not* a big car.

The wrap-around windshields leave me reassured only in the thought that they cannot endure. Oh, they'll do with the people who enjoy café society; that is, those who go out to *be* seen as well as to see; I don't think, however, that housewives who lug the laundry in the back seat once a week are going to care for them. And I should think they will make nervous wrecks out of the back-seat lovers of the kind who park at night in *my* country road; but love, as the saying goes, will find a way, and I expect it will continue to defeat the best efforts of the great minds in Detroit, even if *all* the independents are driven out of business.

Anyway, the new cars are here; all looking very much

ERIC SEVAREID

alike; all equipped with every conceivable gadget to
solve every conceivable problem except, of course, the
usual two: how to get them parked and paid for.

THE MECHANICS OF SELF-
DESTRUCTION

[December 1, 1954]

The junior Senator from Wisconsin will continue along
his chosen road for at least another four years, but it
can never be the same; not after tonight. The road has
suddenly narrowed before him and he will have to drag
with him the weights that the Senate tonight began to
fasten upon his nimble feet; he will bear the load of formal,
official condemnation and censure by his fellow Senators,
a punishment for conduct the Senate has administered to
a fellow member only two or three times before in American history.

It is a heavy vote, an unchallengeable vote, running three
to one against him, including nearly one half the Senators
of his own Republican Party, including every official
Senate leader of that party, save only the floor leader himself, Mr. Knowland; the vote tonight was on the first
count of the two-count indictment, the charge that Mc-
Carthy had repeatedly abused the old Subcommittee on
Elections and thereby obstructed the constitutional processes of the Senate. Tomorrow the Senate votes on the
second count, McCarthy's treatment of General Zwicker.
McCarthy will probably make a voting gain on the second
count, because some Senators were not satisfied with

252

Zwicker's behavior before the McCarthy Committee, but the gain is expected to be a light one. Then, presumably, will come an effort by the McCarthy supporters to kill the entire censure resolution; but judging by the pattern tonight, that has no chance whatever, and will be beaten by approximately the existing three-to-one margin.

This action makes the professional record of the adult McCarthy remarkably consistent; as a lawyer, he was censured by his fellow Wisconsin lawyers; as a judge, he was censured by his fellow judges; as a United States Senator, he now stands censured by his fellow Senators; the extraordinary record of an extraordinary personality, regarded as hero and martyr by some, as merely reckless by others, and, by many versed in human psychology, regarded as a man relentlessly pulled on and on by a powerful unconscious drive for self destruction.

That censure suits this emotional role he plays; that McCarthy really *wants* to be censured is not doubted by many observers here who have watched his behavior since the debate began.

This transaction tonight has raised much political speculation—about the health of the Republican Party if this savage internal feud continues, about a possible breakoff and third-party formation, and about the future role of the Republican floor leader, Mr. Knowland. Knowland is in direct defiance of his President's foreign policy, and he has now taken his stand with the small hard core of McCarthy-supporters in the Senate, but has failed to take any other Republican leaders with him; not Millikin, head of the Republican conference; not Ferguson, chairman of the Party Policy Committee; not Saltonstall, his assistant floor leader.

And in the face of this Republican split, the Democratic

ranks remained absolutely solid tonight, without a defection, in one of the most remarkable exhibitions of party discipline under pressure that even Capitol old-timers can remember seeing. McCarthy's campaign oratory about twenty years of treason came back on his head tonight, with a vengeance; and it was not the liberal, New Deal Democrats who led the solid phalanx against McCarthy; it was the conservative, Southern Democrats. They have roots that go very deep, not only in their party, but in the United States Senate, which they tend to inhabit most of their individual lives. They are men with a strong historical and institutional sense; to them, as with the conservative New England Republicans, these are hallowed halls, peopled with the ghosts of greatness; for men such as these, to make the Senate a place of brawling and slander and hatred is to debase the temple, to debase the meaning of their own lives. Tonight, in the first stage of the long-postponed showdown, the country discovered there are many such men, from *all* sections, in the Senate; far, far too many for McCarthy to cope with, even if he understood them.

ENOUGH WAS ENOUGH

[December 2, 1954]

For the fourth time in the Republic's history, the Senate of the United States has formally condemned the conduct of a fellow member, after as bitter and personal a feud as the Chamber has witnessed in living memory. McCarthy has been condemned on two counts by three-to-one majorities, with half his own party against him; this

leaves him, if not a pariah, almost a lone wolf in the
Senate, in spite of the fact that he has identified himself
with, and claimed leadership of, the safest and most popular
political cause of our time—anti-Communism. It may be
that had he not taken up this cause, he would not have
committed the acts that led to condemnation; but it is also
true that simply because he *is* identified with anti-Communism, the Senators put off the showdown with Mc-
Carthy until the very dignity and order of the Senate were
dangerously at stake.

It is doubtful if the Senate, as an institution, or even as
a gentlemen's club, has ever in its history had to contend
with so difficult a personal problem. The three Senators
previously denounced by the body received that punishment for single acts; two of them for acts of emotional
impulse. In no case has there been such a long train of
abuses laid against a Senator—forty-six in the original
charges filed with the Watkins Committee, covering a
multitude of doubtful acts, over several years, from the
acceptance of interested corporate money to his choice of
adjectives.

The Watkins Committee reduced them to the bare minimum of two counts; and today, in the final voting, one
was replaced—McCarthy's treatment of General Zwicker.
He was condemned, instead, for his abuse of the Watkins
Committee; so, in the test, he was condemned only for
abusing institutions of the Senate *itself;* his treatment of
private individuals, government officials, and military officers did not figure in the final judgment. Nothing has happened to prevent either McCarthy or any other Senator
from treating outsiders the way he treated Zwicker, unless the Senate should, at long last, devise and enforce new
rules of behavior for its investigating committees.

255

The basic arguments against censuring McCarthy came down to three; put in oversimplified form, the Senate majority has answered as follows: to the claim that censure would represent a Communist victory, the majority has said, in effect, this debate has nothing whatsoever to do with Communism; to say that it does is to question the patriotism of Senators, which is inadmissible even as an implication.

To the claim that censure would weaken the prerogatives, especially the investigative prerogatives, of the Senate, the majority has said in effect: censure of McCarthy is a step toward *saving* the Senate's prerogatives and especially that of investigation. It is *McCarthy* who has hurt these prerogatives, by his defiance of committees when he himself is the defendant, by his endless accusations when he is the investigator, so many unproved that he has fatally obscured the line between guilt and innocence and thus diminished the public worth of Senatorial findings.

To the claim that censure would restrict the Senatorial right of free speech, the majority has said, in effect: this *is* a serious argument. The Constitution goes to great lengths to protect this right. But there has always been this risk in judging between freedom and license. We can only go back to the classic judgment that there is no freedom to yell "Fire" in a crowded theater, because demoralization and tragedy result. And McCarthy has yelled "Fire" in so many places—in military institutions, in State Department, in press, radio, and educational institutions, in the Senate itself, with no more than a few sparks at the most as justification for the fear and demoralization that resulted.

Legally, McCarthy has been denounced for just two

items of conduct. Realistically, he has been denounced for
a great many. An overwhelming majority of the Senate
has simply concluded that enough is enough.

LET'S YOU AND HIM FIGHT

[*December 9, 1954*]

Personally, I intend to spend a minimum of time brooding over this, but the ugly truth appears to be that
Hollywood is retaining more of its masculine virility than
is Washington. We had a sign of the approach of this embarrassing condition a year ago when the President was
showing Mamie how the old Wild West heroes used to
fan a six-gun; he cut his hand and had to go to the Bermuda Conference wearing a Band-aid. As a Washingtonian
my confidence revived a bit this morning, however, upon
reading the news that the Hollywood crooner Johnny Ray
got an infection when he stepped on a toothpick from a
Martini glass. I figured this left the political capital a
shade ahead of the celluloid capital.

But then this afternoon the teletypes began to jangle
in wild agitation; when the keys began to spell out the
dateline "Hollywood," I had a premonition that movie
manhood had done something *big;* and, sure enough, the
teletype informed us that Frank Sinatra had been in a fist
fight. It is true that the motivation is obscure; it is also
true that all the enumerated blows went swishing through
empty space and no flesh was marked; but the men did
double their fists, and after all—Sinatra!

257

This dramatic event leaves Washington clearly behind, because we haven't had even a no-hit fist fight around here for years; and with the Senate censuring people for their *words*, with the President refusing even to cuss out McCarthy, I declare I don't know where our next Washington fight is coming from. It begins to look as if there's no hope at all, unless the Democrats should get back into power. On the other hand, if they are getting as soft *out* of power as they got *in* power, maybe that's a vain hope, too.

The whole thing is pretty hard to understand. You take Senators. Historically, especially in the nineteenth century, any U.S. Senator worth his snuff would whang away with fist, cane, or rolled-up speech at any other Senator who insulted his wife or his state or even his party. Today one Senator can even impugn another's patriotism, even imply that he's a traitor, the worst crime on the books, and what does he do? All he does is rise slowly to his feet and politely ask: "Will the Senator yield for a question?" It may be, of course, since the most frequent causative element has been named McCarthy, an ex-boxer with the strength of an orangutang, that the prospective contests have been a bit out of balance.

Another curious thing—even when Senators have been moved to physical violence, they are reluctant to use their fists. You'd think, with all the handshaking they do, their fists would be in condition; on the other hand, maybe that explains it—they've got to *protect* their fists; there's always more handshaking ahead. In any case, the last time McCarthy was in a fight, he used his knee, according to the defendant, Mr. Drew Pearson; and the last time we had a joint, or group, fight at the Senate, not a blow was landed. It was an affair of mutual lapel-grasping, finger-shaking, the push and the shove. That was the fracas in-

258

volving Senators Capehart, Lehman, and Humphrey. Not a blow was landed, but Capehart won, in a sense, because he was first man in the Press Gallery later, with a mimeographed statement. It was the firing of General MacArthur that produced that almost-fight, one of two almost-fights over the same issue. In the second affair the late Senator Wherry shook a finger in this reporter's face; but the finger never did turn into a fist, so there was another chance gone. By the time Wherry found out it was another broadcaster he was mad at, not me, his normal geniality had returned.

The obsolescence of the political fist is alarming enough, but on top of that the art of political vituperation is decaying also. The double-barreled or repeating cliché of the McCarthy kind is a pretty poor substitute for the inspired verbal lines of an Ickes, or a Tom Connally or a John L. Lewis. And with Harry Truman retired, nobody even doubles his fist around a pen any more.

ADVICE, ANYONE?

[December 14, 1954]

The President has proclaimed tomorrow as Safe Driving Day. I hate to be a cynic about such a serious matter, but as age and world weariness creep upon me, I tend to lose my once eager faith in the American custom of special days. Mother's Day seems to work pretty well— mothers like it and the florist business, which started it, according to the history *I* read, thrives on it; but most of the other contenders for special attention have not done well; National Mother-in-Law Day has not improved the status of mothers-in-law, so far as I can see, and in spite of several years of Save the Horse Week, the horse continues to diminish in numbers. Except on television sets between the hours of four and six.

I am one of those fortunate people who can approach the question of safe driving with a clear conscience, fogged up only by a slight touch of smugness; because in twenty-five years of driving, both front seat and back, I have never been involved in a serious accident. (Knock.) There's no wood in this modernistic studio, but my intentions are proper.

The only time I ever disappointed the insurance company I was going no more than fifteen miles an hour. I was eighteen years old. The burning end of my cigarette fell into my shoe, and a parked truck suffered a wrenched rear wheel. But I always blamed that one on my father and his archaic notions about money; if he had promised me a hundred dollars not to smoke till I was twenty-one—the way my pals' fathers did with them—the accident would not have happened. But my father was hopeless; he would never even admit the logic of my argument.

To get back to Safe Driving Day—one is almost tempted to compare it to setting aside a special day for the avoidance of cyanide and man-eating sharks, which would be slightly unfair; but, in any case, the whole idea is based on the evangelistic approach, the attempt to change human nature and habits by exhortation and warning, in the hope that people will *remain* overtly conscious of their duty or their peril.

This is the opposite of the approach that would have some authority fix things, by law, or physical safeguard, so humans *can't* make the deadly mistakes they do. As a fickle and inconstant-type fellow, I have wavered between the two approaches to world problems for a good many years. When I was a college boy and of course knew everything, I was impressed by doctrines of dialectical materialism and "economic man" and so on and had only scorn for the approach of such groups as the Oxford Movement, which would improve human society by improving individual human beings. I was certain that authority of some kind had to *fix* things, from the top, so bad things like wars, or exploitation, couldn't happen. In later years I wasn't so certain, and began to think the only real, long-term solution *is* the improvement of the individual himself.

I notice that seems to be the President's fundamental conception, too. He wants to save lives on the highways by changing the attitude of the human beings who do the driving. Just as he said the other day that the whole dairy problem would be solved if every American would just drink an ounce and a half more milk per day. The trouble with the long-range, humanistic approach is that it takes so *long*. Meanwhile, cars crash and dairy farmers go broke; so here I find myself wavering away from the President and the human-nature approach again.

Both situations need *fixing*. I don't know how to fix the dairy problem—an admission that may get me thrown out of the commentators' club—but I know how the car-crash problem can be fixed. Car-manufacturers have to do just two things: equip all car seats with safety belts, and all engines with governors that prevent speeds above, say, fifty miles an hour. Do those two things, and I'll wager highway fatalities will decrease sixty per cent. I wouldn't wager my *life* on this, but I'd bet a big stack of old scripts containing advice that nobody took.

THE REAL ONES

[*December 15, 1954*]

There are many plaques and monuments and buildings across the country dedicated to military men who died in the country's wars; and so, if one may properly speak of intramural affairs, on public as well as company time, it was good to see, this week, that the Overseas Press Club in New York has now established its new building to the memory of the war correspondents who also died in war; all those, so many of them personal friends, seen alive at breakfast and dead by evening, who tried to stay alive, with no training save the normal instinct for self-survival, with no defense save the useless armor of pencil or camera.

In the televised drama portion of those ceremonies the man who played the part of the immortal Ernie Pyle said that he had come to the point, covering the war, where he felt ashamed that he was still alive. This was not exaggerated sentimentality, nor was such feeling, in the war, confined to correspondents. It was a curious psychological phenomenon that one noted in many, civilian or soldier. Always the heroism or the real worth was elsewhere, in *other* bodies and hearts; the men on the ground thought of the men in the air as the *ones*, the real ones; the men in the air thought of the men on the ground. The whole thought of the wounded, and the wounded thought of the dead.

The war reporter, if nature had accorded him the usual sensibilities, thought of them all. Ernie Pyle, as he himself

262

suggested, came close to cracking up in Europe; and it was this haunting sense of his indefinable and self-appointed duty that made him go to the Pacific theater, where the enemy bullet found him at last. If practically all the combat correspondents, no matter how long they had been there, avoided cracking up, among many soldiers who did crack up, it was not because their fiber was stronger. It was, so it seemed to me, because of an almost unconscious item of knowledge, always lodged in the back of their minds; the knowledge that they *could* go back, could honorably get away from the hell, almost any time they chose. The mere knowledge was enough, whether one acted upon it or not; and therein lay the difference between being a civilian under fire and a soldier under fire. The soldier knew *he* could *not* go back; that knowledge alone, after enough physical wear and tear, was enough to break a man down.

Writers like Ernie Pyle were always aware of this, and from this came the curious, factually unjustified sense of personal unworth that afflicted so many war reporters. Unjustified on the facts because it is doubtful if any other single group of men in the war suffered so high a rate of casualties as did the reporters.

Death is death, but in its manner and form it demands quite differing prices of admission. Most war reporters who died, from my observation, were caught unawares by the death that came. It was one thing to step on a mine while running across a road; it was a different thing to deliberately lift a mine from the ground, as soldiers had to do, and have it go off; it was one thing to be hit by the sniper in the ruined house as you drove through the street; a different thing to go looking for the sniper, as soldiers had to do, and spot him an instant too late.

263

These are, I'm afraid, very intramural thoughts, without much meaning, perhaps, except to other ex-war-reporters and some ex-soldiers.

Suffice it to say that most former war reporters know why it is right and just that many more memorials exist to departed soldiers than to departed reporters. But to say, too, that the new memorial to those departed colleagues of pencil and camera is also just and right; for the old wartime feeling does not pass: that they were the *ones*, the real ones.

THE REVENGE OF J. F. DULLES

[*January 4, 1955*]

It looks as if coexistence is getting off to a pretty poor start, after all. The area for existing co has been shrunk considerable. After sweet-talking us for months, Malenkov has slapped thirty per cent of Russian territory off limits to American visitors; and yesterday J. F. Dulles slapped twenty-seven per cent of the United States off limits to Russian visitors; maybe he did take a three-per-cent loss on the transaction, but this was the first time he's been able to put his massive retaliation into effect, and anybody can be pardoned three per cent failure when it's due to overeagerness on the job.

He certainly did give them tit for tat. They rule out Solnechnogorsk (that's easier done than said); he rules out Kalamazoo. They off-limit Krasnolpolvanski; he off-limits Androscoggin in the state of Maine. They say you can't visit sunny Sevastopol; he takes Atlantic City away from *them*. They keep us away from the Rameshki region northeast of the Moscow and Pechora rivers; and Dulles says, okay, you stay away from the Mississippi from the mid-Iowa line down to Cairo, Illinois.

Of course, the Russians got there fustest with the most-est, but then they had more to git with than we got. I was always weak on percentages—I had the flu during the fourth grade—but by my figures they have snatched away two million five hundred and fifty-seven plus square miles of Russia and we have snatched away one million thirteen thousand plus square miles of the United States. On a real-estate market-value appraisal basis, however, any hard-headed-type statesman like Mr. Dulles knows we're 'way ahead of them. Our whole foreign policy is based on countering aggression with strength, and forcing a Russian relaxation or rollback; and I wouldn't be surprised, when they see they've lost places like McHenry County, North Dakota, if they gradually give way. They'll probably give us back part of Balashikha, as a starter. We'll probably test their sincerity by handing back part of Deaf Smith County, Texas; if the world goes well, if the East Germans and Senator Knowland are quiet, we may get a real *détente*, as the French call it, and pretty soon our folks will be back to their starting-point—at the Metropole in Moscow with a folder of Intourist tickets in their hand; and their folks will be back at the Waldorf with a wallet full of American Express checks. It won't all be easy, though; there are problems. Take Brooklyn. Brooklyn is declared off limits, the only part of New York so desig-nated, and Brooklyn is so proud of this it may not *want* to go back on limits. Take Armstrong County, South Dakota. It's declared off limits, too, but it doesn't exist. It wasn't anything but grassland and gumbo and jack rab-bits anyway, so South Dakota abolished it a year ago.

265

I feel mixed emotions about McHenry County, *North* Dakota, which is graced by my home town of Velva. McHenry is off limits to Russians, but Pierce County, next door is not. This is logical; Pierce never had anything worth hiding anyway, except some thistles and dusty alkali ponds they brag up and call lakes. But I'm a little bothered about how Velva folks are going to like being shut off and mysterious and all. In fact, we always used to say Velva wasn't a bit scared of those Russians; just let them get one good look at the new school and the clinic, and the new north bridge over the Mouse River where the spring rise always used to flood Johnson's chicken yard, and, we'd say, they'd quit being foreigners and settle right down there and be good Americans. Now it looks like we've lost our chance.

Anyway, it's pretty interesting, the way J. F. Dulles has carved up the land of the brave and the home of the free. It sort of reminds me of the fellow who said he believed in Cleveland and Akron and Santa Claus, but had his doubts about Toledo.

CHAMPAGNE FOR BREAKFAST

[*January 13, 1955*]

A fellow called up the other day and suggested this reporter go along on a commercial junket. He had conceived the historic idea of flying a passel of journalists, in the middle of the work week, in the middle of winter, to Nassau in the Bahamas and back the same night. As he described the sunshine, the coral strands and the native girl fire dancer, who has succeeded in applying the Minsky method to voodoo, it occurred to me that I had been derelict in my duty. I had never analyzed the commercial junket, one of the great institutions of our age, for I had never been on one. So yesterday, after explaining to less-principled people in the office that conscience left me no other choice, I stuffed a pair of swimming trunks in my pocket and stepped aboard an airliner, determined to see it through.

It turned out to be the most wondrous junket in the annals of other people's expense accounts since the time another airline flew some reporters from New York down and around Virginia and back to New York, non-stop, with the purpose, as stated by the press agent, of "greeting the spring."

It was a sprightly group that gathered in the plane yesterday for *our* junket, the purpose of which had something to do with a test of some kind. As the hours whiled away, there were some who suggested it was a test of the human liver, but I imagine that should be put down as merely a by-product of the original research. It all began with champagne and caviar for everybody for breakfast. A few regarded champagne for breakfast at thirteen thousand feet as a question; but most, as an answer. Altogether the hospitality on such a junket is overwhelming, a word I use not without deliberation, in view of the fact that by high noon one of our hardy little band was enjoying the benefits of applied oxygen. I believe this was the same client who was found by a searching party, much later, behind a cluster of palms, absorbed in the scientific experiment of seeing how many coconuts could be balanced, one upon another.

As we stepped out into the brilliant Nassau sunshine we

were greeted by a calypso band and hospitality in clear glasses; as we passed from the Customs room the hospitality was in frosted glasses; it was in coconut shells, equipped with straws, at the bathing-beach; in tall glasses at the cocktail club, and in short-stemmed goblets at the hotel dining-room. Periodically, one of our hosts explained that there was something about the sunshine and air in the Bahamas that magically enabled any visitor from the north to accept almost any amount of hospitality without future regrets.

It did not seem polite at the time to question his expert knowledge, but I have had reason, since, for skepticism, because of a phone call this afternoon. This was from one of our fellow junketeers who put a few hesitant questions in an endeavor, he said, to write an accurate account of yesterday's proceedings.

"Is it not correct," he said, "that during the sea bathing a member of the party was attacked by a shark or a barracuda?" After reflection, I explained that what he had seen was a native boy diving for a coin under our glass-bottomed boat in the midst of a school of small bass. "Well," he said, "how about that poor old lady whose clothes caught fire in that thatched hut—did she live?" I explained that it was a *young* lady, that it was a night club, that she was merely stamping out the fire with her bare feet at the end of her dance, and that any flames touching *her* clothes would have died out for lack of material.

"Well," he went on, "when we landed back in Washington—was that a *real* snowstorm?" I said of course it was. He said you never can tell with these junkets, and he had wondered if it was an artificial snowstorm put on by the Nassau Board of Trade for a dramatic climax and contrast. I said the technique of the publicity junket has certainly developed marvelously, though I didn't think it had reached such a peak of perfection as all that.

But I'm not sure I convinced him.

IKE AND THE OLD BATTLE-AX

[February 2, 1955]

Every once in a while, Old Lady Meeker reappears in a dream. Usually it's because I've misquoted something or fouled up my syntaxes, and Old Lady Meeker—we called her Old Battle-ax behind her back—gives me hail-columbia. Old Lady Meeker had pincher glasses, a pinned-up mop of gray hair, and eyes in the back of her head. She taught tenth-grade English and Latin; she made us copy and memorize, memorize and copy. We thought it was corny and a waste of our valuable teen-age time. But I can still repeat the Prologue to *The Canterbury Tales*, and now it seems pretty wonderful. She'd whack any kid with her ruler if he failed to learn the words of the national anthem. Sometimes she'd read aloud from Jefferson or Lincoln and get tears in her eyes, and the guys in my crowd felt horribly ashamed for her.

Well, last night here was Old Battle-ax in another dream, eyes blazing with anger, and I thought I was really for it. But not this time. She was waving a newspaper clipping in her hand, and what do you know?—she was sore at the President of the United States. That was something, for her, considering how she revered the office of the Presidency.

269

She waved that clipping under my nose and said: "Flap-doodle! Pish-posh! The very idea! Shades of Jefferson! Shades of John Adams! Shades of John Quincy Adams, Charles Francis Adams—*all* the Adamses—God rest their souls! What *have* we come to?"

I managed to say, timidly: "Is there something wrong?"

"Something wrong?" she screamed. "By the great horn spoon" (that's from James Russell Lowell, I remember), "indeed there is something wrong. Imagine," she went on, almost hysterical, "the President apologizing to a spoiled little whippersnapper who should have been thankful—yes indeed, thankful. I wish I had her in *my* class, indeed I do!"

I managed to take the clipping and read it, though she kept tapping her shoe, and that unnerved me almost as much as it used to when I would recite for her. The clipping said a sixteen-year-old high-school girl in Michigan was punished for prattling away while the class was listening to the President's State-of-the-Union message the other day. Her punishment was to write out the seventy-seven-hundred-word message in long hand. Took her a week, no less. What does she do but send the manuscript to the White House with a note informing the President he should have said it all in fewer words. And what does the President do but write back to her saying he apologized "profoundly" for the length of his address.

It was hard to tell who Old Lady Meeker was madder at, the girl or the President. "Imagine," she said, "the little whippersnapper taking up the President's time like that. Where's the respect? And I suppose she called him 'Ike.' Oh, dear, dear me! And the child is complaining—complaining, mind you, because she's obliged to carry a few facts in her silly little head about the state of her country.

I suppose the burden will warp her precious personality or something and they'll send her to a psychiatrist. Faugh!"

I tried to say something, but then Old Battle-ax lit into the President. "Sometimes he tries my faith, I declare if he doesn't. Why, just the other day I was telling Mr. Jefferson how proud he must be about the President's speeches on mental discipline, and strengthening the moral fiber of our youngsters and all. And now this—*apologizing* to the lazy creature for his state-of-the-Union speech! Think what Mr. Lincoln would have told the little whippersnapper. Or Mr. Wilson, or Teddy Roosevelt. They'd have told her a thing or two, I declare if they wouldn't!"

Well, I never did manage to say much—only nod and mutter the way I used to in front of her desk when she was on the warpath. The dream got sort of fuzzy then, and all I remember is Old Lady Meeker marching back up there, clutching that clipping, to show it, I suppose, to Jefferson and Jupiter and the others in her present classroom. But I hadn't forgotten about those eyes in the back of her head, and I didn't dare let my face down in a smile until the clouds had swallowed her up.

THE FUN AND GAMES OF
HARVEY MATUSOW

[February 7, 1955]

The federal grand jury in New York now opens its inquiry into the weird case of the "double witness," Harvey Matusow, and the Justice Department has dispatched one of its top officials to help out; in the interests,

271

not only of justice, but of the Justice Department; for the astonishing Mr. Matusow who doesn't seem to care what he says about anybody, himself included, has the Justice Department, as the *Washington Star* puts it tonight, "over a barrel." And the Department is accompanied in that undignified position by those various Congressional investigators who have used Matusow over the years.

Matusow, as you probably know, is the ex-Communist —at least it's assumed the prefix is accurate—who turned "expert witness," so called, and put the finger on scores of Americans as Reds, pro-Reds, or fellow travelers in hearings and court trials, and who now calmly states that his testimony was malarkey in big part, given out for personal publicity and, apparently, a general love of fun and games.

How many respectable citizens he may have injured over the last three years is anybody's guess; maybe quite a few, if you believe he's now telling the truth. The trouble is nobody can be *sure* he's now telling the truth; the only thing you can be sure of is that here is a real mixed-up kid, which means that his previous testimony as well as his present testimony is thrown into doubt as dark as the most neurotic recesses of the Communist mind. So he is being investigated by the Justice Department, as he should be; the only drawback is that this almost amounts to the Justice Department investigating itself. The happiest result for the Department, as for the various committees who used the man, would be to prove that he was telling the truth before, but is lying now.

Matusow, one would think, has got to be punished somehow; but if he is convicted for perjury, it won't much help the Department or the committees whether it's for previous perjuries or present perjuries. Either way the country is told that officials whose sworn duty it is to find the guilty and protect the innocent have for years been exposing or convicting people with the aid of a plain liar. Either way officialdom has got to explain to the country how it could be so thorough in exposing the lives and characters of so many defendants and so careless in accepting at face value the character of its own "expert" witness.

It will not be enough to establish that the Matusow testimony was merely incidental in all the cases involved, that the results would have been the same without his words. That in itself may be very hard to establish—who can say *what* bits of testimony are the straws that tip a balance in the mind of a juror or a committeeman? Various officials, political and juridical, will still stand convicted in the public mind of the grossest carelessness in the most delicate kind of cases, involving the personal honor of individuals.

The Justice Department is over a barrel for other reasons besides those that concern its own prestige; for some technical reasons involving the requirements of corroboration, it may prove impossible even to prosecute Matusow for perjury. Furthermore, because of the Matusow mess, future prosecutions involving the use of other ex-Communists as witnesses may be weakened; the latter contingency, no doubt, is quite evident to what is left of the Communist Party, which must be rubbing its hands in pleasure.

In any case, the whole unsavory business would seem to endorse the instincts of those leading lights of the law who have always been profoundly uneasy about the wholesale use of professional, paid informers. They have their valuable uses, in many investigative areas, including tax and customs cases; some have no doubt served well in Communist cases. But these cases often involve not only acts and associations but also the vague, unverifiable area of thoughts and ideas; and in this area, professional informers obviously must be used with the utmost caution. They have not been so used, in this administration or the last one.

Maybe now they will be.

BENSON SHOULD OF STOOD IN
A FEATHER BED

[February 11, 1955]

Quail-hunting is the most important item on the President's mind today, so I see no reason why I shouldn't analyze quail-hunting. It's true that I am a first-season amateur at quail—Virginia quail—and never have tried those Georgia quail the President is after; but then I've never shot a commissar either, or even *been* to Russia, but this has not prevented me from talking about the Kremlin all week.

If a faint trace of bitterness creeps into this account, it is due to the fact that the Virginia quail season is all over, while Georgia's is still on, apparently; and the daily limit in *my* neck of the woods is only eight, whereas the President can take twelve a day. But I doubt that the general behavior of the quail is any different for Presidents than for garden variety shooters; the quail is a bird of character —a noble bird. It has dignity, and settled habits; you can depend upon the quail, except that sometimes it will flush eighty feet off single, and other times a whole covey will flush at your feet with a paralyzing roar of wings. The quail is a monogamous bird; this is a pity, for otherwise, presumably, there would be *more* quail, for Presidents and commoners; but it means you can shoot cock or hen, indiscriminately, which is a good thing because they are too fast and too much alike to differentiate, anyway.

I must say today's dispatches from Georgia are distressingly incomplete. We know the President is using a twenty-gauge double gun; this is the mark of a true up-country quail man. The twenty has plenty of power and pattern for quail; it is light and short, for quick swinging in briar patch and woods, where the canny quail is bound to lead the President a scratchy and exciting chase. But there the dispatches leave off; not a word about whether the President is a snap shooter or takes his time and is content with one bird per flush; not a line on whether he works around between covey and woods to try the tricky overhead shots; not a word whether he uses the swing-through system or the pointing-out system when he pulls the trigger.

Well, the White House correspondents under Truman weren't required to study Chopin, so I suppose we can't force them to take up upland gunnery; still, it would be a help. A million fellow sufferers like myself are getting edgy waiting to find out if the President uses number-eight shot or nine, high speed or standard, an improved cylinder with a modified barrel, or a modified with a full.

I'm not hinting, or anything, but if it's all right with the President, and the press corps would like to deputize me to sort of represent them, next time, for the technical details—why, I guess I could leave the Russian situation to the other experts for a day or two.

Some of us ordinary heel-and-toe quail men are a little disappointed that the President rides in one of those mule-drawn "roadsters," so called, carrying the dogs and all; no doubt it's *comme il faut* in upper Georgia quail society, but still it's a little too much like his riding around the golf course on that jeep. After all, part of the fun is seeing who gets worn out first, you or the quail, and even the President's eighty-four-year-old friend Barney Baruch does it on horseback, at least.

Well, anyway, the President is getting a crack at the quail, with Secretary Humphrey. This is more than he got six weeks ago when he was up in *my* quail country one day with Secretary Benson. They were at a big ranch near my forty-acres-and-no-mule. The back country grapevine works fast, and next day an old codger said to me: "Dangdest thing. The fellas they salted out twenty-five pheasant from Fred Sharp's game farm and spotted all the quail coveys, in case the President wanted to go huntin'. Well, the President he was clear achin' to go, but Benson, he didn't want to go. So you know how the President spent the afternoon? Lookin' at Benson's movies about the Mormon church."

REVOLVING NON-SEQUITUR

[*February 18, 1955*]

Pundits and commentators don't live by catchwords alone, but the slogan tends, at times, to become the staff of life in this political center, and people have to draw from it what nourishment they can, depending up their individual metabolism. Gastro-intellecto disturbances arise, however, when these special diets are suddenly changed without advance preparation; so it is probably a good thing that we all have the quiet week-end in which to nibble cautiously on the latest exotic dish from the Presidential table—"dynamic conservatism."

Mr. Eisenhower threw this one out for grabs yesterday in addressing his party's assembled leaders. They, of course, are a hardy breed, and they downed this rare morsel without the bat of an eyelash, or the knit of a brow. It has been a little harder for others among us; we had just got our systems accustomed to "progressive moderation" when the President coolly announced that he was changing his mind; he said that "at the moment" he rather favors "dynamic conservatism" to define his party's domestic policies. There was a threat implied in this statement. He may switch to still another definition at any time; there is nothing to do but hang on and wait, newspaper copy desks hoping to high heaven that the next definition will fit more easily into a one-column headline than the existing two.

That was one of the great things about Teddy Roosevelt's Square Deal, or Truman's Fair Deal. Nobody could prove just what *they* meant, either, but they were short, they were crisp; they fitted headlines nicely, and they bandied good in conversation. You could, if you wished, transpose them into verb forms, like Deal Square or Deal Fair, though it sounds pretty silly. You can transpose Ike's slogans too, but you can't work up much active verb sense out of them. In fact, nothing happens to them at all. What is the difference between "progressive moderation" and "moderate progressivism" or between "dynamic conservatism" and "conservative dynamism." Either way, they just sort of sit there and don't *go* any place. The fact that they sit there, fixed, imperturbable, does, however, give you a chance to work around them, squint at them through one eye at a time, and measure them like a fish that *didn't* get away. I don't mean like a dead mackerel that both shines and stinks in the moonlight, but like a dead tuna, say, that is neatly mounted, its mouth closed in a satisfied expression, the whole thing covered with a careful coat of shellac.

A slogan defining administration policy is a pretty serious thing and you can't let just any old slogan in the official house. You'll notice the administration is taking its time about replacing "massive retaliation" and "unleashment" for its foreign policy and has turned down various gratuitous offers from the Press Club Bar, like "spiritual values and no ground troops" or "a warm chuckle and air power." Of course they still have "peaceful coexistence" around, but it didn't seem very impressive when they first fished it out, so it's been tossed back in to see if it will grow a little.

On domestic policy, though, the President seems to be striking out pretty boldly, like a fellow who will try anything not only once, but twice. And we'll just have to see how the country responds to "dynamic conservatism." I'm not going to go so far as to say the two words add up to a revolving non-sequitur, though they do seem to sort of turn around and butt each other; it may be more accurate to say this slogan contains the built-in retraction or escape clause. It's a little bit like "make haste slowly," or Damon Runyon's "medium hello," or the old vaudeville gag: "If we had some eggs we could have some ham and eggs, if we had some ham."

Classicists, no doubt, will be reminded of the Red Queen, I guess it was, who said something about running faster to stay in the same place.

But I'm afraid the thing defeats me, owing to my lack of learning. I quit school at the point where we worked with definitions that defined something. Never did get up in the higher echelons where they worked with definitions defining definitions.

EVERY MAN TO HIS OWN
RED MENACE

[March 11, 1955]

Politicians, like columnists and commentators, would have hard going without those handy words "the public." Right now, some Republicans tell us "the public" is outraged because Democrat Paul Butler mentioned the health of the First Lady in a political context; Mr. Butler is telling us "the public" feels one way about the President as a man, but quite another way about him as a political leader. One set of columnists assures us "the public" wants a showdown with the Chinese Reds, while another set is confident "the public" wants no more war in Asia.

"The public," of course, consists entirely of *other* people. I never met a man who considered himself part of the public; so perhaps there is no such thing as the public, but only persons, who coalesce in certain attitudes in varying degree and from time to time.

Still, you have to generalize or you can't communicate about general ideas; so it's interesting to see the latest analysis of what's on the mind of the American public, meaning all of us, but in our various groupings. The latest attempt, financed by the Fund for the Republic and published in *Look*, is one of the best attempts; it is not based

279

ERIC SEVAREID

on the quickie public-opinion poll technique, which assumes, falsely, that attitudes can be *extracted*. They can only be *detected*, through long conversations conducted by skilled conversationalists, and that is what has been done here, with a carefully categorized cross-section of the public; that is, the people; that is, us.

The first thing it shows is that the great majority of us are chiefly worried about personal problems, of money, marriage, health, and so on. It strikes me that this is natural, and eternal. Even in prosperity, almost none of us feels *completely* secure; if most of us did, the whole social machinery would probably slow to a crawl. The Lord has probably always prohibited utopias because he knows they would prove fatal.

This study reports that almost nobody volunteered any concern about internal Communism; if people were jogged a bit, however, and asked specifically, then a large minority said they *were* worried about domestic Reds. But the queer thing about it was that very few worried about possible Communist espionage or sabotage, the real areas of concern for this country, and many more worried about Communist *ideas* converting others, the area in which the American Reds' success has been microscopic.

This curious response was explained by additional probing, which revealed that only a fraction of our people have any clear and cohesive notion of what Communist ideas *are*. To some, a fellow always talking about war was a Communist; to others, a fellow always talking about peace was a Communist. The study concludes that many Americans use the label "Communist" simply as a convenient synonym for something they dislike or distrust. For quite a few people Communism seems to resemble weather. They said that even if the President assured them

280

there was no danger from Communists within government; even if a school board assured them there was no such danger within the schools—these people would refuse to believe it.

On the big international questions of the moment, far more Americans would rather try to talk things over with Russia than ignore or fight Russia; a majority would rather fight Russia than let Communism take over in Europe or Asia, but for every American who would let Europe go without a fight, there were *two* who would let Asia go without a fight. Which must be somewhat disturbing to those political leaders who believe our ultimate fate rests with the course of Asia, not that of Europe.

SQUATTER'S RIGHTS FOR
SQUIRRELS

[March 25, 1955]

After days of struggle against the elemental laws of nature and politics, the White House has thrown in the sponge, or the divot, and has decided to let the squirrels stay, whatever they do to the President's putting green. Any politician or any hunter could have told them; but, as the teachers say in the moderate progressive schools, pupils learn best by doing. The last thing you can do with squirrels, as with many other wild creatures, is get rid of them; and the last thing a politician should ever *try* to do is to take the opposite side from pets or wild creatures in a public argument. You can oppose peace, universal brotherhood or the Bill of Rights in this political age, but

281

you cannot oppose churches, organized veterans, or our furred and feathered friends and hope to get re-elected. Our finny friends, yes; fish don't count, but don't ask me why.

So the White House has yielded to these elemental laws and will let the squirrels stay; they were there, first, anyway, when Republicans were Whigs. Not that they *could* have been eliminated. The wildlife folks over in the Interior Department could have told the White House folks that much. Governments can erect iron curtains that keep humanity in or out; but the genius of man has not yet devised a fence that a determined American squirrel cannot get under or over. Not only can you not keep squirrels out of places they want to be in; you cannot eliminate squirrels, any more than you can eliminate starlings, as the District Sanitation Department well knows.

This opens up the whole question of the national illusions about wildlife. I am only about half-informed on this subject, but gambling on the assumption you are only about half awake at this point anyway, I will proceed. So far as I can gather, the Lord determines the supply of wildlife in His own mysterious ways and neither the hunter nor the humanitarian can affect the situation, save in specific areas for specific periods of time.

Anybody who spends much time in woods and fields soon discovers that the whole existence of wildlife is a furious struggle between life and death the clock and the year around. Nearly every set of wild creatures is prey for another set; all are prey for weather, disease, and curious cycles of scarcity and plenitude that even the experts cannot entirely explain. There are exceptional situations, of course, but over the long haul, man with his gun and trap or man with his feeding station and sanctuary affects the situation only in minor degree. Sometimes a hunting season is curtailed, because quail, say, are short; but next season they are even shorter. Sometimes a season is prolonged because rabbit, say, are too thick; but next season they are even thicker. States pay out vast sums in bounties on fox, because fox kill game birds; and they often find the expenditure useless. Deer are rigorously protected in some regions and still disappear; in other regions, with less protection they become so thick they starve, and are decimated by disease. Some years ago the number of killer animals on this continent like fox, mink, and weasel suddenly and enormously increased; did it mean a decrease in the game birds they kill? It did not; they, too, suddenly, enormously increased and in the same period—no one knows why. Sometimes the humanitarians are quite wrong about how to increase the life and happiness of wild creatures; sometimes the hunters are wrong—the story of the buffalo and the passenger pigeon seems evidence of that.

But there's no mystery about the White House squirrels. The laws of politics and the laws of nature take care of them. They stay.

THERE WERE GIANTS IN THOSE' DAYS

[March 29, 1955]

Mr. John W. Davis was buried yesterday at the age of eighty-one; another of that dwindling group of towering Americans from a past age of event; great men, like Henry Stimson, who never achieved the pinnacle of public life, the Presidency, when lesser men did; men whose dedication to their country was whole-souled, nevertheless, and for whom the supreme frustration of personal ambition never deflected them away from public services of a monumental nature. The small band of true elder statesmen is dwindling; their counsel will one day soon be entirely lost, and sometimes one wonders how and when they are to be replaced. This may be illusion, but it always seemed to me they represented an influence in our public affairs fundamentally different from the mental and emotional promptings of most men now of the prime and middle age. Because the minds of men like Davis and Stimson—one could add others, like Learned Hand or the poets Sandburg and Frost—were formed in a quite different era.

Their views of life were rooted in the long American past, anchored in what seemed to be rock; their principles of conduct and action, their faith in the American vision, were matured before the First World War, which began the present process of anarchy in personal and public principle. Nearly all who have matured since that first world slaughter matured in *doubt* and the short-term view. *They* matured in faith and the long view. On behalf of their eternal principles of the free mind, they would join in no hasty rationalizations in the misused name of security; they would today, I think, in the face of possible war in Asia, look to the lessons of history, not to the alleged compulsions of strategy, where so many lesser men direct their eyes.

There were eternal verities for a man like John W. Davis, and one was the meaning of the American Constitution. He was probably the greatest constitutional lawyer of his time; and he would, if his verities were involved, defend a so-called security risk other men would shun, or even an acknowledged Communist.

Always, the principle was the thing, not the individual, not the pressing needs of the harried present, nor the fleeting charms of popularity. Such men would not bow to the icons of public opinion, knowing the majority can be wrong; one cannot quite imagine them scrutinizing the public-opinion polls, sending careful trial balloons into the air to see where safety lay; or surrounding themselves with ghostwriters weighing each calculated word to offend no possible pressure group. They proceeded from principle and hoped the needs of the moment would fit; they did not proceed from the needs of the moment, inventing or adjusting principle as protective coloration.

Such men had a positive effect on their country's course, beyond, sometimes, the influence of those who had taken the great offices in their stead. One wonders, sometimes, what the course of Reconstruction would have been—that period of public disease—had Horatio Seymour not lost the Presidency to General Grant, so vastly inferior to Seymour in intellect and vision. One wonders what would have been our course through the frantic twenties, ending in the depression collapse, had John W. Davis not lost the Presidency to Calvin Coolidge, who sat on the White House porch and rocked, impervious to a new idea. Those are the might-have-beens of history, indication in themselves of how wrong the majority can be.

But Davis's life and works were not might-have-been in themselves. Private life did not frustrate the great lawyer; his works were many, important; and the country is the better for his long and enviable life.

FRIDAY NIGHT, THANK GOD

[*April 1, 1955*]

Well, the Capital has got through this April Fools' week; God's in His heaven, Ike's in his farmhouse, congressmen are clearing out for the Easter recess, and all's right with the world of Washington; at least until Sunday and the television interviews, when the congressmen still hanging around will doubtless send up a few more gaily colored trial balloons, to be shot down during the course of *next* week.

Washington got through the week, but it was a near thing; there were times when the nerves were pretty strained and sanity sorely tried.

Admiral Carney caught the dickens because he told reporters he thought the Chinese Reds would probably attack those islands very shortly; this is almost precisely what Secretary Dulles has also been saying privately, but he *didn't* catch the dickens. The President said his subordinates like the admiral have a perfect right to express their opinions, but no right to cause embarrassment to the administration by so doing. This cleared everything up; an officer can talk provided he knows in advance what the effect of his words will be; rush orders for crystal balls are expected to flow out of Washington in consequence.

One set of senators said the way to save the peace is to get out of those off-shore islands; another set said the way to save peace is to tell the Reds plainly we will defend them; meanwhile the official policy remains, to leave the whole issue in doubt. One set of officials said if we fail to defend those islands, we lose prestige all over Asia; another set of officials said that if we intervene for islands right on the China coast, to which we can make no legal claims, we lose prestige all over Asia.

General MacArthur declared he never advised getting Russia into the Japanese war and knew, in fact, that that would be a fantastic move. Whereupon the Forrestal diaries are produced stating flatly that MacArthur not only advised but urged Russian entry into that war; whereupon MacArthur says Forrestal could not have dictated that passage, or if he did, he must have been mentally ill at the time. Which led the *New York Post* to propose Mac-Arthur for a new position, to be known hereafter as the Commissioner of Past Policy; he will officially decide what should be done in all crises that are definitely over.

Senator Neely opened an attack on the President's personal conduct of his office, which some other Democrats were itching to join, but lacked the nerve; whereupon Mr. Neely sent *all* his colleagues fleeing for cover by beginning with the one thing you *cannot* attack—the President's churchgoing motives and habits.

Senator Knowland made the cheerful statement that it would be worth a third world war to defend those islands of Quemoy and Matsu. He didn't add: "April fool," either.

Senator McCarthy contributed to the week by a change in his phraseology; he freshened it up a bit. Last fall he said something or other was the "most unheard of thing he had ever heard of." This week he said Harold Stassen's refusal to let his subordinates testify was the "most unheard of thing he had ever *seen*."

The most unheard of thing the *women* of Washington have ever heard, or seen, occurred at a reception for Mrs. Eisenhower. A lobbyist's wife showed up wearing a copy of the same dress the first lady was wearing. The wife quickly threw on her mink cape, having left her good Republican cloth coat at home, but it was too late. "I was so embarrassed I could die," she said. The lady who designed the dress tried to join her in *rigor mortis*. "I would just like to drop dead," she said. As the First Lady merely chuckled at the contretemps—French for "unheard of"—the two women remain alive.

But for them, like the rest of us, it was a near thing, and Friday night didn't get here any too soon.

LEAVE MY SUBCONSCIOUS ALONE

[April 15, 1955]

As self-appointed protector of the public weal, it is time I give warning that the advertising man is after your last, secret possession. He's felt your pulse till it's off-beat; he's extracted your thoughts about his product till you feel subversive, and now, so help me, he's after your innermost *feelings*, your subconscious mind, no less. If the deep, subconscious truth is that you dislike his canned corn because you were frustrated in your desire to caress the corn-colored hair of the girl who sat in front of you in grade school—why, he'll find it out.

The whole process is the newest thing among the sales and packaging boys; it's called "motivational research." And personally, as a fellow recently conditioned to buying nothing unless it contains *both* lanolin and GL 70, it's making me feel old-hat, a fading old soldier in the great crusade for consumption. I've given the best years of my life already, trying to get my subconscious to explain why I approve stuff like holidays, women, and money and why I

288

disapprove work, blisters, and mosquitoes; and it just seems too much effort to find out why I squeeze a tube of tooth-paste at the front end instead of the rear. The thing is, though, that the motivational-research boys will find out *for* you; in fact, they don't care if *you* know the answer as long as *they* know it. Then they've got you. They know just where to aim their ads. They're already at it.

Know why they don't advertise beer as a healthy *food*, any more? The researchers found people subconsciously thought of fat and waist-lines. That's why beers are now "always refreshing, never filling." Know why the ads on cigarette-holders don't emphasize the holder in the picture? Because the motivational boys fished around in the sub-conscious and discovered people are afraid they'd look conspicuous using a holder. Know why airline ads are now directed at the *wives*—telling them how much quicker hubby will be back with the family? Well, the motivation-ists discovered a lot of hubbies didn't fly, not because they feared a crash; what they *really* feared was that if there was a crash their wives would think: "Silly fool, he should have gone by train."

The Corning Glass Works found a lot of engineers wouldn't buy glass pipe; the deep, subconscious reason was a childhood fear of breaking glass and getting spanked. How they'll get around that one, I don't know. Probably advertise "the new, no-spank" glass pipe.

The other day a motivational psychologist told kitchen-range manufacturers they should call it a "stove" again, and not let it disappear under the counter any more. Said today's woman is no longer the efficiency-minded careerist dame of the thirties, but is part homemaker again and sub-consciously wants a big, busy, warmhearted stove as a center of family life to express her own personality.

They find out all this with what they call the "depth interview." Now I understand that fellow who asked me all those questions about what I thought of when I thought of the meat industry. I said: "Oh, steers, dust, Gary Cooper, Texas lobbyists with Stetsons and loud voices." The fellow nodded, looked wise, finally tiptoed out as if he was afraid he'd drop and bust all that sensitive, subtle information.

A great idea for boosting auto sales has just occurred to me. Rip off the name of the car. Nobody is forced to wear a sign on his *suit* saying "Hart, Schaffner & Marx"; or the word "borsolino" on the crown of his hat. Bet the motivationists will find millions of men subconsciously resent exhibiting a trade-name on the way to work. Why not replace it with the name of the *driver?* Personality-expression, see?

As soon as I'm through talking to the Patent Office, I think I'll ring up Charlie Wilson.

THE GREAT WHEEL TURNS

[April 18, 1955]

The conference at Bandung, Indonesia, opened today; no matter what it may do, the very fact of its being is a thing to challenge the imagination, to set anyone's historical pulse to beating. Here are the leaders of twenty-nine separate nations gathered, representing more than one half the world's population; here are the new independent governments from a great geographical arc extending from Japan down and around as far as Africa. These are the non-whites of the world; these are the peoples so long dominated directly by Europeans, the peoples who could only try to adjust to a political world others made, now setting out to make their own world, to see, at the least, where they stand, in relation to the West, in relation to one another.

For fifty years perceptive Westerners have been warning the world that the next great turning of history's wheel would occur in Asia and Africa; it has happened already, still is happening before our eyes; no Western statesmen sit in the Bandung Conference; no Western government, even one so powerful as our own, can do anything but watch and wait, daily more conscious of how little the Western centers of power can really do, in our time, to effect its desires in this vast, awakened Eastern world. The "voiceless ones," as Sukarno of Indonesia put it today, the voiceless ones have now found their voice, and the rest of the world has no choice but to listen.

But it is not one voice heard in Bandung this week; it is twenty-nine voices, and they are bound to speak as anything *but* one voice; they are speaking of "unity in diversity." They *are* united in a common kind of *past;* they are not united in their present views and problems, nor in their desires for the future. One may doubt that *their* peoples desire peace any more than the peoples of the West; one may doubt that they are more steeped in what they call "spirituality" than what they think of as the materialistic West; but they are united in a common feeling of standing apart from the West and its deathly feuds; a feeling of inhabiting a different *stage* of history; these governments represent the most ancient centers of civilization, and yet, in many political meanings, it is they who are new and fresh; we and the remainder of the West who must seem old, in our political institutions, and in our quarrels. There is much truth in this, for we in the West are caught up in the continuing troubles of much past history; they are caught up in troubles that are new; they are unsure what their relationship should be with us; and we, including our own country, have not yet found an effective working pattern with them.

Their common past of colonialism, exploitation, and submergence give them a certain unity, but they are divided by the same force that divides the rest of the world —Communism and what to do about it. The Communism of Russia and China, lying as an endless weight against their borders for tens of thousands of miles is their problem too, however much it poses as anticolonialism and freedom. It was the Arabs who told Bandung today that Communism is a new form of colonialism much more dangerous to them than all the old forms put together. If they should be equating Communism and America's influence in Asia, they would do well to compare the historical record of Communist aggression in ten short years with the story of America in Asia since Admiral Peary; our record has been quite different from Europe's record in Asia, and in any case Europe's old story there is coming to the end of the book.

DREAMS OF A FAIRY
GRANDMOTHER

[*April 20, 1955*]

Coming events cast their sunbeams as well as their shadows before them; and there was a little story ticking out on the Associated Press wire today that seems to throw at least a faint, flickering light within the dark passages of the daily news of trouble and stress. No doubt it will alarm some men who harbor doubts that women are here to stay, but it will also relieve other men who are getting so tired in the terrible tempo and pressures of modern life that they doubt *they* are here to stay, themselves, and sometimes don't much care.

It has long been apparent to social thinkers and doers that the American male in business and professional life has been losing his authority and effectiveness within the family; partly because he's so confoundedly tired when he gets out of that subway or commuters' train that disciplining a teen-ager, or re-doing the wife's accounts, is just more than his beaten spirit can contemplate. It's long been evident that the American business and professional male is giving up his mortal shell well before his wife simply because modern competitive tensions are too much for his nervous system to stand very long. And he cannot properly discharge his *civic* responsibilities either. This is one reason the professional political machine in most communities has a high, considerably justified contempt for the reform movements put on, from time to time, by the so-called good people of the community. Generally the moves are just a brief sprint, very soon abandoned. As young Mayor Quigg Newton of Denver used to put it, the good people want to *buy* good government the way they buy electric power, without taking the trouble to find out how it is manufactured or delivered to them. They're too busy.

So, as one who has often brooded upon this condition to no purpose, today's little story on the ticker seemed to me at least one sunny straw in the social winds. It concerns the *women*. More particularly, it concerns *one* woman, named Mrs. Nellie Broderson, of Palo Alto, California. Mrs. Broderson has just been named Clubwoman of the Year;

what a woman like Mrs. Broderson can do, brandishing one good, strong woman's club, has been enough, apparently to strike terror in the hearts of the most cynical politicians.

Mrs. Broderson says, "Pshaw, just five determined women can clean up any community." Once women get started, she said, they'll dig out the truth. Mrs. Broderson moved to Palo Alto only four years ago, and she and her determined confederates have already dug out the truth about the local juvenile detention home, the local jail, the *lack* of a home for the aged. Not only dug out the truth about these institutions, but started an unstoppable local movement to build *new* institutions. The county fathers said it was impossible, but the women forced through a three-quarter-million appropriation for a new jail, alone.

"Men," said Mrs. Broderson, "are too busy to find out what really goes on in the town and the nation; but women have time, and they can do it." Not the *young* women, so much—they're busy, too, rearing their families—but the older women, whose children are grown. This may raise the specter in some alarmed male minds of a *grand*-matriarchial political society; but I can think of a lot of fellow commuters to whom this is no specter but a very pleasant dream, of a fairy grandmother, and if she has to wave a club instead of a wand, why, these guys, at least, are too tired to care.

THIS TELEGRAM SMELLS

[May 6, 1955]

Sunday is the day set aside to make mothers happier, with the by-product of increased happiness among florist, telegraph, and telephone companies; and if the President

can issue a statement about Mother's Day, I see no reason
why a fellow who makes a living out of statement-issuing
shouldn't tag along.

I've been looking over the new Western Union form
telegrams for the occasion; I know the company means
well, but—well, it's like the political movement to make
the rose the national flower. What I mean is, filial sentiment, like the rose petal, is a pretty delicate thing, which
flourishes better in quiet and private passages. I can't help
thinking officialdom is a pretty heavy burden for so tender
a thing as the rose; men and women who become national
institutions get gray and solemn, I've noticed; and I should
think the institutionalized rose might wither pretty fast.

I hope Western Union won't feel hurt or anything if I
suggest that one's feeling toward his mother is also a
special, private sort of thing that doesn't do too well under
conditions of mass or public manufacture, though, goodness knows, every politician, editorial writer, and popular
preacher is in the business along with W.U.

What I mean is, don't you think you've gone a little too
far this year, Western Union? I mean this Mother's Day
telegram form bearing the picture of a carnation and giving
off the *perfume* of the carnation when you sniff it closely.
Your publicity release says: "Western Union people are
excited about the idea of adding scent to sentiment on
Mother's Day telegrams." Well, I'm not. I won't argue
with you about the carnation being the Mother's Day
flower; I don't know who passed such a law, though if you
say so, I suppose that's official, too; but mothers are differing individuals and you take my mother for example. As
I recall, she doesn't *like* carnations; allergic to them, or
something. Furthermore, she's the old-fashioned-type
mother, and telegrams still frighten her. You go and hand

her a telegram that smells like a flower and I know just what's going to happen—she'll think somebody *is* dead, this time, and faint away. On the whole, I think you did better with those singing telegrams; I imagine your success with that just carried you away, and if W.U. people are allowed to *telephone* maybe you better get the board of directors together for another look at this thing—for Operation Re-think, as my advertising pals would call it.

I notice you're covering a lot more territory this year, including Mother's Day messages for grandmothers, aunts, and even girl friends' mothers. It might be better if they had their *own* days—I'm sure you wouldn't object—but lumping them all together this way sort of blurs the lines of authority, and if I know anything about women I think you're going to mess up some relationships that were doing all right up to now.

And take those thirty-one suggested messages—some, as you point out, in rhyme—where the sender just makes an X. Don't you think that makes it a little too much like an election or a public-opinion poll? I noticed your footnote saying: "for only a few cents additional the word 'love' can be added to any of the above texts," but even so . . .

Another thing. That first message is pretty neat, the one that goes: "You don't need satin to be pretty; or perfume to be sweet; you're a very dear mother; who simply can't be beat." That one. *My* mother used to teach English and she was a bear on punctuation. She's going to notice right away that you've cluttered it up with semicolons where commas ought to be and I'm afraid it might spoil her whole day.

THE RETARDED STUDENTS

[May 12, 1955]

China's Defense Minister spoke today at the Warsaw meeting of the Communist military leaders; the current interest lies in his pledge that Red China will fight alongside Russia if war should erupt in Europe. But he went on to accuse what he called American monopoly capitalists of trying to drive the world into war, with the old, old Marxist argument that capitalism must expand and dominate for reasons of profit. For some time it has been difficult to think that the hardheaded rulers of Soviet Russia still believe the tenets of Marxist fundamentalism; it is quite possible that the rulers of the raw young China do so believe, and important to find that out for sure.

If they do, they will change one day; cynicism is bound to set in among them as it has in Moscow long since and they will be trotting out the fundamentalism only for mass exhortation purposes as the Russians do. But to rational men it remains extraordinary that the old Marxist doctrine still serves even for propaganda purposes. Its hold is fantastic, in view of a whole century's undeniable lessons, as to both the causes of war and the real nature of internal social progress. It seems baffling to free men accustomed to the free flow of facts that millions do not understand that free capitalism has no need of aggressive expansion; that the great wars were brought on by pseudo-capitalist fascist regimes, which resembled Communism far more than democracy, by peoples not rooted in the civil democracy the Marxists profess to despise.

297

It seems baffling that they will not face the truth, after a century's experience, that virtually the whole Marxist analysis of the future has proved false prophecy. It did not come true, as Marx predicted, that under capitalism the misery of the workers would increase; it has vastly *de*creased; it did not come true that under capitalism inequalities in wealth would spread farther and farther apart; in every modern Western society they have come closer and closer together. It did not happen, as Marx predicted, that the middle class would be squeezed into dissolution; instead, they have immensely expanded in numbers and power until they are the dominant and cultural class of modern Western nations.

What of Marx's ten point program, to come about only through proletarian revolution? Nearly all of it—the progressive income tax; abolition of inheritance rights (through the tax weapon); free education for all children in public schools, and so on—nearly all of it has come about, and it has come about by peaceable, democratic means, along with the whole accompanying apparatus of pensions, medical and unemployment insurance, public housing, and all the rest. And this immense structure of progress and security has been built and enforced without the sacrifice of the individual's personal freedom, which the Communist states have never been able to accomplish, and their leaders have long since abandoned any wish to accomplish.

Even Marx, in his last years, admitted the possibility that these advances might be accomplished in some countries by peaceable, non-revolutionary means. For obvious reasons of their own, the nationalist Communist leaders forget this. But why do the run-of-the-mill Communists close their minds to the plain, demonstrable lessons of history? The

Indian philosopher Devaraja puts it this way: they are not interested in the *substance* of social progress, but in its form: not in progress *achieved*, but in its making. Orthodox Communists persuade themselves they want the *ends*, that the means are secondary. The reverse is the truth: they live for the means alone.

THE MONSTER'S MAW

[*May 24, 1955*]

The country's radio-TV owners and managers are in town this week, looking, for all the mystery and magic of their medium, pretty much like other rumpled conventioneers, bothered by the heat; today, they heard that useful citizen of Louisville, Mr. Mark Ethridge, describe TV as "a voracious monster which consumes Shakespeare, talent and money at a fearful rate." I couldn't, as our British cousins say, agree with him more.

It has long been the fashion among some to complain that the percentage of high-quality programs on TV or radio is low. But when you look at the business from the inside out, you often wonder that the percentage is as high as it is. For there's never been a media monster with an appetite like this. A book lasts, a play lasts; a magazine lasts, at least for a week. But in five, fifteen, or thirty minutes the radio or TV program is gone and can't be repeated. Every few minutes the maw of the monster must be fed a new dish, for eighteen to twenty-four hours a day, three hundred and sixty-five days a year. Make your complaint to the typical program director, and if he doesn't stab you with his letter-opener, he will say: "Look, friend, there isn't even enough *mediocrity* around, let alone high-class stuff."

This is the thing that stops me, or anyway slows me down, in pondering the proposed subscription TV, a very hot topic on which I am otherwise a moron. You drop in a coin and get a very superior show on your set; but what shows and how often? Suppose you get every hit play on Broadway. That's ten or twelve evenings out of your year. Hollywood produces maybe one superior picture a month; that's another twelve evenings. There are maybe three nationally important prizefights a year. Add a few odds and ends; if you have thirty-six, that is, ten per cent of your evenings in the year graced by really superior programs not otherwise obtainable at home, programs with enough popular demand to warrant the production costs, you would, I suspect, be doing well.

Mr. Ethridge today went on to express the plaintive hope that TV may someday be free of the shackles of the *ratings;* that sword of Damocles, the worry of the sponsor, joy of the advertising men, terror of the talent, the ratings. The other day the producer of a popular nighttime TV show said to me: "Over forty million people see it every week." The ratings, he said, prove it. I was duly impressed, but then the subversive habit of pondering began to gnaw at the vitals of my faith.

Let's see. Total population is a hundred and sixty-five million, of all ages. Take away the forty-three million kids under twelve who'll be in bed; Triple A estimates maybe sixteen million people in cars at that hour. FCC figures sixteen million people have no television sets or stations to listen to. There's about a million on trains, planes, and busses at that hour.

How many million people are in hotels, hospitals, theaters, movie houses, restaurants, ball parks, bridge games, PTA meetings; how many are chinning with the neighbors, walking the dog, reading a magazine or book? How many million are listening to the radio? How many are carpentering in the basement, rocking on the front stoop, or just sitting and thinking, or just sitting? How many million are working at night jobs or already asleep? How many are watching TV but not *that* program because it isn't carried there or are watching some *other* program, even if it is?

The thing gets obsessive, like counting, or rather subtracting, sheep. I would love to believe that one fourth of the entire American population watches my producer friend's show. But my love of producers, otherwise unlimited, doesn't seem to stretch that far.

GREAT OAKS FROM LITTLE
ISMS FALL

[June 16, 1955]

It's beginning to look as if something will have to be done about the state of Oregon if time-honored traditions are going to be kept intact on Capitol Hill. The Hill suffered quite a jolt when Senator Wayne Morse calmly switched from Republican to Democrat in mid-trout-stream; and it was adding insult to injury when this one-party state sent to Washington Democrat Senator Neuberger. Not only was he an author—every sound statesman knows an author

301

is practically as suspect as a poet—but he showed no proper respect for his seniors, began making unmaidenly floor speeches at once, and even clobbered the Vice President.

But now another Oregonian, a Republican at that, has mocked ancient tradition, kicked over the traces, and broken the unwritten rules. So the warning flags are up, the alarm bells are ringing, the fat is in the fire, and all congressmen will have to close ranks and march shoulder to shoulder in order to repair the breach. What has happened is that Representative Walter Norblad of Oregon has recommended that a post office in his own district be *closed down.* Costs the government more than it takes in, he calmly announced, seemingly unaware of the revolutionary step he is taking. As everyone knows, you let one bad apple get its head into the barrel, and before you can say: "my deserving constituents," the tent show as we have known it will be no more.

I'm against meeting trouble more than halfway or crossing any bridges before we get to the crossroads; but if this is not a whither-mankind question, it is certainly a whither-Congress question; and if this newfangled notion of Norblad's should infect other stalwart sons of Congress, it is easy to imagine the consequences that will, as they say, flow.

Happier minds may shrink from contemplation of the prospects, but I can detect oncoming calamity, to say nothing of catastrophe, as quickly as the Alsop brothers any day in the week, and this is what my crystal ball, full of dark clouds larger than a man's hand, foretells:

A Senator refusing to be photographed with the beauty-contest winner from his home state on the grounds that he's busy and has no time for damn foolishness.

A Republican Congressman scotching the rumor that he plays golf with Ike every week; admitting, in fact, that he's not even a member of Burning Tree.

A Senator rising to say: "I'm voting against this river and harbors appropriation for my state; boondoggling is boondoggling wherever it's done."

A farm-state Congressman getting up and saying: "If it's creeping socialism to give free vaccine shots to all children, then it's also creeping socialism to give federal subsidies to farmers and I'm agin' 'em." A New York City Congressman declaring the Irish are no better than anybody else, a Nevada Congressman declaring that gambling is sinful, and one from Iowa admitting that just as many bums, crooks, and deadbeats come from the small towns as from the big cities.

If Norbladism takes hold, we may even get to the awful point where Congressmen tell the American Legion it's wrong on something, question the omniscience of J. Edgar Hoover, tell the home town that it's a dull place compared to Washington, argue that a drafty log cabin is a lousy place to be born in, and admit they know only the first stanza of *The Star-Spangled Banner*.

But even under Norbladism run rampant, *some* traditions, thank heaven, will be safe. The crystal ball does not predict any Texas congressman explaining that Texas joined the Union, instead of the other way around.

GENEVA AND AFTER

[September 9, 1955]

This reporter has been talking all week about the great shift of political gravity in the Western world; this move from cold war, when the powers acted as if they were at war but stopped just short of waging war—to the cold peace, when they will act as if they are at peace but stop just short of ratifying peace. One senses that the implications are many and profound, even if one can only grope among their meanings.

America seems ready to accept, however cautiously, peaceful coexistence with the Communist world. Once set upon this path, we are a people who will not easily draw back; indeed, some among us seem ready to run down this path headlong; it is a little breathtaking, for example, to see the arch-conservative Senator Malone telling us to trade more and more with Russia, to stop broadcasting to the Russian masses over the heads of their rulers. But what is important is that acceptance of peaceful coexistence means acceptance, by and large, of the *status quo*.

Our government is moving steadily toward acceptance of a spheres-of-influence world; the reverse of our stated policy the last ten years, the very attitude, it may be remembered, that cost Henry Wallace his Cabinet job when he expressed it. The Geneva Conference marks the end of the liberation-of-captive-peoples policy, of the "dynamic anti-communist foreign policy," as restated in the Republican platform of '52. That is the reality, as to both Europe and Asia, but our public statements have not yet been trimmed to match our acts. The words and the music do not yet go together. We will continue to preach freedom and self-determination to the world, but we will not, apparently, do anything about it; whether it is the native peoples of French North Africa at stake or the captive people of Russia's Poland.

One is not in Europe very long before discovering that this suits the deepest instincts of our allies. Most of them, certainly the French, are tired and a little afraid of America's penchant for mixing moralisms with world politics. They know perfectly well that we have changed the music of our policies; they would like to see us change the words.

Perhaps one day we will; continuing contradiction between tongue and hand is not only confusing to the world, but corrupting to the nation that indulges in it. Because we ourselves are still confused about what we are doing, this contradiction is not yet hypocrisy, but it can become so.

America is slowly coming to terms with the reality of the world. Maybe this is inevitable; maybe, indeed, it will hasten, not foreclose, the day of liberation for the captive peoples as a sense of security grows upon the Russians as well as upon ourselves. And yet there is a certain sadness in the present process. It marks, one might say, the end of America's youth in the world; the crusading fires, alight since the Declaration of Independence, may well die within us. Something wonderful may pass away, as something wonderful goes when youth leaves a man and he comes reluctantly to terms with life.

A NOTE ON THE TYPE

This book was set on the Linotype in Janson, a recutting made direct from the type cast from matrices (now in possession of the Stempel foundry, Frankfurt am Main) made by Anton Janson some time between 1660 and 1687.

Of Janson's origin nothing is known. He may have been a relative of Justus Janson, a printer of Danish birth who practiced in Leipzig from 1614 to 1635. Some time between 1657 and 1668 Anton Janson, a punch-cutter and type-founder, bought from the Leipzig printer Johann Erich Hahn the type-foundry that had formerly been a part of the printing house of M. Friedrich Lankisch. Janson's types were first shown in a specimen sheet issued at Leipzig about 1675. Janson's successor, and perhaps his son-in-law, Johann Karl Edling, issued a specimen sheet of Janson types in 1689. His heirs sold the Janson matrices in Holland to Wolffgang Dietrich Erhardt of Leipzig.

Composed, printed, and bound by KINGSPORT PRESS, INC., *Kingsport, Tennessee. Paper manufactured by* S. D. WARREN COMPANY, *Boston, Mass.*

Typography and binding based on designs by WARREN CHAPPELL.